Parenting
Mentally Ill Children

Parenting
Mentally Ill Children

Faith, Caring, Support, and Surviving the System

Craig Winston LeCroy

 PRAEGER

AN IMPRINT OF ABC-CLIO, LLC
Santa Barbara, California • Denver, Colorado • Oxford, England

Library of Congress Cataloging-in-Publication Data

LeCroy, Craig W.
  Parenting mentally ill children : faith, caring, support, and surviving the system / Craig Winston LeCroy.
    p. cm.
  Includes bibliographical references and index.
    ISBN 978–0–313–35868–5 (hard copy : alk. paper) — ISBN 978–0–313–35869–2 (e-book)
  1. Mentally ill children—Care. 2. Parenting. I. Title. [DNLM: 1. Mental Disorders.
  2. Adolescent. 3. Child. 4. Parenting. WS 350]
  RJ499.L355 2011
  618.92′89—dc22   2010053263

ISBN: 978–0–313–35868–5
EISBN: 978–0–313–35869–2

15 14 13 12 11   1 2 3 4 5

This book is also available on the World Wide Web as an eBook.
Visit www.abc-clio.com for details.

Praeger
An Imprint of ABC-CLIO, LLC

ABC-CLIO, LLC
130 Cremona Drive, P.O. Box 1911
Santa Barbara, California 93116-1911

This book is printed on acid-free paper (∞)

Manufactured in the United States of America

To All Parents of Mentally Ill Children

Everybody is a story.

—R. Naomi Remen

Contents

Acknowledgments

During the course of my work, many parents took the time to speak to me about their lives—and the conversation was often emotional and difficult. I deeply appreciate the opportunity I had to listen and learn about lives of the parents I interviewed. Your courage and compassion, your honesty, inspired me to complete this book, although it took more years than I had imagined. Through stories, laughter, and tears, we have shared a storytelling journey together. I hope that this coming together can be the start of a pathway to greater hope, wisdom, and valor as you navigate life's waters. My goal was to merge enough common themes to create something of value to all parents who might read this book. I also hope that professionals will peruse these pages to learn, to question, and to commit to a high moral standard of help.

I have been teaching social work for more than 25 years now. Along the way, I have been privileged to work with some of the brightest, most committed, and most genuinely helpful students in my final year of preparing this book. Eric Bradley conducted a number of the interviews in this book and wrote a master's thesis that became a prelude to this book. His thesis was masterfully done and is well represented in these pages. Danielle Demailo was the primary contributor to the policy chapter (Chapter 8). Her research and writing were invaluable in helping me finish this book. Mia Zamora made significant original contributions to Chapter 7, Faithful Acts of Caring: Lessons on a Meaningful Life; her research and creative writing added significantly to the final product. Christina Leber was the primary contributor to the Appendix. My academic colleagues, Jose Ashford and Judy Krysik, read drafts of some chapters and advised me along the way. Together, all of you helped me plow through and meet my final deadline for completion of the manuscript.

I started working on this book seven years ago. I was honored to receive financial support for much of this effort. Arizona State University provided me with a Dean's scholarship to get the project going and also supported my effort when I went on sabbatical. I was honored to fill the Zellerbach Visiting Professorship at the School of Social Welfare, University of California–Berkeley, which provided me with some funds and an office in Haviland Hall on Berkeley's intellectually stimulating campus. The sheer number of bookstores in Berkeley greatly added to the reading list I created for this work. I lived in a small apartment in a large historical house that was managed by the Berkeley Historical Society. With the blessing of my wife and son, I had moved to Berkeley in retreat mode to work exclusively on this project. However, after my six-month stay there ended, we all headed off to New Zealand, where I was supported by the University of Christchurch, School of Social Work. I continued my effort on the book and, eventually, the project landed back home in Tucson, Arizona, where I finally completed it.

I appreciate the support I received from Debbie Carvalko, my editor at Praeger Publishers. After reviewing my prospectus, she immediately understood my purpose in writing this book.

I hope these printed pages offer something of great value for each of you who read them.

CHAPTER 1

Introduction: The Crisis of Children's Mental Health

Cole is no good, and for a mama to say that, for a mama, I wish I could be dead. Used to be all I ever wanted was a child of my own.... But now I think about doom, what it is to be doomed. Cole is living proof ill winds blow in out of nowhere and stomp out love and mercy. But why is that? I gave years trying to figure it out and I guess there are years ahead of me to come. I won't ever let up wondering what went wrong.

—E. Clark, *Biting the Stars*

"My daughter has punched me, kicked me, and slapped me. She threw a lamp at me and cut my index finger deep to the bone." Julie, a 45-year-old, composed mother of four, continued her story, recounting many events that have thrown a dark shadow over her life as a parent. Initially there were problems with compliance, as daughter Tammy refused to shower and resisted the bedtime Julie set. Tammy would begin screaming in an effort to avoid being controlled by her parents. Her screaming was so loud that the family was eventually evicted from their apartment.

At a very young age, Tammy showed signs of being a violent child. One time she locked herself in the bathroom for four hours, explains Julie. "After the first hour, I'm thinking, what's going on? After the second hour, I really started to get agitated. After the third hour, I was saying, 'Tammy, get out.' I finally forced my way through the door. The bathroom floor was wet and as I turned to leave, she shoved me, knowing that if I fell on my hand, I'd need more surgery, because it was recently broken." Julie looks up at me, adding, "We didn't even have medical insurance at the time."

She sums up her feelings about Tammy with a sense of conviction: "When you stand before a judge, and you hear things like, 'She's a danger to herself. She's a danger to the general public,' you're thinking, 'That's my child.'"[1]

In the last several years Tammy went from what some would consider a difficult child to what can aptly be described as an out-of-control child. She was arrested at a motel, where police found drugs. Julie thought, "Sure, marijuana"—but the hotel room was actually lined with cocaine. Her son heard someone on the street call Tammy a slut. Another parent told Julie that she saw Tammy flashing construction workers. Julie confesses that Tammy does not understand the difference between love and sex and Julie knows she's "very sexually active."

Tammy is 14 years old and suffers from a mental disorder known as bipolar disorder. She's been on and off medications and in and out of treatment agencies. Some of it helps; a lot of it doesn't seem to make any difference.

Right now Julie does not have to contend with Tammy; she's run away. But this is not the first time she has left home unexpectedly: Tammy has run away 29 times in the last 8 months. Julie qualifies this behavior a bit, "Some of these are walk-aways because she did come back home within 24 hours," she explains. But the runaway periods are getting longer—her last one was 2 weeks, the one before that was 3 weeks, and the current one is at 3 weeks.

As she reflects back to these events, I can see the desperation in Julie's tired face. She tells me about how a parent deals with a runaway child: "I hunt her down. I bang on doors. I ask the police to help me find her, but the police won't do anything unless I can tell them where to find her."

Last week Julie got a tip from someone about where her daughter might be. When she knocked on the door of the ramshackle trailer, a large man answered and feigned an inability to speak English. She confronted him immediately, "You understand 'Policia'?" she quickly asked. "My daughter's in this house." As she spoke those words, Julie wedged her way past the man and spotted her daughter bailing out a back window. She lowered her voice and looked down. "I looked inside and began to cry. Tammy would rather be in filth with nothing, no food, no clothing, than to be at home with her parents. We aren't the best parents in the world, but we do provide her with food, love, and the basic necessities of life. That's really hard. To realize that here's this man, twice my age, laying in a bed in the living room of this trailer, with three inches of dirt, no linoleum or carpet. Three inches of dirt and beer cans. A tiny TV set. I don't understand that."

Even though as a society we have always been grudgingly aware of the fact that there are a substantial number of individuals in our midst who suffer from mental illness, we have historically overlooked the fact that many of those who have this kind of disease are, in fact, children and adolescents. It was not until the publication of Knitzer's 1982 landmark study entitled *Unclaimed Children: The Failure of Public Responsibility to Children and Adolescents in Need of Mental Health Services* that we began to comprehend the immensity of this issue.[2] Knitzer's study served as a catalyst to focus national attention on the numerous gaps in mental health services for youths, created a growing awareness with regard to children's mental illness, and stimulated more research in this area. However, even though this book was well known in 1982, more than 25 years later the field feels like it is barely scratching the surface.

Just a few years ago, interest in mental health research and service delivery became popular again with the release of the Surgeon General's *Report on Mental Health*, which outlined the status of mental health research and services in the United States. In this report, an entire 70-page chapter entitled "Children and Mental Health" addresses the current status of children's mental health services in the United States.[3] One outgrowth of this publication was a similar document entitled *Report of the Surgeon General's Conference on Children's Mental Health: A National Action Agenda*, which outlined a number of specific goals for the field of children's mental health and presented a number of action steps that would facilitate the accomplishment of these goals.[4]

Perhaps what is most striking about these documents is the estimate of just how many youth in the United States are suffering from the effects of mental illness. According to the Surgeon General's report, the Methodology for Epidemiology of Mental Disorders in Children and Adolescents (MECA) study estimated that almost 21 percent of U.S. children ages 9 to 17 have a diagnosable mental or addictive disorder associated with at least minimum impairment. When broken down into more specific mental or addictive disorders, the percentages are as follows: anxiety disorders, 13 percent; mood disorders, 6.2 percent; disruptive disorders, 10.3 percent; and substance abuse disorders, 2 percent.[5] Alan Kazdin, one of the nation's leading researchers on children's mental health, explains that if you consider the approximately 68 million children and adolescents in the United States and a prevalence rate of 20 percent, then approximately 13.5 million of our nation's youth have significant impairment due to an emotional or behavioral problem.[6]

The overriding conclusion in the United States today is that one in 10 children suffers from mental illness severe enough to result in significant functional impairment. That means approximately two children in every classroom across America are suffering from a mental illness. At almost every child's birthday party in America, one of the guests will be struggling with a mental illness. Additionally, the Surgeon General's report explains that children and adolescents with mental disorders are at much greater risk for dropping out of school and suffering long-term impairments such as an inability to attain and maintain employment.[7]

This bleak analysis is not limited to the United States. The World Health Organization (WHO) indicates that by the year 2020, childhood neuropsychiatric disorders will rise by more than 50 percent internationally to become one of the five most common causes of morbidity, mortality, and disability among children.[8] WHO's report states the case for addressing children's mental health issues emphatically: "These childhood mental disorders impose enormous burdens and can have intergenerational consequences. They reduce the quality of children's lives and diminish their productivity later in life. No other illnesses damage so many children so seriously."[9] Twenty-five years after the publication of *Unclaimed Children*, there is recognition of the increasing prevalence of mental disorders in children and adolescents and the need for governments, researchers, clinicians, and families both in the United States and around the world to start thinking critically about how to *reclaim* these children and address their problems.

At the beginning of this ordeal with Tammy, Julie was constantly questioning herself: "What was I doing wrong?" Like a lot of parents I spoke with, Julie has a difficult time with excessive worrying and questions herself repeatedly about her parenting skills.

You can see the exasperation welling up in Julie. She has recently been evicted from her apartment because of Tammy's behavior. "It's never been a thought of mine to get rid of my child. But right now, I'm more ready to put her into some kind of drug rehabilitation program. Let her do some time and straighten out." I can see irresolution in Julie's face as she assures me, "If I don't, we're going to find her in a ditch dead, and I know it. If not, raped or heaven forbid what. This is what goes through a parent's mind." And then, as if she is trying to convince herself, Julie quickly claims that Tammy is choosing to be where she is at and choosing to do what she wants to do. Julie's pretext is that Tammy understands the consequences and the potential risks of her actions.

Throughout the interview, Julie's emotions and the mental anguish she lives with are revealed. She readily admits she has had a lot of counseling—counseling that is focused exclusively on dealing with her daughter and the ways she manages to cope with it all. "What am I supposed to do, dump my child? That's the only thing I cannot do." Too often, Julie finds herself in situations where she simply does not know what to say or how to act in response to Tammy's out-of-control behaviors. She describes feeling ashamed and hurt and having "a hundred billion emotions at once."

Julie confesses, "I'm worried about her, but all the tears in the world won't bring her home. It took me forever to realize, and a lot of tears, that it isn't me. It's her. She is responsible for her own actions." As she reflects on what she has learned from her experiences, one question haunts her: "My God, what could I have done differently?" Mixed in with all the questioning, I can sense one confident perspective that surfaces. "If you have a bipolar child, you're going to have problems," she concludes.

And, as Julie realizes, these problems do not go away. While many people think about raising children until they reach 18 years of age, Julie knows that "a mother is a mother forever" and that while other parents may look forward to a life of their own after their children are adults, that will not be her fate. "The way I see it, if I allow myself, I'm bound down with grandchildren, because my child is obviously not able to take care of any children. She's not protecting herself—to not have babies, to not catch AIDS, to not catch STDs. That's a lot for a parent to worry about."

As I sought parents to interview for this book, the significance of the opportunity to tell "their story" became more and more clear. My initial attempt to recruit parents for this study included going to mental health agencies and meeting with groups of therapists to explain my study. I was almost universally confronted with mental health professionals who did not believe parents would have the time or inclination to talk with me. They felt if I paid the parents to participate in the study, perhaps a few would contribute. They were not optimistic, and because the mental health professionals believed parents wouldn't participate, there was little follow-up on my requests to contact parents. This observation is, in itself, an example of how little understanding most mental health professionals have about the needs and experiences of parents of mentally ill children.

When this process did not result in very many referrals for me, I posted flyers in agencies inviting parents to talk with me about their experiences in parenting and obtaining mental health treatment for their child. I was quickly flooded with calls from parents who wanted to describe their experiences being parents of a mentally ill child. In contrast to what the mental health professionals told me, parents *were* interested in taking the time to talk, to share their experiences. Ironically, it is this sharing of experiences, this storytelling, that is a critical and an important process absent from the mental health service delivery system.

There is something very basic and fundamental about telling one's story.[10] In discussing the sociology of illness, Arthur Frank discusses the "wounded storyteller," noting that ill people's storytelling is guided by a sense of responsibility and represents one way of living, as he says, *for* the other. According to this author, "People tell stories not just to work out their own changing identities but also to guide others who will follow them."[11] Frank puts his finger on a critical aspect of storytelling by recognizing that it has an element of testimony and that such testimony is inherently valuable—even therapeutic. People who suffer *need* to tell their stories.

It may, indeed, be difficult for professionals to listen to what parents have to say about their experiences. It is, in many respects, narrative or storytelling about suffering. The voices are varied, yet the pain is a persistent theme. Professionals may have turned away from this pain because it may be too difficult for them to hear. The vulnerability it provokes in the professional may challenge his or her true commitment to help.

In the end, such listening is a moral act. To hear the experiences of parents can bring sanity and reduce suffering. To bear witness is an act of caring for another.

In many respects the process I experienced, as parents told me their story of their child's mental illness, was a call to tell their story. Such experience of narrative encounters may in some small way help repair the damage done to a mother's (or father's) sense of self, her esteem, her ability to feel like a good mother.[12]

Why is it that so many parents told me they had never had the opportunity to "tell their story"? I can only surmise the answer to this question. Perhaps storytelling is disregarded in mental health treatment because the initial purpose of a visit is for the practitioner to take a "pychosocial history," which is different from hearing the story the parent has to tell. True, such storytelling can interfere with proper assessment and diagnosis of the client—a key part of "proper" treatment on the mind of the therapist or clinician. Perhaps the helper does not want to entertain the prospect of hearing a story that he or she might not be able to make sense of, or that the practitioner does not have to time to listen to, or that may reveal aspects of living that the helper would rather just not hear.

When I teach my "Introduction to Social Work Practice" class to university students, I stress the need to "hear" and "listen" to the client and not just do the assessment or complete the psychosocial history. I often tell students about a client I saw at a child outpatient clinic where I was working. She was a victim of domestic violence and was living with her children at a shelter. However, staff at the shelter did not want to "hear" her doubts about leaving her husband, her concerns about surviving financially, and her ambiguity about whether she could strike out on her own—so she came to see a therapist at another clinic who might listen to her. It is commonly accepted that without listening, without having a level of empathy with another person, the change process is more likely to halt than begin. An important goal of this book is to help mental health practitioners listen better to their clients—the parents of mentally ill children—as they reveal important aspects of their true selves, and relay heartfelt experiences about people presumably trying to help them.

Because I am a social worker by training and interested in how people receive and accept social services, I look here for patterns or interpretations that may be of benefit to mental health practitioners. Because I have gotten close to the parents I interviewed, I may be overly critical, but I am committed to helping change how parents are helped by mental health professionals. If nothing else, I hope to describe how mental health professionals interact with the mental health system.

What is most critical about capturing parents' "quest" stories, as Arthur Frank calls them, is that they are in essence manifestos, public declarations. A quest story addresses suffering directly, and people are motivated to share their stories by their belief that something is to be gained from the experience.[13] An important narrative quest story will seek to use the parent's experience of suffering to move others forward to an action agenda. Doing these interviews, I could tell that some parents had a quest story underlying their interest in talking with me. They were, in essence, saying: "I am experiencing this crisis now, I am living through it, and I can share this with some hope that other parents will find some meaning in it." An important reason for writing this book is to bring these messages to witness, because maintaining silence about such messages can only lead to little or no resolution.

For many of these parents, there is an important subtext to their stories: How have I managed to deal with this problem? One goal in documenting their accounts is the moral purpose of providing experiences of other parents as an example (or witness) of how they have coped with the burden of love they feel with their child, developed a sense of faithful caring, or managed to find meaning in sorrowful events. Parents will be able to affirm their similar feelings and experiences, and they may also gain a better framework for making sense out of their own experiences.[14] After reading these accounts, parents may experience the "looking glass self," a reflection of many aspects of their lives. Ideally, parents will also be able to look at their circumstances through new windows. If I am successful here, I will be able to open up windows that many parents have not really looked through but that, at the same time, seem strikingly familiar.

I met Chris on a sunny afternoon in my office. She is a soft-spoken woman, with long blond hair flowing down her shoulders. Chris would be the first parent I interviewed for this book. As I shut the office door, she began telling me an intense saga that would reverberate deeply for me as I contemplated her life story. We talked for hours and covered her experience with John, who had notice-able difficulties at birth. Chris's first encounter with professionals came when she enrolled her son in school. She tried to place him in preschool but described it as a "nightmare" because John had so many behavior problems—running around, eating things, breaking things, and stealing toys from other children. When he was five, she tried again and enrolled him in the local public school. "I can remem-ber going to the school and watching him go through the gates and just sitting and crying, because I knew that the school would call me and tell me about his behav-ior problems." Eventually, they put John in a special education class and attempted to teach him to read, but he simply could not focus long enough to learn much.

Chris described the common pressure many parents feel to medicate their children because of behavior problems. At five years old, John began what would become a lifelong involvement with psychiatric medications. He was diagnosed with attention-deficit disorder and prescribed Ritalin, the drug commonly used to treat this disorder. Chris described how John at that young age already knew that he had a problem unlike other children: "He knew something was wrong him-self, and that he had to take medication. I clearly remember him sitting in bed sev-eral months after he started taking the medication, and he looked up at me and said, 'Mama, I just want a big knife and stick it in me and die.'" Chris gets a com-plete look of absorption on her face and exclaims, "This is a five-year-old asking to die!" John could explain that he did things he wasn't supposed to do, but he just didn't understand why he did those things. At this age, John was getting into everything and was breaking, crushing, and smashing things on a regular basis.

At this point, Chris is describing the normal progression that many parents face with children who have serious behavior problems, but her story reveals per-haps the darkest side of what can happen with children who are difficult to man-age. Her marriage was clearly strained from all the problems the couple encountered with John. Although Chris found a protective love for John and developed a meaningful relationship with her son, her husband was not so forgiv-ing of John's misfortune. Her husband would not allow for any "help"—no counseling or therapy—but for a while he agreed to the medication. At some point he decided even that medication was not acceptable, because it made John "retarded." His father's response to the situation was to become harder on John—what he needed was to "straighten up." But John continued to have problems. He was still not consistently potty trained, and Chris tells me about a time when John had an accident and the father was furious. He grabbed John's pants from the floor and stuck them on his head, then rubbed John's face in the mess he had created. As Chris speaks, I can see a tinge of guilt. She explains her behavior: "To this day, I can't believe I allowed this to happen, out of fear. I should have intervened; sometimes I did and ended up having to hide my face for a week because I was black and blue."

The severe stigma Chris faced as a mother began at home but did not end there. She describes a lifetime of isolation that continues to this day. The rejection and isolation she feels are because of John—specifically, society's nonacceptance of him. She tried to get help from day-care providers and friends, but the story was always the same: "We cannot handle him. He writes on the walls, wets his pants, we can't stand it. You have to take him." Chris got accustomed to the immediate wall that would go up upon any encounter with other acquaintances. She did not get invited to other people's homes for dinner. There were no play dates for John. No one sent invitations to birthday parties. She retreated alone with John to the only place she could go—her own home.

Chris's encounters at the school contributed to her sense of inadequacy as a parent and reinforced the stigma she felt. Whenever she went to visit the school, she felt as if she was the target of disdain. "You can feel the looks, the way people respond to you." School personnel quickly became frustrated with John and responded to Chris with a lot of defensiveness. Whenever she was called into a teachers' conference meeting, there was never any problem solving involved. Chris explains the mantra she heard from school officials. They didn't ask, "What can we do to support John and you?" The message was, "You need to get him on more meds. He has behavior problems."

Things progressed and in many ways got worse for John and Chris. Chris is a single mother now, like almost all of the parents I interviewed. Eventually after witnessing her husband mistreat John, and being regularly beaten herself, she broke free of her marriage. But she endured physical and verbal abuse, the multiple affairs her husband had, and experienced many encounters with Child Protective Services.

When John was in the seventh grade, he tried to commit suicide. He attempted to set himself on fire, but ended up lighting a field on fire. He was not taking his medications because, unbeknownst to Chris, while John was in the care of his father he was not allowed to take the medication. Chris believes this practice led to John smoking, as he self-medicated with cigarettes. When John's father found out about the fire, the child was given a beating. John reported his father to Child Protective Services two weeks after the abuse. The investigation did not turn up anything, however, because by the time Child Protective Service workers examined John, his bruises had healed. Chris remembers the call from the agency workers: "They told me, if you do not report these abuses, we are going to take your kids away from you." What was disturbing was that at that time Chris did not know John's father had hit him. As a result of these events, the family got a referral to receive social services—the first time Chris and John were referred for other services. Not even the school district had helped the family find any additional services, other than the medication. And no one had suggested that Chris obtain any professional help for herself.

Chris and John represent many of the families who not only suffer from the impact of mental illness, but even more disheartening, need mental health services and do not get them. One of the primary conclusions of the Surgeon General's report on mental illness is that many children who need services go without them.

Of those children with a serious emotional disturbance, an estimated 75 to 80 percent fail to receive specialty services such as individual treatment, and the majority of the children receive no services at all.

What is even more overlooked and in great need is individual support and guidance for the parents. This aspect of mental health treatment is rarely mentioned—even the Surgeon General's report does not identify it as a critical need. The most "help" John will ever receive is from his mother. Chris has faced guilt, shame, and stigma—alone, with no support from anyone. She has suffered physical abuse. Her everyday life is consumed with caring for her son, yet no agency, no school, no professional reached out to her to provide the help she needed, until her circumstance became dire. At one point, Chris attempted suicide. "I thought about dying for a long time. I thought about killing myself. I needed to just do something. Somehow, God reminded me that Christmas was coming." Chris made it out of her deep despair, but not all parents do.

Many of these parents live in a world filled with chaos—and it is most certainly a world where they have lost control. Without control, there is no sense of resolution.[15] The parents' lack of control over their child's symptoms is complemented by the mental health system's inability to control the symptoms. For many mental health professionals, there is a denial of the limited extent to which their work can impact the child. This refusal to acknowledge these shortcomings borders on a breach of ethics because no one helps the parent confront the awful truth about the likely prognosis for his or her child. When there is a pretense of successful treatment, there is denial of the suffering of what it cannot treat.[16]

Julie, after a lot of suffering and sorrow, finally realizes that her daughter's fate is not in her hands. She continues to reconcile her efforts to do "enough" and not beat herself up too much. Chris talks about the utter lack of control in her life. She finally figured out (by herself) that to get any sleep, she had to unplug the phone and simply not worry about her child (who is now living in a group home and old enough to be "independent") until the next morning when, after a full night's sleep, she could address whatever presented itself. She recounted the long weeks that went by, where she cried herself to sleep every night.

These are only two of the many parents whose stories this book will present. Surely their stories bellow a need to be heard and understood, not as clients or patients, but as parents in their everyday efforts to survive.

In spite of the difficulty of dealing with mentally ill children and the incidence of mental disorders in children, there is simply far too little written about *parenting* mentally ill children. One obvious example is Marc Bornstein's series, *Handbook of Parenting*.[17] This five-volume set addresses the topics of children and parenting, the biology and ecology of parenting, being and becoming a parent, social conditions and applied parenting, and practical issues in parenting. It contains 86 chapters and 3,216 pages of text, none of which addresses parents of mentally ill children. There are chapters on parenting infants, parenting adopted children, single parenthood, gay parenthood, parenting talented children, even psychoanalysis and parenthood, but not parenthood and mentally ill children. Some chapters come close: parenting and child maltreatment, parenting the ill child, and mentally ill *parents*. The 2002 publication is the second edition of Bornstein's book. When *Parenting Mentally Ill Children: Faith, Caring, Support, and Surviving the System* is published, I will send Marc Bornstein a copy and hope for an invitation to write a chapter for the third edition—these parents need their story told, too.

How can mental health professionals provide help if they do not understand the experience of a parent? It seems rather obvious that any effort to think about services or therapy for a family would need to be preceded by an understanding of the parental experience. Consider that mental health professionals and researchers often lament the issue of premature termination from treatment—when "children" drop out of treatment prior to the treatment being concluded. This well-known problem in therapy has not been considered from the parent's point of view. It is as if the professional does not recognize that the *parent* brings the child for treatment, whether that therapy consists of individual or family treatment.

My aim in conducting these interviews with parents was to present the point of view of the parent, to understand how parents attempt to make sense of their lives.[18] While the federal government and other researchers have called for more studies of children with mental illness, few efforts have been put forth to hear the voices of the parents themselves. What does it feel like to be a parent of a mentally ill child? What does it mean when your child is given a diagnosis of mental illness? What experiences do parents have in their efforts to get help? What are the meanings that parents associate with their child receiving medication? Do they accept the illness as it is explained? How do they cope with the chronic sorrow these experiences bring?

This book is a compilation of voices—of parents speaking about their feelings, thoughts, attitudes, and perspectives that have been affected by being a parent of a mentally ill child. While there is a long history of accounts or memoirs of individuals with mental illness and some written by parents of mentally ill children, this book differs from those earlier publications in its attempt to look across the many parents with whom I spoke.[19] Also, overarching themes and issues for parents will be identified, a feat that cannot be accomplished on the basis of a single account. The in-depth interviews were conducted with more than 40 parents who have children with an "official" diagnosis of mental illness.

Although the sample is not random and can be questioned in terms of its ability to be representative of all parents with mentally ill children, I do believe enough interviews were conducted to reach "saturation," so that this work presents consistent themes that all parents are likely to experience. The parents in this sample are almost all low-income individuals and represent poor and working-class families—those with the fewest resources available to address their difficulties.

The interviews were conducted primarily at the homes of the parents, or sometimes at another comfortable, convenient location. All interviews were tape recorded and professionally transcribed. My approach comprised the research interview as conversation. This methodology is aptly described using a traveler metaphor to illustrate the process of the interview.[20] In this metaphor, the interviewer is a traveler on a journey that leads to a story told on returning home. The interviewer-traveler explores new landscapes by having conversations with the people along the way. The traveler may seek to find certain places by following a method—a path that leads to a goal. As the traveler wanders and meets the locals, he or she asks questions that bring forth their stories of their everyday world. The conversations I had with parents were consistent with the Latin meaning of the word "conversation"—namely, "wandering together with."[21]

As I spoke with parents, I used the following framework to interpret my experiences:

- *Life world*—to enter and understand the everyday world of the parent and his or her relationship to it
- *Meaning*—to understand and interpret the meaning of central themes in the life world of the parent
- *Specificity*—to obtain descriptions of specific situations
- *Focus*—to focus the interview on themes as they emerge
- *Qualitative knowledge*—to obtain qualitative knowledge as expressed by parents
- *Deliberate naiveté*—to be open to new and unexpected information[22]

What emerged from these interviews is a better understanding of how parents make sense of their faithful acts of caring for their children, their acceptance of mental illness in their child, their struggles to obtain needed help, their efforts at managing everyday life, their chronic sorrow, and their quest to find meaning from their experiences. We make sense out of our lives by looking backward and we live our life looking forward.[23]

Much of what is written here is the "pedagogy of faithful caring." This term refers to what parents of mentally ill children have to teach parents with mentally ill children, parents without mentally ill children, mental health professionals, and society at large. While all can benefit from this analysis of what it means to have a mentally ill child in today's society, the most direct benefactors will be other similar parents and those whose mission it is to help such parents. It is important to understand that this book is not meant as a replacement for what students learn in classes about children's mental illness, or what agencies train mental health professionals to know. However, it is indeed critical that such students and professionals learn things *beyond* what is taught in textbook descriptions of *Diagnostic and Statistic Manual of Mental Disorders* (DSM) diagnosis for children or therapy models for treatment.

These children and families need to have a real "face" put on their lives. Any effort to provide a humane response to this social problem requires this level of understanding.

CHAPTER 2

Accepting the Verdict: My Child Has a Mental Illness

> In the end, I found that I had written a recovery story after all. What is recovered is a family more resilient, forgiving, and loving. Like the characters in the *Wizard of Oz*, we have made a journey through a perilous land, and we have discovered in ourselves the gifts that prepare us to seek the future beyond the fear, the darkness. After the earthquake, wind, and fire, a still, small voice of peace.
>
> —D. E. Burns, *Saving Ben: A Father's Story of Autism*

I'm thinking about my first interview with a parent and already feeling uneasy. How can I open myself up to the kind of hurt and disappointment I think I'm likely to be exposed to? Having my own child makes the experience more difficult. I can still remember the nervousness I felt prior to his birth. Would there be any problems? How would I handle it if he was born with a developmental or neurological problem? I'm not sure if all parents have such thoughts, or if my anxiety was related to my work in the human services field, where I am exposed to a lot more human pain and suffering. Whatever the case, I realize that I now have to enter into the parents' experience of having a mentally ill child and I know it will be difficult for me, both personally and emotionally. I also realize that this is important: Parents are so crucial in understanding a child's mental illness that an understanding from their point of view is seriously needed.

Weeks before I began the interviews, I thought about what I was likely to hear and the impact it might have. What would it be like to care for a child who had additional needs, who needed more protection, more caring? There is a stirring feeling, knowing that I will take this journey into the hearts and minds of parents. Parents who had been, for years, the object of other people's reports would now be telling their own stories. However, telling does not come easy; neither does listening.

COMING TO A NEW REALIZATION

The initial response to comprehending fully that one's child has a mental illness can only be characterized as a cry from the heart. The sorrow that follows evokes existential questions such as "Why me?", "Why this child?", "What did I do wrong?", and "What good can come of this?" Of course, there is no answer to such questions, but parents must live through the sorrow if they are ever to accept that some questions can never be answered. For many parents, what emerges is what Arthur Frank calls a "quest story." There is a pressing effort to assure this experience is not all for naught—to find meaning, contribution, and some way of bringing understanding to others.

An important part of the journey parents take is coming to terms with "how it all started," when they realized that their child was different. This beginning process is described with tension and suspense in Valerie Paradiz's memoir *Elijah's Cup*.[1] As the book begins, Elijah, still a toddler, starts experiencing seizures. Is Elijah seriously developmentally delayed? Or is he just starting slow, or experiencing a slowness due to a disease? The parents resist admitting that a problem exists, but struggle with their impending realization that Elijah truly has a problem. The seizures lead to a brain scan that shows nothing abnormal. The searching plays out in dialogue as the parents drive home after their first visit to the hospital, "questioning ourselves at every stop light . . . Questioning the past and Elijah's complicated birth."[2] These parents express the searching process, and for many who suffer the same fate the answers become necessary and urgently needed.

In her memoir *Tell Me I'm Here: One Family's Experience with Schizophrenia*, Anne Deveson recalls her experience in accepting that her child has schizophrenia: "Had I been equipped with my present knowledge, it would have been clear that Jonathan had been heading for a breakdown for months, even years before it occurred. . . . But I was grappling with that age-old parental dilemma of balancing the danger of being over-reactive with making sure that I was not guilty of benign neglect. And then his father brought Jonathan into the kitchen and said, 'I think he's sick.' After that, the days that followed were never quite the same."[3]

For some parents, the final acceptance that their child is mentally ill emerges from an intense experience that breaks down the barrier of "this isn't happening to me" and allows the realization to set in. One woman describes the difficulty: "The very nature of serious illness lends itself to second guessing. I've done this; I think most family members of the mentally ill do. Because we feel helpless to cure, we look to see if there was, instead, some triggering event we should have taken seriously. And we nearly always find something that we feel ought to have clued us in."[4]

In this instance, there was a telling event: The 17-year-old boy, Daniel, emerged from his bedroom one evening completely naked, exposing himself to his mother and two sisters; he was smiling and oblivious to the inappropriateness of his behavior. In a similar manner, Anne Deveson describes seeking help when she was attacked by her son because he thought that rats were eating his brain, a dramatic event that she never forgot.[5] For other parents, like Peter Wyden, author of *Conquering Schizophrenia*, care is finally sought because of concerns that things aren't going normally, that the child seems shy or socially awkward.[6]

The parents I interviewed shared their frustration at the ensuing diagnostic process:

> When James came along, we noticed when he was 2½ that he had way beyond the terrible two's. As he got older, going into three, it didn't get any better. We knew something wasn't right. The part that frustrates me even now is when we starting going to "experts," describing things that were going on in our house, how the first reflex of most of the psychiatrists, social workers, therapists is to shift blame back, try to find something you're doing as a parent to cause this child's behavior. We had no idea what was going on, what we were doing or not doing. We also had another child—Amy was then about 9 or 10—so we knew we weren't totally stupid.

> I said we needed a second opinion. The physician we were seeing at the time got angry with me for asking for a second opinion. As a parent, that's my right. If you tell someone that your child has some weird disorder and they don't believe you, you're going to get another opinion. At that point, we did get a second opinion from someone who wasn't affiliated with the hospital, and [that person] had a different opinion. So when that report was given to the primary physician, he again was saying, "Well, I haven't seen him enough." I said, but you're not listening to what we're saying. Finally we left that physician.

This parent received an accurate diagnosis only after her son was hospitalized and the psychiatric consultant listened to her descriptions and tried to understand why so much of the diagnostic puzzle didn't fit. Eventually it became clear that he had obsessive–compulsive disorder (OCD), but that he had been very good at hiding it.

Another parent describes her desire for practical information:

> Why don't we call it what it is, treat it the way it's supposed to be treated, give the parents the education they need to deal with it, give the parents the support they need to deal with it, and go on. In our family, I have seen a great difference in children having a real diagnosis and being treated for it.

IT'S TOO HARD TO BELIEVE

Many of the parents I talked with were cognizant of breaking through the barriers of "this can't be happening" by acknowledging their children are acting in ways that are concerning, listening to others who commented on the child's behavior, and paying attention to the overwhelming feeling that the parent isn't doing a good job because of the child's behaviors. As one parent says, "All I could think of in the days that followed was getting Alex home, getting him better. I wanted this problem fixed. I wanted Alex back in school, and I wanted to forget this horrible thing. I didn't want to write down what happened. I didn't want to think about any of it again, ever. We were having a bad week. I was sure it would soon be over, and we would move on. I was wrong."[7]

This same parent explains how he moved from denial to acceptance: "This simple act of picking up a book and deciding to learn more about Alex's condition was an important step for me. For the first time, I admitted to myself that Alex's illness was not going to magically disappear, that he wasn't going to grow out of it. I abandoned, finally, the idea that we would pull together and get through this."[8]

Having certain expectations about a child's future is a part of every parent's thought process at some point, be it at their child's birth, at his or her high school graduation, or on an everyday basis. The parents interviewed described a variety of reactions to first hearing of their child's mental health diagnosis. For some, it was a relief; for others, fear; and almost always confusion and uncertainty. One mother explains, with regard to her son's first diagnosis:

> At that time, it was like death. All of a sudden you're told your child has a mental disability. Wow! What a loss. He's not going to change. His brain is pretty much hardened this way. I felt lost. I felt like I lost a boy that was supposed to go to college and have girlfriends and dates. I had this vision of my son coming home and saying, "Hey, Mom, I met this girl. I'm going out with the guys for a beer, Mom." Just looking forward to him having a great time, being a part of a life I don't think I had. Get out there with your friends. Do things. He didn't have that. It's been painful for him to this day.

Another parent struggles with the process of diagnosis and what it might likely mean for her child:

> I have to get everything I can for my son now, because if he gets everything taken care of then by the time he's in first or second grade, he can go to a regular school. I don't want him to be labeled "learning disabled" for the rest of his life. He doesn't have full-fledged autism. He's smart. If he can teach himself to control his impulses—it's learned behavior—he'll have a better chance. And I don't want to put him on any medication. I want to exhaust every other option I can find right now. I don't think it is fair to put a four-year-old on drugs. There's not enough studies about it. You never know, 10, 20 years from now, what he's going to be like. He has good days and bad days, like everybody.

Parents may feel compelled to "hide" or, at least initially, deny the problems. But before long, friends and neighbors will talk about the child who is not quite "right." This stigma, a sense of disgrace, will infect parents and intensify the problems that come along with it. Mentally ill children become tainted and confused by such events. Initially they cannot understand their situation, this formless difference. They may live surrounded by the complications that the mental disorder brings and react with anger, sadness, guilt, shame, worry, and isolation.

For some parents, rejection will become a part of the process. Many parents divorce. Some parents will not accept what has happened, will not believe what the other parent says, or will blame the other parent for the child's misfortune. But the children alone must, for all time, bear witness to the unfortunate circumstances. The deep love present in most parent–child relationships can carry the child through lifelong difficulties, but still "His shadow falls before him, wherever he goes."[9]

At some point parents become aware that their child is, without a doubt, different. No matter what they do to avoid admitting what they witness everyday, sooner or later they awaken to the truth. The process is difficult: What parent wants to admit his or her child has a mental disorder? Does that mean abandoning hope or potential for help? A lifelong struggle for normalcy? Such awareness is different for different parents and child problems. For some, it is immediate; for others, it occurs gradually, over a period of time. Often parents know something is wrong but cannot make sense out of their child's difficulty until it has a name or becomes a recognized reality. Prior to this confrontation with reality, there is often a nagging sense of uneasiness, consternation, and discontent.

In their interviews, many parents were able to describe their memories of early events that hinted something was wrong. Many suggested as much to pediatricians and school officials, only to be reassured that things were fine. But over time, the evidence became substantial and overwhelming; the picture was too vivid and clear not to notice strange, inappropriate, or even risky behavior. Many mental disorders mark their presence with a dramatic event—lipstick smeared all over the individual's face without acknowledging that this is a problem, an uncontrollable outburst that leaves a house in ruin, an unsuccessful attempt to take one's life. As one parent explains:

> *The problem started escalating when one day at the day care, he had hit a little boy or girl, whacked her upside the head with a metal truck, which was really dangerous. So they started saying we really need to have someone look at this stuff. So he got referrals starting in kindergarten for his aggressive behavior. He got suspended in the first grade, and the second grade, and in the third grade for his aggressive behavior.*

AFTER THE DIAGNOSIS

For many of the parents I interviewed, it was clear how welcome a diagnosis was for them. When faced with the burden of not knowing, confusion, and uncertainty, obtaining a "clear" diagnosis represents progress. Once a name is attached to the child's condition, parents feel they can begin the process of coping and moving to action. But for too many parents, their child had multiple and conflicting diagnoses that caused their uncertainty to linger. In the end, most parents, whether correct or incorrect, felt they found a diagnosis that fits, one that they could accept as valid.

It was a big relief to hear that there was a name for his disorder. Because now I know it's just not me. I had been assured that his behavior and all the things that he was doing had nothing to do with bad parenting. He's just spoiled. That is what I would hear: "You spoil him. You don't discipline him." And none of these things is true. That's not what it was from. It was great to understand that.

He was diagnosed with ADHD [attention-deficit/hyperactivity disorder]. We were happy with that, because we were given something that had a label. Everybody wants a label for something, and he gave us some options about how we could treat it.

Warren was diagnosed in December. Throughout his schooling, I was told that he was immature, that I babied him. He was spoiled. Nobody really saw any problem, no doctor, no psychiatrist. No one saw any problem until a doctor did a chromosome test for fragile X. Then we found out he had Klinefelter's syndrome.

I went online and looked at all the different signs that I was seeing, and I kept thinking it does sound like ADHD, except for the fact that he can focus when he wants, which I guess a lot of ADHD kids can't. There were so many symptoms he was not fitting. And then as soon as we hit on the bipolar [disorder diagnosis], I thought, well, that fits it to a T, because we have the really high anxiety and then we have the really low [phase]. For example, one day one of the CDs wouldn't play in his computer and he had a total meltdown. He just started bawling. And I thought this isn't normal. This is an extreme low. Now there's a name to his problem. And so now we can work on it, because we know what it is. Overall, I'm glad to get a diagnosis.

Once we went out of the public system to see a private system psychiatrist, he was diagnosed with schizoaffective bipolar type, given medication for schizoaffective bipolar type, and he's been able to maintain better, [though he is] not 100 percent. He doesn't have a concept of what this is and what it makes him do. But when you have a real diagnosis, it helps to be able to focus in on what is the problem, how do you deal with it, and get real support.

When parents first learn of the diagnosis, they are often at their most vulnerable point. They are often taken to the brink of what they can manage and realize that help must be sought. Often a crisis situation brings them to this state. Their emotions are up front and personal. At times, they are in touch with the primal love and caring that is required when a parent surrenders his or her child to professional help. Often it is a hospital, sometimes the police, or an agreement between parent and child that moves them to action.

Sometimes, in the aftermath of the diagnosis and acceptance of that diagnosis, coupled with exhaustion there is intense sorrow, but also guilt. These deeply emotional times reflect the unmet needs of parents—alone, isolated, and without assistance in managing a flood of conflicting feelings. The process that emerges in this early phase for parents includes their first reactions of existential angst coupled with beginning sorrow. How could this happen? Questioning and self-blame may become the forum in which they seek to sort out their mixed emotions.

> When I took him to his pediatrician, she referred me to a neurologist in New York. He talked to me for 5 minutes; he checked my son Caleb for like 10 minutes, made him walk back and forth, and asked me some questions. Does he rock his head? Does he clap his hands? And sometimes he does do that, especially if I catch him doing something he's not supposed to do; I will yell, "Caleb!" and he gets nervous. The doctor looked at him and asked, "What's your name?" Back then, Caleb didn't have good eye contact. So the doctor told me right then and there, "He's autistic," and I got very upset. I was crying. I never expected that, and when I left, I was not satisfied. He was fast talking, and I think he just labeled [my child] too fast. I spoke with my mother and teachers in the school, and they all said to get a second opinion.

> Depression and anxiety tend to run in a family, and I've had it for a long time. I wasn't diagnosed for a long time. I kept seeing signs of what I had when I was younger in my oldest daughter. I had it clear back then and didn't know it.

After they establish confidence that they have a reasonable diagnosis, parents often become freed to be more focused. Their parenting becomes learning and understanding so they can make the decisions that need to be made based on the best information. This drive is motivated by an underlying belief that they can cure the illness, that medical science can produce a remedy. Most parents experience failures with both mental health counseling and with medication—neither seems to really address the concerns. This low point is where the parents feel very vulnerable, and can lose hope. Eventually the parents come to terms with acceptance of a chronic condition. While they remain resentful and sometimes angry, this is a point where parents can "let go" because they realize that they cannot control the ultimate outcome with their child. Many parents get to a point where they can shift their perspective from hopeful and optimistic about a future for their child to a realistic perspective about maintenance without crisis and chaos. The parents also realize that for them, life will be different. They will be responsible for caring in a manner they did not expect and have not prepared for.

> Once they explained to me what ADHD was, I could see the problem. They can't sit still. It started making sense, and I started getting books and reading—that definitely fits him. I did a lot of research to learn about it so I can help him along the way. I don't know if it ever goes away 100 percent, but I want to try to cure as much as I can.

ACCEPTING DIFFERENCES

One of the most notable stories about the difficult issues parents face with the care of "special" children comes from Pearl S. Buck, who in 1950 courageously wrote about her experiences raising a mentally challenged child. Her words spoke clearly to parents who were on the same path, who were trying to cope with the same difficulties. She was most likely the first renowned person (winning both the Pulitzer and Nobel prizes for her writing) to publically acknowledge having a child with a developmental disability. A developmental disability such as mental illness carries a significant stigma, and is not well understood by the general public. As one parent describes his experience:

> No parent wants their child to be noticed as different from the norm. You want a healthy, happy child who fits in and makes you proud. But what do you do when your child is different? Speaking for myself, I had a hard time when my son was diagnosed with autism many years ago. I walked around looking out of the corner of my eye, ready to pounce upon people for their reactions. Actually it was more my perceptions of their reactions—not to mention the perpetual knot in the pit of my stomach. Like many parents whose children are different, it felt to me that I was battling the whole world.[10]

> When I was about 9 years old, my father and I went to visit an acquaintance of his from work. I vividly remember entering the man's house and being introduced to his child, who had Down syndrome. The boy took me to his playroom and showed me many of his most prized toys. That event may well have influenced my ultimate decision to pursue social work as a career for myself. Whether it did or not, it was an important first exposure to "difference" and I had to, from that point forward, reconcile how other people could be significantly different from me. This process wasn't easy for me as a child and it isn't easy today even for adults.

Despite being a practical issue in everyday life, relationships with "special" people have not been addressed much. A useful resource is Cathy Sammons and Nancy Miller's book, Everybody's Different: Understanding and Changing Our Reactions to Disabilities, which tackles head-on the issue of differences and describes how we as a society can function to accept and accommodate those who are different from us.[11] Parents of mentally ill children have to face this "difference" in a society that is not well prepared understand it.

BIOLOGICAL DETERMINISM AND PARENTING: THE BLANK SLATE THEORY

Steven Pinker's The Blank Slate is a scientific review of what he refers to as the modern denial of human nature. Pinker traces the cultural history of our belief in the "blank slate."[12] The denial of biological determinism (or at least the denial of aspects of such determinism) has created negative and damaging implications for how we think about everyday issues such as parenting. With regard to parenting, Pinker notes that "Many policies on parenting, for example, are inspired by research that finds a correlation between the behavior of parents and the behavior of children. Loving parents have confident children, authoritative parents (neither too permissive nor too punitive) have well-behaved children, parents who talk to their children have children with better language skills, and so on. Everyone concludes that to grow the best children, parents must be loving, authoritative, and talkative, and if children don't turn out well it must be the parents' fault. But the conclusions depend on the belief that children are blank slates."[13]

What are the implications of this thesis for parents with mentally ill children? Pinker says these notions have harmed the lives of real people: "The theory that parents can mold their children like clay has inflicted childrearing regimes on parents that are unnatural and sometimes cruel . . . and multiplied the anguish of parents whose children haven't turned out the way they had hoped."[14] Mental health practitioners may be the most rigid in their insistence that they can "reshape," "treat," or "counsel" children, reprogramming their "blank slate."

The blank slate doctrine "calls to mind the old-fashioned notions of born criminals and bad seeds, and it was blotted out by twentieth-century intellectuals, replaced with the belief that all wrong-doers are victims of poverty or bad parenting."[15]

REFRIGERATOR MOTHERS: A FORGOTTEN NOTION?

Infamous therapists of the past declared children mentally ill because of "refrigerator mothers" or "schizophrenogenic mothers," as they were known. From the late 1940s to the early 1970s, the concept of the "schizophrenogenic mother" was popular in psychiatric literature. Especially well known was Bruno Bettelheim's claim that autism was the direct result of mothers who were cold and rejecting, unable to "bond" with their child. It was only a short time ago that all mental health practitioners believed that the "double bind," a further elaboration of the schizophrenogenic mother concept, was surely the cause of schizophrenia. According to this theory, if a mother barked out a communication that had two meanings and repeated this style of communication, it would spark the underlying mental illness in the child.

Research later confirmed that the mother who could cause mental disorders such as autism or schizophrenia in her offspring did not exist. Such a blame-leveling concept, which had no basis in scientific fact, caused a great deal of harm.[16] This harm is poignantly filmed in one documentary on seven resilient women who refused to be crushed by this burden of blame.[17] The legacies of these early psychological theories still remain but are no longer so clearly identified.

In 1998, Allen Rubin and his colleagues published a study that sought to determine if students and practitioners had outdated views about family culpability and mental disorders.[18] Are the old days of blaming parents for their child's mental illness gone? These researchers noted that the current shift in better understanding of the biological causes of mental illness is important in shaping how we deliver services to families. In fact, research shows that when families are made to feel culpable for the mental disorders through psychotherapeutic treatment, they are not helped, and this factor may, in turn, exacerbate the child's illness.[19]

Current research-based practice focuses on what is termed "family psycho-education," which provides families with education about mental illness, outlines social support, and teaches skills in managing difficult behaviors. The approach is aptly described by McFarlane, who states, "Family members are not only blameless but in fact secondary victims of a biological illness, and are partners in treatment and rehabilitation—a group of lay collaborators with special knowledge of the patient."[20]

The Rubin study sought to compare this psycho-educational perspective with the current attitudes and understandings of students and practitioners. When asked if "getting families to understand how their family dynamics have helped cause their relative's severe mental illness should be an aim of therapy," 49 percent of students and practitioners indicated they agreed either slightly, moderately, or strongly with this practice. When asked whether "parental dysfunction is a primary cause of serious mental illness in children," 57 percent of students and practitioners agreed at one of the three levels. Finally, when asked if "family resistance to change is usually an important obstacle prolonging the illness of clients with a serious mental illness," 68 percent agreed at some level.

The conclusion? Mental health professionals have not made much progress in understanding the etiology and treatment of mental disorders. They do recognize that biological factors are important, yet they also believe that parents are culpable. Rather than alleviate the parents' sense of blame, their focus is more directed toward having parents recognize their own culpability as an aim of treatment. While the authors of this study struggled to explain this finding, my analysis of how we as a society understand these parents makes the explanation of how parents are held culpable easier to understand. Mental health professionals may need to take specific steps to help parents on an *ongoing* basis deflect what will likely come their way in terms of blame and culpability.

If I were to ask my students in a social work practice methods class what is the best predictor of a child's development of a serious mental illness such as schizophrenia, most would agree today that the major risk factor is heredity. However, what they say and how they will act toward parents, as we will see throughout this book, are two different things. But why this disconnect between knowledge and action? Pinker suggests the answer: The prevailing cultural belief that is deeply rooted says children are blank slates, that we can imprint serious problems on them.

Both Steven Pinker and Judith Harris (the author of *The Nurture Assumption*, which criticized the belief that parents are the most important factor in child development) have written massive volumes where they challenge such prevailing norms as blank slates and the notion that we can imprint serious problems on our children. They exclaim that children simply do not allow their personalities to be shaped by parents in any fashion—not by nagging, not by criticizing, and not even by serving as role models.[21] The evidence for such claims is straightforward: Children who grow up in the same home are no more alike in personality than children separated at birth, and adopted children (who are separated) grow up to be no more similar than strangers in spite of living in different environments.

Parents almost always react negatively to the blank slate theory. As one parent put it, "I hope to God this isn't true ... the thought that all this love that I'm pouring into him counts for nothing is too terrible to contemplate."[22] In his reassuring style, Pinker reminds us that sometimes the truth can help us revisit our hopes in a liberating way. The everyday implications of this thesis are difficult to grasp, but as Harris has noted, it is not about absolving parents of responsibility for their children's lives as many fear. In fact, the notion of adult parents complaining about how they were treated as children turns it all around—everyone needs to take responsibility for their own lives, not blame their parents. Perhaps the liberation is a loosening of the control so many parents are afraid to let go of. Parents can stay away an extra night without the kids or spend additional hours working without consigning children to poor outcomes and bad personalities. What these researchers would like parents to do is to be ethically responsible (this is their moral duty) and create good environments for the present. Harris sums up her view by exclaiming, "We may not hold their tomorrows in our hands, but we surely hold their todays."[23]

This new scientific information can help parents better understand that their child's mental illness is not their fault: Nature is imperfect and genetic factors are largely responsible for disease. In the past, and even today to some extent, many parents believe that they could have prevented their child's mental illness. The primary message from Pinker and Harris is simple: It matters how you treat your child, but you may not be able to change who that child is. Stop trying to change the child and start learning how to live with the child.

CHANGING VERSUS MANAGING

The significance of this perspective is that therapists and parents who subscribe to the blank slate theory will have a hard time accepting children with mental illness as they are. Their focus will be not on managing these children, but on the relentless pursuit of changing them. This endeavor may, understandably, be difficult to give up. But when well-meaning professionals bring this perception to bear on families, much is left out—in particular, help for the parents and the parent–child relationship. Professionals must become more aware that the parent needs to put the reality of a child's mental illness into a perspective and develop a sense of harmony in a chaotic day-to-day existence.

The mental health community has always been preoccupied with the notion that all "disorders" are treatable or fixable. Indeed, some disorders do respond well to treatment, but many, many others do not. In *What You Can Change and What You Can't*, author Martin Seligman outlines some of the different outcomes one can expect. For example, he suggests that phobias are treatable but indicates that schizophrenia, obsessive–compulsive disorder, and depression are only partially treatable. An important therapeutic implication looms over these observations: The attempt to rid patients of "bad feelings" is a misplaced effort.

The humane therapeutic approach to addressing sadness, aggressiveness, and anxiety is to help individuals live more comfortably with a range of controllability. Seligman puts it more bluntly, and attaches a label to this perspective: "dealing with it." While this label may sound harsh, ultimately the approach may just be more practical and helpful to parents. In fact, Seligman's current research on happiness suggests a beneficial direction for parents and mental health practitioners—namely, to focus on helping individuals function well when they are feeling bad. He describes his recent work, which places an emphasis on using one's "signature strengths" rather than trying to eliminate weaknesses, as a means to move closer to happiness.

Years ago, Talcott Parsons noted that the social expectation of being ill means surrendering oneself—or in this case, one's child—to the care of the medical community. The child, the family, must accept the verdict of the problem being reduced to a medical explanation. It is a critical moment that signifies a problem beyond oneself. At the same time, it also represents the medicalization of the difficulty.[24] This reduction is rarely questioned by parents, as it has obvious immediate benefits. As Frank says, "The colonization of experience was judged worth the cure, or the attempted cure" (p. 11). Yet, what happens is that when the disorder is recognized as chronic, not curable, the family wants greater individual understanding, a process Frank refers to as "reclaiming."

LABELING AND SOCIAL PERSPECTIVES

Many movie and book plots have shown how normal individuals have been labeled and treated as mentally ill. Once the initial diagnosis is established, everyone begins to see any behavior as less than normal. The classic study on "being sane in insane places" proved this point: Normal individuals were admitted to mental hospitals when they claimed they had "heard voices." Once admitted, the eight individuals in the study acted like themselves and did not complain about any psychiatric symptoms. Most of the patients were diagnosed with schizophrenia, however, and staff continued to perceive them as mentally ill despite their return to their normal behaviors. Eventually, they were discharged from a hospital with the conclusion of "schizophrenia in remission."[25] The author of this study commented: "Such labels by mental health professionals are as influential on the patient as they are on relatives and friends, and they should not surprise anyone but the diagnoses act on all of them as a self-fulfilling prophecy. Eventually the patient himself accepts the diagnosis, with all its surplus meaning and expectations, and behaves accordingly."[26]

Further documentation of the impact of labeling came in the form of a study that divided 25 psychiatrists into two groups and had them listen to an actor portraying a person of normal mental health. The experimental group was told the actor "was a very interesting man because he looked neurotic, but actually was quite psychotic"; the control group was told nothing. Sixty percent of the psychiatrists in the experimental group diagnosed the actor as having various psychoses, most often schizophrenia, while none of the psychiatrists in the control group did so.[27]

These studies suggest that professionals who are expected to be objective are mis-guided by labels and preconceived notions. The science of putting people into mental health categories is far from what you might expect. This ambiguity is, in part, why parents have revealed over and over how different psychiatrists have labeled their child differently. It doesn't mean that psychiatric categories aren't real—there is good evidence that they are. Rather, this lack of consistency emphasizes that the science of accurately assigning diagnosis is pretty dismal. Nonetheless, the significance of a diagnostic category is critical to the life course of the child.

How mental health professionals label children together, as part of the system, influences how we think of them.[28] As I talk with parents, it becomes clear that in their daily lives they interact with many people in the community with regard to their child. To act together, they have to cooperate; when cooperating, they share the label used to explain the child's behavior. When an incident occurs, the parent calls the therapist and explains it. The therapist acknowledges the child's mental state and suggests its influence. The police arrive and speak to the parents, who explain, "He's bipolar." The police haul him off for commitment to a hospital (sometimes a jail), and they explain the cause of the child's behavior as it relates to his illness. The shared definition of the problem takes into account the responses of others to the child's actions. The label doesn't cause the behavior. However, it is reasonable to assume that the repeated labeling makes it more difficult for the child and the parent to continue normal routines of everyday life; as a consequence, their own redefinition begins. Everyone begins to act together according to how they understand the child's behavior.

To fight back against labels, two pediatricians suggest that the use of anti-quated terms like "eccentric" or "quirky" is a better alternative than mental diagnoses. "Quirky" can be a way for parents to talk about their diagnosed child without fear of prejudice. As one parent of an autistic child says, "Whenever you mention your son has a mental disorder, people think he's retarded. He becomes undesirable, but 'quirky' gives a comfortable nickname to his diagnosis that people accept."[29]

UNDERSTANDING OCCURS IN A SOCIAL CONTEXT

When I teach my Foundation to Social Work course, I tell the class, "If a therapist calls a child a giraffe, everyone looks strangely at the therapist. If a therapist calls a child bipolar, everyone looks strangely at the child." It is important to understand that labeling, which indicates how we understand a problem, is influenced by social conditions. This point is not emphasized enough in our training of professionals.

A child's crisis provides a context to examine the labeling process, which has all too rarely been subjected to analysis. A crisis often isn't directly related to the child's mental illness. It isn't a hallucination or hearing voices or some other clear symptom of mental illness. It is "acting out" or aggressive behavior, extreme noncompliance, an emotional outburst of uncontained feelings. The crisis, while perhaps preceded by some facet of the child's mental illness, boils down to

unexpected behavior problems not unlike a child's uncontrollable temper tan-
trum. At some level, these behaviors can be developmentally "normal" although
they might be at the extreme level.

For example, three weeks ago my 16-year-old son became consumed with
emotion, was feeling very angry, and smashed a wine glass on the floor. He has
no signs of a mental illness and rarely displays behavior problems of any kind.
We have not labeled him anything, except to say that he is a normal adolescent.
The point is that after a label is attached to a child, the child's behavior—all
behavior—is viewed from within the context and meaning of the label. The
implication for mentally ill children is that all the behaviors and actions that
are "difficult" cannot be understood as normal or developmental, but rather are
understood only as a part of the child's mental illness. Because of how we collectively perceive the child, assessing a child's progress becomes extremely difficult.
I don't mean to suggest that most of the behavior problems that mentally ill children display are not real or not part of the mental illness. The difficulty arises
from the fact that there is now no way to separate any behavior problem from
the illness. As this parent explains, it is often difficult to separate what is the
mental illness and what is a developmental difficulty due to circumstances:

> When we finally sought help, a therapist worked with him on his anger manage-
> ment. At the time we had separated and his behavior got worse. But rather than
> understanding the developmental sequence that emerged, the therapist thought all
> the behavior problems were due to the separation and that his aggression was sim-
> ply due to this. That led me to be even more confused. But often things happen
> like families divorcing and therapists misread this, assuming the events are what
> is most significant rather than understanding the child has a mental disorder that
> is aggravated by a series of difficult events.

Now let's turn this analysis to the parents themselves. How are parents of mentally ill children labeled by others? Are they seen as "problematic," "disturbed," or
"deviant"? In the same manner, how mental health professionals label parents
together as part of a system influences how we think of them. This analysis is more
difficult because parents don't get overtly labeled, but the covert processes that
take place are likely to shape future interactions with parents. Here we might look
to case files and descriptions of how parents are characterized. The files or descriptions are collectively acted on by mental health professionals, as the therapist com-
municates with the psychiatrist, the school officials, and others involved in the
child's care. One hopes that professionals reading this book will see the enormous
but sometimes subtle influence they have while attempting to help parents.

DEVELOPING AN IDENTITY

Parents of mentally ill children eventually reach a point where they reexamine
themselves or their identity as a parent. How do parents come to recognize themselves not as parents of a child but as parents of a mentally ill child? They

develop a new vocabulary of motives.[30] Parents move into a new, albeit isolated, realm of how they respond to others. This new self emerges in response to those who increasingly interact with parents about their mentally ill child. Having taken action to obtain professional help for their child, the parents have started a process of redefinition for both themselves and their child.

Every parent with a mentally ill child feels compelled to explain how the mental illness happened, and in every conversation parents wrestle with what their role might have been in contributing to the child's condition. Most mentally ill adults explain their condition by recognizing a biological basis for their mental illness.[31] For children, the line to biology is not as easily drawn.

Accepting that a loved child is mentally ill is difficult to assimilate into one's worldview and into one's family. It doesn't seem possible. How can she be a danger to herself? It's not fair. God wouldn't do that to us. We've done nothing wrong to deserve this. We read about this in newspapers, but it doesn't happen to us. Parents go through stages: shock, disbelief, bargaining with God, anger, depression, acceptance. But these stages are not necessarily encountered in any order, and it can take months and even years to finally accept that your family has a mentally ill child. When that acceptance finally comes, your family adopts a new normal, and your identity includes mental illness. As David Karp points out, "Diagnosis is a pivotal moment in the lives of both patients and caregivers because both then typically embrace a medical version of what is wrong."[32]

> I just couldn't believe there was a name for it. That was when I first heard of it. That began our journey. And it's hard when you get diagnosed, because all of a sudden you have a label. I now see that as just a part of who we are.

DIAGNOSIS AND THE MEDICALIZATION OF CHILDHOOD

The large number of children now diagnosed with mental illness may represent the "medicalization" of childhood. This high prevalence may result, in large part, from the psychiatric and medical establishment defining what is and is not a psychiatric illness in childhood.[33] This thesis was put forth by Peter Conrad, who argues that deviant behavior in children has been "medicalized" by labeling it ADHD and assigning a medical drug for its control.[34] From this perspective, certain behaviors in children have become defined as medical problems, and medication has become the major agent for exercising social control over the behavior. This is not to say that children don't suffer from clear psychiatric illnesses—they do.

A devastating critique of the *Diagnostic and Statistical Manual of Mental Disorders* is Herb Kutchins and Stuart Krik's book, *Making Us Crazy: The DSM Bible and the Creation of Mental Disorders*.[35] In this book the authors argue that the *DSM* is mainly a tool intended for the insurance industry, noting how every illness comes with its own diagnostic code that is used on insurance claim forms. Their book provides good evidence to suggest that the *DSM* is not based on science and does not hold up when science is applied to its categories of diagnosis. It also provides a warning for society: Anyone with objectionable views or behaviors that deviate from social norms is "crazy."

What's important to understand is that the increased diagnosis of children's mental health problems is coupled with an aggressive pharmaceutical industry and parents as well as society are struggling to figure out what is normal, what isn't, and what should be seriously treated as a psychiatric disorder. Are we as a society reducing our capacity to tolerate "difficult" children? Are we being encouraged to frame difficulties as psychiatric issues, thereby changing the social and cultural expectations of "normal" childhood behavior? When G. Stanley Hall wrote about adolescence in the early 1900s, he identified three common aspects of development: conflict with parents, mood disruptions, and risky behavior. While we now believe these aren't *universal* experiences, they do represent what many young people experience.[36] Would these youth of the late 1900s be classified as having mental disorders? As Hall noted, adolescence is the "age of rapid fluctuation of moods . . . with extremes of both elation and depressed mood."[37] We have lost the edge of understanding what does and does not count as a serious mental disorder with children, and this fuzziness has only made the situation for parents more difficult.

Parents sense this loss of understanding, as the media have increasingly portrayed the misguided interests of the pharmaceutical industry that preys on "difficult" children. What parent in America doesn't believe that ADHD is overdiagnosed? In the end, the medicalization process doesn't help parents get a handle on whether their child does, in fact, have a "real" diagnosis. The future for increased understanding looks grim with the mass marketing of drugs and the decreased tolerance of the community for anything less than "normal" behaviors.[38]

When children are given a diagnosis, it is based on the American Psychiatric Association's official diagnostic handbook, *Diagnostic and Statistical Manual of Mental Disorders*. The fifth edition of the DSM is due out in 2012. One of the topics of much discussion is the controversial diagnosis of childhood bipolar disorder. This diagnosis has seen a steep increase in recent times—a 40-fold increase in less than 10 years.[39] The controversy over this diagnosis is a reminder of how the diagnostic system functions. Illnesses are now put in categories based on symptoms—which is a lot better than the system used in the first edition of the DSM, which was based on a now discredited psychodynamic perspective.

A diagnosis exists if the symptoms match the criteria outlined in the manual. That leaves room for assessing the reliability of the diagnosis. Many studies find very low agreement between two people categorizing the same symptoms. The diagnostic field still suffers from a lack of understanding on what causes the symptoms. All of this is to say the diagnostic system is severely lacking.

Consider the issue of multiple diagnoses. Many children probably do have co-occurring psychiatric disorders, and many children are labeled with two or three disorders because the system is imprecise. For example, many children are thought to have both depression and anxiety. Do they really have both conditions, or is the problem made up of a combination of these things that represents something else?

The following parent's story presents a good example of how confusing obtaining a clear diagnosis can be:

> "It's ADHD," and I said, "What the heck is that?" So you go through the steps. He started school, and we started him on meds, and we put him on Ritalin, only he had hallucinations with Ritalin. We went on from there, and he was the youngest child ever to be admitted to the hospital at the time. Because he would freak out and go running up and down the streets. He was five years old the first time he got hospitalized. Then I started my research. ADHD does not say your child can run around and try to stab you with a knife. That's not typical. Then we went to another doctor who diagnosed him with ADHD, oppositional defiant disorder, parent–child conflict. They also gave him sexual identity crisis. He had seven diagnoses.

As I talked with parents, it was exceedingly apparent that children were misdiagnosed, overdiagnosed, underdiagnosed, and that most of the diagnoses changed with every new psychiatrist. It is worth noting that many professionals attempt to link the diagnosis and treatment. If a child is responding to a medication for ADHD or depression, then the conclusion is that he or she had that diagnosis. However, the medications are not precise. Antidepressants are used to treat depression, panic disorder, obsessive–compulsive disorder, eating disorders, and phobias.[40] That is why understanding the symptoms may be more important than the diagnosis.

CHAPTER 3

The Burden of Love: An Everyday Reality for Parents

I've spent my life wondering why Cole was born to me, how much was my fault, how much we just are who we are even before we come into this world. I hoped if I held up moments to the light, studied them like sparkling diamonds, sharp to cut glass, stars in a boy's eyes, I'd know why—something that ought to shine darkens to black.

—E. Clark, *Biting the Stars*

The most difficult thing about writing this book was listening to the stories that parents told me. As a researcher, I'm accustomed to taking notes and conducting interviews. But from my very first interview with a parent, I left dumb-stricken after listening for upward of two hours. Parents were describing pain, frustration, blame, guilt, and suffering. In every interview I conducted, I heard the suffering. And it was no secret. In every encounter except one, parents retelling their life experiences broke down in tears. Some cried a lot, some shed only a few tears, some worked hard to fight back tears—but what I saw was the tremendous burden they all experience. In many ways these parents are exceptionally tuned in to the love they have for their children. Yet, because these ill children are more vulnerable than "normal" kids, the burden of parenting is an everyday reality for them: a burden of love.

These parents accept the challenge of caretaking and learn to adapt to the burden that is an everyday occurrence. As the very first parent I interviewed, Christina, told me:

Being a parent of a child with a mental illness or behavioral health challenge, or whatever we're going to call it, is a full-time 24/7 job, no pay, very little gratitude or kudos. You don't get any vacation time. But it's also not a choice that you've made . . . it is the roll of the dice.

Other parents were aware of the burden they faced and their struggle. Here is how several of them dealt with it:

I started off with the best intentions, and it was very upsetting, and I couldn't deal with it for a while. But he only has me, so I had to do what I had to do. Feeling sorry for myself wasn't going to help him. It's been rough. I have to study. There are days when I get no sleep. It's rough, because he takes a lot of my time, and I have to have something for school and passing tests. Sometimes it's hard. Many times I thought I was going to have a nervous breakdown. We try to be strong, and I try to have patience. I ask God every day for patience. Some days, I don't have patience and I yell at him a lot. We just try to make the best of it. This is my son. This is what I have. I wouldn't trade him for anything in the world. I think he has a good future. It won't be easy.

I'm still not the best [parent]. But if I have to correct him in everything, no matter what he asks, it would be, "No. Stop. Don't. You can't." You can't live like that. I know there are things I could do better, and I will. We didn't get where we're at overnight, and it's going to take more than overnight to change it. With him, it's got to be gradual, not sudden.

I've had a lot of counseling. The counseling that I get personally for myself, she still tells me to this day, it's your daughter. Your daughter seems to be causing the issues and problems that you're having. Well, what am I supposed to do, dump my child? That's the only thing I cannot do. So what do you suggest?

It's really hard, because sometimes you get so mad. The frustration level is very high. It feels sometimes like you don't exist, because all the energy that you have is going toward them, so you don't have any left for yourself.

FAMILY BURDEN: WHAT WE KNOW

A fair amount of evidence suggests that the parents and caregivers of children with mental illness tend to experience significant levels of continuous or chronic strain and stress.[1] In the broadest terms, these experiences of strain have been discussed in relation to family burden. Burden is commonly defined as the negative consequences to families related to their caregiving roles.[2] Researchers who have investigated the family experience of mental illness have found strong and consistent support for the presence of family burden. In fact, such findings are so common that the concept of burden has come to define the family experience of mental illness.[3]

While the literature that addresses this concept has a long history,[4] it was not until 1982 that researchers first found it meaningful to distinguish between objective and subjective family burden.[5] *Objective burden* refers to tangible stressors related to the care of persons with mental illness, such as financial hardships, limitations on social life, and difficulties in the coordination of services. *Subjective burden* refers to the extent to which the presence of the person with mental illness, his or her behavior, and his or her dependency are perceived by family members as constituting sources of worry and strain on the family.[6] While the concept of family burden is a familiar one, this division into objective and subjective burden allows us to further understand and relate to the specific stressors associated with caring for a loved one with a mental illness.

While a considerable amount of research has documented the burden associated with the provision of care to an adult relative who is suffering from a chronic mental illness, much less attention has been paid to those who are caring for children and adolescents with a mental illness. Thus it is worthwhile to review some of the key elements of the literature on adult family burden, as many of the issues that arise for adult caregivers are easily translated to those who are actively raising children with a mental illness. The following discussion regarding the adult family burden will serve as a backdrop for a more focused discussion of the burden experienced by parents and caregivers of children with a mental illness.

One of the more frequently quoted experts on family burden in relation to mental illness, Harriet Lefley, describes family caregivers as "a stressed and potentially at-risk population whose quantitative problems may equal or even outweigh those of the persons around whom they revolve."[7] In other words, having a relative with a mental illness is associated with increased risk for psychological distress among family members.[8] Lefley identifies three basic sources of family burden: situational stress arising from daily interactions with the mentally ill individual; societal stress arising from negative attitudes and lack of support; and iatrogenic stress (iatrogenic illnesses or symptoms are those caused by medical providers) arising from inadequate or misinformed service providers. Clearly, the concept of family burden is a complex and multifaceted one, any one segment of which could potentially cause a great deal of strain, let alone several of the components combined.

Psychologist Herbert Gravitz argues that five core factors bind families to the despair of their loved one's illness.[9] The first of these is *stress*, which Gravitz suggests serves as the foundation of the family experience of mental illness, in part due to the ongoing fear, dread, and worry that the negative symptoms of the illness could strike at any time, forcing the family to "walk on eggshells." The second factor that he cites is *trauma* (an emotional or psychological injury), which Gravitz argues is at the core of the family's experience and can "erode members' beliefs about control, safety, meaning, and their own value."[10] The third factor is *loss*, which encompasses such areas as one's personal, social, spiritual, and economic lives. Consistent with loss is the fourth factor, which Gravitz identifies as *grief*. He argues that those who care for someone with a mental illness often grieve the loss of a life that will not be as expected. The fifth and final factor is *exhaustion*, which is defined as the natural result of living in an atmosphere that is fraught with stress, trauma, loss, and grief. Given the great variation in the severity of mental illnesses, not every family will necessarily experience all of these factors concurrently. Nevertheless, Gravitz argues that all families will be touched at some point by each of these factors, and that adjusting to such adversity is a significant task with which families must cope every day as they try to make sense of their own lives.

Frank Karp wrote an engaging book on family burden, titled *The Burden of Sympathy: How Families Cope with Mental Illness*.[11] This ethnography of families examines what it is like for families to be caretakers of mentally ill family members. Karp's main concern is with the obligation family members feel toward their mentally ill relative(s) and how these family members cope with fulfilling their obligations toward the ill person(s) while trying to live their own lives. His book relies on two guiding questions: What are our limits in caring for another person? What are the boundaries of sympathy that people confront in their quest not to be consumed by the day-to-day suffering of a loved one? Karp captures the essence of caregiving and its struggles, and imparts a sociological perspective to help us understand caregiving and burden. His book is primarily about caring for adult family members, where the limits and boundaries are relevant. In contrast, parents of mentally ill children cannot yet ask these questions, because they feel bound to provide and care for their children. Later in life, the ongoing burden with their adult children will lead them to these questions.

FAMILY BURDEN: ISSUES FOR PARENTS

Although in general little attention has been given to the experiences of parents who are actively raising children with mental illness, the concept of grief—one of Gravitz's primary factors of burden—has received some recognition in the literature. Marsh and Lefley state that "at the core of the subjective burden is a powerful grieving process."[12] Family members may mourn for the relative they knew and loved before the onset of the illness, for the anguish of their family, and for their own losses. This grief is accompanied by strong sentiments of sorrow and empathic pain as the family as a whole goes through their own grieving process over hopes and expectations that have not come to fruition.

Peggy MacGregor, in a poignant paper that appeared in the professional journal *Social Work*, entitled "Grief: The Unrecognized Parental Response to Mental Illness in a Child," echoes the need to address grief and loss issues as part of family burden.[13] She explains that for parents, countless forms of both internal and external grief and loss exist, such as loss of self-esteem and sense of competence as a parent; loss of control; loss of pleasure in a child's success; loss of hope; loss of security and certainty; loss of religious faith; loss of a positive sense of the past life of the family; loss of privacy; loss of social network; loss of financial resources; loss of freedom for caregivers; and loss of faith in mental health professionals and the health care system. While this is just a preliminary list of the many forms of loss that parents of children with a mental illness experience, it serves to summarize the gravity of the situation that many caregivers must face.

MacGregor is not content with just identifying the various forms of loss that parents experience, but instead goes on to question why these issues have not been systematically addressed by both researchers and practicing professionals. She asks a challenging question: Why is it that the discipline of social work—whose major focus is feelings, thoughts, and relationships—has nothing to say to parents about grief and loss? She explains that after her own experience with a mentally ill child, she found that "most of the psychiatric world does not acknowledge family grief and is not really prepared to deal with mental illness as an honest family tragedy."[14]

MacGregor argues that this professional lack of acknowledgment is mirrored in the greater society as well. She explains that affected families have joined an "underclass of grievers" who are disenfranchised by society from the normal grieving process because their loss is not "openly acknowledged, publicly mourned, or socially supported."[15] MacGregor concludes that such "grief occurs because society does not recognize and validate the existence or importance of the relationship, the loss, or the griever."[16] While this type of subjective burden is not always immediately apparent, nor does it receive much attention in the literature, its underlying existence can have a profound effect on the public and private parenting experience for many individuals who care for children with a mental illness. Hence, it appears that many parents would greatly benefit from some form of acknowledgment and validation of their loss, so that they can begin to come to terms with the reality of their situation.

UNCERTAIN GRIEF

In my interviews with parents, I found an experience of what I label *uncertain grief* that appears to gnaw at parents over time. My review of literature on children with mental illness did not turn up any discussion of this concept, which is not surprising given that parents are rarely considered a central part of the therapeutic process and, in fact, are too often ignored during their child's "treatment."

The difficult aspect of uncertain grief is that it is *uncertain*. In other words, it is unclear to the parents why or how they may be experiencing it. I don't think a single parent whom I interviewed described being helped because someone recognized there was an underlying grief to their existence, something not being addressed, and helped them with it. Yet I repeatedly heard remarks about the experience of uncertain grief in their stories. The uncertainty arises because the parent knows the child and loves the child just the way the child is, but still feels something is missing, both for the parent and for the child. Without labeling and understanding this phenomenon, parents may not know it is there, and that it is something for which help might be available. Instead, such parents grapple with a profound but unidentified sense of grief—and the unidentified aspect makes it impossible to understand. How can they recognize and address the grief if it is not understood?

The following parents searched deep within themselves to reveal some of their more difficult feelings and the underlying uncertain grief they have experienced:

> It's hard as a parent. You're real torn. Most of her life I thought, "I love her; she's my child," but she's so difficult that I don't want to deal with it sometimes. That's a hard thing to admit. But it's okay to know that. Sometimes I can't and don't want to deal with her.

So was I wrong in keeping him? Was I right in keeping him? Am I responsible for him? He probably knows about my guilt and pushes my buttons. I have no doubt. Because he's so lonely and so desperate, so hopeless. And I don't have any answers, and I feel bad. . . . And there's nobody to talk to about it, really. I keep getting, "But you're doing the best you can, you're . . ." The doctor said at the last visit I should be up for sainthood. I'm the strongest mother he knows. Yeah, that's nice. You know, I don't have a choice. I'm not giving up on him, but there's no one to help me with the agony. That's why I don't know who you [the interviewer] are, or what you're doing, but somebody had to hear. I cry at night. I worry every day. I probably overindulge, because I feel so bad there's no way to make him well. He doesn't connect with people. He's difficult. He lives in a world of fear you and I will never know.

With so many parents I heard the desperation in their voices, the gnawing uncertainty they were experiencing. One mother stated it this way:

Words cannot describe what it's like. [These kids] die but they never get buried. Then they come back for a while, but you lose them again. And you think, "I can't go through this again."

A similar process was identified by Pauline Boss when she sought to understand how people cope with a loss that has no physical presence,[17] such as the loss people experience with missing soldiers or kidnapped children. This kind of loss is also experienced by those dealing with psychological loss like Alzheimer's disease. As she notes, "An ambiguous loss may never allow people to achieve the detachment that is necessary for normal closure. Just as ambiguity complicates loss, it complicates the mourning process. People can't start grieving because the situation is indeterminate. It feels like a loss but it is not really one."[18] Parents of mentally ill children don't experience physical loss, as with death, but many of them do experience the similar process of uncertain grief. Their child is present, and he or she is still the same child they have loved all along, yet these parents must come to terms with the fact that the child has changed in a way that is substantially different from what should be the normal course of development.

Acknowledging and understanding that the child has changed represents a good step toward addressing uncertain grief. If parents recognize that a significant change is happening to their family, they can shift from the crisis of their everyday life to a focus on managing the change and beginning a new process of coping with the changes. The process of coping and even finding strength from caring is addressed in later chapters of this book.

THE BURDEN OF BLAME

Another common theme that emerges from the family burden literature is the experience of stigma and blame that many parents and families must cope with as a result of caring for an individual with a mental illness. Many parents, and especially mothers, feel judged by both the clinicians who work with their children and the larger social system. In her article "Motherhood, Resistance, and Attention Deficit Disorder: Strategies and Limits," Claudia Malacrida reports the results of her interviews with 34 women whose children were diagnosed with ADHD. According to Malacrida, "Mothers in this study were acutely aware that they were judged as lacking or worse when their children began to encounter problems."[19] She articulates many parents' experiences when she states that "Women who pressed too hard to achieve a diagnosis, or who insisted that there was something that their children needed in order to achieve their full potential, were named by teachers, psychiatrists, psychologists, and physicians as over-protective, over-achieving, or simply in denial of their children's true limits."[20]

As Malacrida reports, women who were reluctant to have yet another assessment or therapy session, or who were loathe to medicate their children, were accused of being negligent or in denial of their children's difficulties. They constantly encountered questions from family members, friends, and professionals about their disciplinary practices, their parenting skills, and their personal lives. These women were told by professionals, friends, and family members that their marriages, their employment, their frequent changes of residence, their divorces, their other children, and even (in the case of a child whose language problems were seen as the root of his behaviors) their foreignness were "really" the cause of their children's problems.

The study by Malacrida focused on women—and my study, too, primarily involved women. It would be remiss to ignore the issues of gender and caretaking because they are intertwined. Strong feelings of obligation and assumption of the caretaker role are not evenly divided between men and women.[21] Women are seen by men, society, and themselves as primarily responsible for caring when a family member becomes ill, whether from a physical disease or a mental illness. As the quotes in this book clearly show, it is the women who express feelings that it is their responsibility, their role, and their obligation to provide most of the caretaking. There are a few exceptions, of course, and perhaps society is moving slowly toward a more equal distribution of roles. Nevertheless, as most women know only too well, they are socialized to be caretakers, and their families expect them to be caretakers when the need arises. After all, women are often more in tune with feelings than men, and can feel an obligation to monitor other people's feeling states to ensure their emotional well-being. The work of being a mother is taking care of her child.

Gradually, the accounts and testimonies of male caretakers are making it into the professional literature, but so far these voices are relatively few. While I have not done enough interviews with men to make a comparison, it is likely that this chapter would be very different if I had interviewed only men. They would probably not experience blame at the same level, be more devoid of guilt, and be less burdened by the entire experience. I do not mean to suggest they would not suffer in this situation—just that would more likely be a different kind of suffering.

Whether male or female, all caretakers seem to suffer from the burden of blame. Jeri Baker, in her essay "The Heroine's Odyssey," which draws from her series of interviews with mothers of emotionally disturbed children,[22] states:

In addition to frustrations arising from the separation of services, parents suffered personal pain from the effects of a long-standing belief among both professionals and the general public that parents were to blame for children's emotional and behavioral problems. These beliefs created an additional burden of guilt and often meant enduring accusations that were hard to refute and treatment interventions aimed at correcting parents.[23]

In our society, when a person or group of individuals is stigmatized because of their struggles with mental illness, we are often quick to assign blame for their behaviors and struggles. Such assignment of blame is often aimed at the individual with mental illness, in the sense that society perceives he or she should be able to "fix" the problem. However, this appears to be less true when the person with mental illness is a child or adolescent. In those cases we are more likely to hold the parents of these children responsible, thereby further stigmatizing not only the child but also the parents and other family members. It is within this cyclical interaction of stigma and blame that many of the parents interviewed for this study constantly found themselves trapped within.

In Malacrida's and Baker's studies, as well as in my own research, many of the parents of mentally ill children expressed not only a sense of feeling blamed, but also a translation of this sensation into significant feelings of guilt. While some parents in my study explained that some feelings of guilt were inevitable, what is particularly concerning are the reports that such baseline levels of guilt were often elevated by the blaming behaviors of professionals and laypersons. It appears, then, that blaming parents for their child's behaviors has a variety of negative consequences.

As I talked with parents, the sense of blame they experienced was easy to identify, along with undertones of anger:

My husband will not go to any meetings for his children. He's had it. He's tired of being called an alcoholic. He hasn't drank in 13 years. He's tired of feeling as if he's an inadequate parent. He's tired of [treatments for which] no matter what you say to the doctor—"It makes my kid nauseous"—they say then, "Give them a bag to throw up in," and give them the same meds. The apathy for parents is sometimes [unbearable;] it truly comes from outside.

How many times can you be told you're stupid, in how many different ways? When we tell our children they're stupid, it's abuse. But all of this [outsiders' comments] sounds like, "You're inadequate. You're stupid. You're no good. You shouldn't have been a parent in the first place." And then [there is] your own guilt that you may be carrying around. So it doesn't give parents a whole lot of desire [to seek help]. [Parents face the prospective of] blame from the system and then your own self, your own inability to cope.

What I feel like they were afraid of, as soon as you say the word "schizophrenia," is "Wow, he's going to come in and kill us all." He's different. He's an odd duck, and it's hard to mix him in. He's also very bright, and they just didn't want

anything to do with it. They heard "schizophrenia," and they went forget it. . . .
You could feel it.

I'm saying to myself: What's wrong? What mistakes am I making again?
Everywhere I went, it's what I was doing wrong, but I'm like . . . if I were really
screwing up, why am I coming for help? It's like, "Blame me, but blame me for
getting help." It was really a difficult situation for many, many years up until last
year. My fault. Okay. Well, I got all the fault.

In her article entitled "Family Burden and Family Stigma in Major Mental Illness," Harriet Lefley notes that "the professional community and the society that reflects its values have given [parents] a message of their own culpability in generating or precipitating the devastating illness of a loved one."[24] Lefley describes how parents try to determine how, when, why, and under which conditions their behaviors could have led to their loved one's illness, thereby further exacerbating their feelings of personal guilt.

Peggy MacGregor, who has a child with a mental illness, offers a first-hand perspective of the parents' dilemma when she states that "the mental health professionals that we spoke with volunteered very little, while at the very worst time in our life I knew our family was being observed for pathology."[25] "Over time I experienced their silence as deliberate, a conscious refusal to offer information, consolation, and validation because I didn't deserve it."[26] Lefley echoes these sentiments when she describes the mental health risks of an overburdened caregiver who is "suffering from the pain of her child's illness, the stigmatization of having 'caused' it, and the burden of overseeing a treatment plan that may be unrealistic in terms of time, energy, and money and demands from the rest of the family. At the same time, she is trying to balance conflicting advice from professionals."[27]

The majority of those parents whom I interviewed reported asking themselves at one point or another, "What am I doing wrong?" When one considers how such thoughts are often reinforced by professional and lay opinions, it is easy to see how these parents could find themselves in the midst of a "Kafka-esque nightmare" as Lefley describes. Much as Peggy MacGregor felt that as a parent of a mentally ill child she was being "observed for pathology," many of the parents I interviewed expressed similar concerns.

The data on subjects' experiences of feeling blamed by family members give tentative support to Rubin et al.'s concept of a "spiral of blame," in which family members become more critical and over-involved in caring for the child in part due to their own feelings of culpability and responsibility for the child's mental health struggles.[28] The spiral of blame occurs when "the treatment intensifies the guilt and sense of blame felt by the family, which in turn increases family members' anxiety and preoccupation with their relative's problems. Increased anxiety and preoccupation are likely to intensify the level of expressed emotion in the family and the level of criticism and over-involvement by family members who, feeling blamed for causing the disorder, are less able to be supportive and philosophical in the face of its long-term persistence."[29]

For example, a number of the parents interviewed for the present study reported being blamed and criticized by their own parents, and particularly by their mothers, regarding their ability to raise a healthy child. One might speculate that the grandparents' entrapment in this spiral of blame may be due, at least in part, to their own feelings of guilt and responsibility and their inability to correct some of their own parenting mistakes.

It appears that not only do many families feel blamed by the practitioners who are supposed to help them, but the loved ones they care for may actually experience an increase in negative symptoms as a result of that blame, thereby leading to the development of a negative cycle. Much of the literature points to the fact that assignment of culpability and blaming of parents and caregivers by professionals and society often go hand in hand with an increased sense of isolation and loneliness for many caregivers. While a more detailed investigation of this theory is beyond the scope of this book, this subject area certainly warrants further study and investigation.

One family whom I interviewed described their dilemma of never knowing to whom they could disclose information about their daughter's disorder. Like many parents, they had the experience of professionals and school personnel initially not believing any of their descriptions of what Jenny was like. Even though she was in treatment at a special education school and received after-care treatment from a local hospital, the staff did not encounter the same level of difficulty experienced by the parents. This dichotomy can be fairly typical: The child may work hard during the day to function as best as he or she can, but then "let go" upon arriving at home. These kinds of behaviors on Jenny's part make it difficult for her parents to feel comfortable sharing information about her mental illness with others. They fear others will not believe them or, at the least, will not understand the seriousness of her disorder. In this way the experience becomes quite insular for the family, who receive little support from the outside. As I listened to Jenny's parents describe this issue, I could sense their level of frustration—"People should know what we and Jenny are dealing with"—while at the same time they fear being labeled as not being strict enough or not parenting their daughter properly.

In 2006, *The New York Times* ran a series of articles on "troubled children" that addressed many of the issues parents face with childhood mental illness.[30] After the article was published, 122 comments about it were posted at the *Times* website. I read all 122 responses, and they gave a clear sense of how many people react to the problems of parenting mentally ill children. Most disturbing is that many readers still wanted to point a finger at the parents as key causal agents in the illness: "Missing from the [*New York Times* "Troubled Children"] article is a consideration that emotional and behavioral upset in children may be a manifestation of normal reactions to difficult family and environmental situations. It is very convenient for the community of child psychiatrists, as well as for a subset of parents, to locate the source of the child's difficulties within the child in the form of biologically induced mental illness. Perhaps the reason that psychiatric diagnoses don't 'stick' in children is that children's problems are part and parcel of their larger environment."

Another reader also saw parenting as the primary cause: "Isn't it possible that many of the behaviors are due to years of enabling the behaviors and lack of firm and consistent discipline? Many parents are afraid to discipline their children and end up with out-of-control young adults." Still another reader exclaimed: "Has anybody looked at the dynamics of these kids' families? It is a truism that bad parenting and dysfunctional family dynamics do affect a child's self-esteem and emotional development. So why do we have to find a label and medicate every time a child exhibits some troubling behavior? Rather than observing the child alone, perhaps a psychiatrist should be required to spend a week at the child's home observing how a troubled child is spoken to, listened to, comforted, disciplined, validated, and loved. The psychiatrist might walk away with the understanding that a child's 'mental illness' is a brilliant coping mechanism."

Unfortunately, the tendency for many people to ascribe mental illness to "bad parenting" is unlikely to go away soon. As discussed earlier, Pinker's notion of the "blank slate" is appropriately subtitled "the modern denial of human nature." Many people strongly believe that parents "imprint" behavioral problems and mental illness on the child's blank slate, even though research suggests that children's major mental illnesses are more likely to be rooted in behavioral genetics. Although poverty, child abuse, and a cruel environment may play a role in these conditions, they likely play a much lesser role than most people realize.

When I hear the arguments about parents creating their children's behavior problems, I am always struck by how little discussion centers on how many children in the worst of situations end up without difficulties. The existence of these "resilient" children suggests that even under dire environmental circumstances some children can emerge as competent and happy adults. I'll never forget one college student who did some part-time work for me when she entered college as a freshman. She was very competent and bright, and we worked together for a number of years. As I got to know her, she shared her personal story of growing up. Her father was an alcoholic who could not keep a full-time job and her mother was a heroin addict. She left home during her senior year of high school to live with another family. Amazingly, she said, her family didn't even notice she was gone—that was the level of dysfunction. Yet this woman was as "put together" as any student I have ever known. And now, after knowing her for a dozen years, I can report that she never varied from her well-formed goals and functional lifestyle. Recently she graduated from law school and is involved with a wonderful man and ready to start a family.

BLAME AND SERVICE PROVIDERS: WHY PARENTS OFTEN FAIL TO GET THE SERVICES THEY NEED

As many reports have documented, there is a growing concern in the field of child and adolescent mental health about the lack of service utilization by children and adolescents with mental health needs.[31] Similarly, the dropout rate for those in mental health treatment programs is surprisingly high. According to the U.S. Surgeon General, one of the main causes of the low frequency of service utilization by children with mental illness is the amount of stigma and blame that they and their families often experience. Such stigma and blame may cause families to shy away from environments where they will feel further blame and opprobrium, such as a mental health agency or clinic. Similarly, the high treatment dropout rate might be partly explained by these same experiences of blame and the subsequent guilt that is experienced.

A number of the parents who were interviewed for this study related how they often jumped from agency to agency seeking a respectful relationship with a mental health provider. In some cases, this constant shifting and relationship building further contributed to the parents' feelings of exhaustion and their being overwhelmed by the greater system. A few parents reported that they terminated their child's treatment altogether because of their feeling of being constantly blamed by professionals, and because of the lack of consistent treatment for their child. These stories resonate with Allan Kazdin's statements regarding the influence that parents have over the amount and type of treatment that mentally ill children receive.[32] As I spoke to parents, it was clear that they had also experienced enough blame and guilt to sometimes limit their involvement with the mental health system. The problem is likely more widespread, because it is the parents with whom I *didn't* talk—those most hidden from the mental health system—who are of most concern. It should be an axiom that the importance of parents' perceptions regarding their child's mental health treatment cannot be overemphasized.

The final connection that resonated with me as I read literature on this issue and conducted interviews with parents pertains to the issue of blame, especially the link between stigma and blame and an increase in social isolation and withdrawal. Validating what other authors have asserted,[33] many of the parents whom I interviewed attributed much of their social isolation to the level of blame and stigma that they experienced. This perception of blame can negatively impact parents and families in countless ways, inhibiting some parents from seeking out new relationships or even going out to a restaurant as a family.

The professional literature has reflected a growing awareness regarding the treatment of parents by professionals; this issue was mentioned in the Surgeon General's report on children's mental health as being a part of a larger problem that currently requires reform. The report called for a need to "understand the reasons for underutilization and compliance," and noted that "stigma is an important factor. Parents are fearful about bringing the social and emotional difficulties of their children to the attention of medical professionals, perhaps afraid they may be blamed."[34] While many theories have been proposed regarding parents' failure to fully use mental health services, much of the problem boils down to parents not feeling respected. If parents cannot develop trust and a respectful relationship with a professional, they will not be motivated to continue treatment. Further, parents too often receive "help" that is poorly conceptualized— they are, after all, looking to obtain practical information they can use. Many parents may also leave the system knowing that there are no real alternatives, no levels of service, no assistance beyond the basic counseling. As Senora

Simpson, a family member at the Surgeon General's conference, notes: "Real parent involvement, and attention to family satisfaction, family practice, and quality of life are left to chance."[35]

One other reason for parents' failure to take advantage of mental health services is the totality of the overwhelming experience of caring for a child with a mental illness. Delaney and Engels-Scianna explain that, in addition to the everyday burden of caring for a child with a mental illness, the parents interviewed for their study faced the challenge of consolidating a huge volume of information and opinion.[36] Often they tried to integrate professionals' opinions, relatives' perspectives, and the school's input, all of which might offer different recommendations for how to handle the problem. Parents were frustrated that often none of these recommendations incorporated any complete explanations or led to any real solutions. It also was difficult to integrate professionals' opinions when they differed from parents' experiences of their child's problems.

ISOLATION

It is not surprising to find that "the stigmatized nature of psychiatric illness contributes to isolation or withdrawal" by caregivers.[37] Peggy MacGregor further supports this concept: "Parents believe that something has happened to them that is out of the natural order of things, and thus they feel separated from the rest of humanity."[38] Such feelings of isolation and separation from others would fall under the category of subjective burden, in that they are often experienced in private and can remain hidden from others. Although such hidden emotions can have a significant negative effect upon the caregivers' own mental health, this issue has received very little attention in the literature.

One parent explained that when her son's illness became more serious, "Support systems just dissolved all around us. I had lost so many friendships . . . even his godparents who were supportive, but just didn't understand. They'd be like, 'You need to give him a good spanking.' "

Yet never was this the kind of advice that parents wanted or felt they needed. In most cases, friends' and relatives' suggestions represented temporary solutions to a long-term problem. For a variety of reasons, those trying to give the advice and understanding gradually drifted out of the families' lives, further contributing to the subjects' sense of isolation.

Another parent further details the effects of the combination of blame and isolation

I was isolated from everything, and I continue to be isolated even now. For example, [I was] trying to get a job and place him in the care of child-care providers, people who I knew who were neighbors and who had day care in their homes. He would be there about a week, and they would say, "We cannot handle him. He writes on walls, wets his pants, I can't stand it." Immediately a wall goes up. Invitations to come over for dinner stop.

FAMILY MEMBERS AND BLAME: IT HURTS

It appears that in many cases the behavior of the child has consequences that extend far beyond trouble at day care or school. In fact, because of a rush to judgment by friends and family, and even those outside of the immediate social circle, the child's behavior can have an indelible impact on the individual social lives of his parents and siblings. One of these sources of blame that greatly affected the parents whom I interviewed, perhaps because of their literal and figurative proximity, was their own families. Much of this blame came directly from the subjects' parents, and it took a variety of forms, ranging from doomsday predictions to advice on how to better "control" their children. One parent stated:

> I remember my mother telling me one time that "If you don't do something, he's going to be one of those people who gets on the Texas tower and kills a bunch of people [referring to sniper Charles Whitman, who killed 16 people in 1966], or be a mass murderer." That was really hard to hear from my own mother.

Other parents related similar stories about how family members had predicted that their child would "be the next Charles Manson." In some cases, parents already felt bad that their child "was not like everyone else" and such blame-laden predictions from family members merely enhanced these feelings of self-blame. Another parent related how her parents told her that her son was having so many behavior problems because the mother worked outside the home:

> They were telling me it was my job, that I was making him miserable, that it was my fault that he was acting up. And they always gave me this "When he's with us, he never does anything wrong." And I'm thinking, you know, "Okay, so it has to be me." ... they've been kind of real negative on the whole thing in general.

Often coupled with these expressions of blame and wrongdoing were unsolicited suggestions by family members on how to best manage the child's behavior. For some parents, what makes such blaming patterns even harder to bear is the fact that few family members ever offered more tangible solutions to these problems or actual assistance in caring for the mentally ill child. As one parent put it, "My family has been very hard on me. They say you need to discipline him more. He needs to be punished. He needs to be spanked. This, that.'" This same parent explained that while she feels many family members are quick to point fingers and tell her what she should be doing differently, they never offer to assist her with child care or other kinds of objective support, which she explains is the kind of support she can really use: "My family was not very understanding. And to this day they have a hard time. There's no 'Okay, we'll take him for the weekend' or 'He can spend the night.' It's just been me and Wyatt."

A number of parents articulated similar frustrations. It is often hard to tell which is more difficult for the parent: being told what you are doing wrong without any realistic solutions as to how to change, or not receiving any physical or other support.

THE PUBLIC FACE OF BLAME

Another form of blame that many parents reported experiencing often came from complete strangers in locales such as shopping malls and grocery stores. Nearly every parent interviewed related a story about how at one time or another when their child was hyperactive, violent, or aggressive, they were told to "Control your kid," "That kid should be locked up," or "They have places for kids like that," or were simply glared at by other adults. One mother, whose son has been diagnosed with ADHD, states that people often ask:

> "Why is that kid acting like that?" I've had arguments with people in stores and restaurants and on the bus, all over. Sometimes I just say, "He's attention deficit." Right away people say, "Shut that kid up" or "Control that child." We've been kicked out of restaurants. We've been told not to come back. You ought to see him in the movies, and if the movie's something he wants to see, he's running up and down, he's in front of the screen, popcorn everywhere. When they start talking, at least you can understand them. It's definitely been hard. It's been the hardest cross that I've had to bear in my life. I get into a lot of arguments with people.

One could argue that caring for a mentally ill child is burden enough, let alone having to deal with the accusations and scorn of others in public. Some parents reported that such treatment further contributed to their feelings of isolation and social exclusion. Another parent related that when his son had an outburst in public, he often felt others suspected him of abusing the child. He explained, "He'd be in the middle of the store and start throwing a fit. We were taught how to do care holds. We'd be sitting there doing a care hold on him in the store, trying to get him to calm down, and you have all these people looking at you, like you're abusing your child."

A number of parents related similar stories, yet none felt that they had any other option at the time than to hold or discipline their child in public. Therefore, some parents felt that they were being blamed on two fronts—on one side for not "controlling their child" and on the other side for "abusing" their child by doing a care hold or arranging for a time-out. Undoubtedly, such conflicting messages from society further contributed to parents' confusion and uncertainty about their behavior management techniques, adding to their ongoing experience of burden.

MENTAL HEALTH PROFESSIONALS AND THE EXPERIENCE OF BLAME

The third and final source of blame that many parents reported as having contributed to their experience of burden came from the very professionals whose mission it is to help such children and their families. Much of the blame from professionals that parents experienced came at the time of the original diagnosis of their child with a mental disorder. Understandably, the assessment of a child with a potential mental disorder is rather complicated, and consequently a fair amount of confusion and conflicting evidence often surround the process. A number of parents adamantly stated that they were told directly by mental health professionals that their child's behavior problems and mental health issues were their fault. As one parent revealed:

I was doing everything that I needed to be doing, and in three months he was kicked out of his first day-care center. So I said, "Okay, what's wrong with this kid?" Then I went to [a publicly funded mental health center], and they said, "Oh, it's your fault. You're a bad parent." They told me I needed to sign my rights over to the state and give [my son] away. I told them they could put it where the sun didn't shine. His therapist told me that.

Another parent relates that, "As far as mental health professionals go, I would think that they should know better than to try and point the blame on parents and put it to poor parenting skills. They never gave us suggestions on parenting or how to parent. They said, 'It's nothing wrong with your child. It's your parenting skills.' "

While these may be extreme examples, undoubtedly many parents feel that they have been "written off" by the system and that the behaviors that they see at home on a daily basis, which they perceive as being detrimental to the health of the child and the family, are of no interest to the clinicians. Not only do many of these parents feel that little credence is given to their viewpoints by professionals, but many have come to believe that they are, in fact, wholly at fault for their child's illness.

Many parents express how frustrating it is to be actively seeking services for their child when those in positions of influence and authority choose to minimize their concerns and instead place the onus for the child's behavior on poor parenting skills. This perceived lack of understanding and concern for the child's well-being that many parents experienced greatly influenced their sense of self-effectiveness, thereby further contributing to the cycle of blame.

Another arena in which a number of parents reported feeling blamed by professionals was in the school system. Many parents felt that the teachers who worked with their children took out their frustrations with the child's behavior on the parents by blaming them. One parent relates:

When you come to the school, you can feel the looks, the way people respond to you. They become defensive and frustrated with him [her son]. When you sit down for a teacher's meeting, there's no problem solving involved. It's not like, "Let's talk about what we can do to support Jonathon and you." It's, "He needs therapy." A lot of accusations. Implications that I'm not a good parent.

While we do not know the other side of these stories, such as the teachers' or mental health professionals' perspectives, the very fact that parents even perceive so much blame is cause for alarm. Those interviewed reported experiences of blame and accusation from a number of sources, ranging from family members to mental health professionals to complete strangers, which further contributed to their sense of isolation and confusion about where to go for professional assistance, personal support, and hope for their child. There is little doubt that such experiences had a profound effect on these parents in a number of areas—from their personal relationships to the family dynamics to their own mental health. It is hard to imagine how such experiences would not have some kind of negative impact on these individuals' parenting abilities.

GUILT

In my interviews, I heard about the blame experienced by parents, but I also heard about parents' struggle with guilt. The experience of guilt by parents was often closely tied to the various episodes of blaming and accusation that were discussed earlier in this chapter. A number of parents related how they often felt that their child's illness was at least partially—if not wholly—their fault. Such self-blame was often related to parents believing that they had "faulty" genes that they had passed on to their child or that they had made parenting mistakes that had a negative effect on their child's overall mental health. Moreover, the gravity of such feelings of guilt and self-blame appear to have had a profound influence on the parents' own mental health and sense of well-being.

One mother, disturbed by hearing numerous reports from teachers about her son's aggressive and overactive behavior, as well as what she experienced at home, sought out the assistance of several mental health professionals. This mother stated that these professionals "didn't find anything abnormal." When asked if this outcome was a relief, she stated:

> It wasn't a relief. It was like, "Okay, if it's not that, then what is it?" I was looking for an answer. I wanted to know: "Okay, what's wrong?" And then there was a lot of guilt. I was thinking, "Did I do something when I was pregnant that I shouldn't have done? Did I get exposed to something? Did I cause this? Was it the way we were raising him?"

While one might think that the absence of a diagnosis would be a relief for parents, this particular mother found that the lack of a name or a category for her son's behavior actually produced more anxiety and strain concurrent with her feelings of guilt and self-blame. Interestingly, another mother whose son was diagnosed with ADHD by a mental health professional was not comforted by a name finally being given to what she had been observing and experiencing for years. When asked how she responded to the diagnosis, she stated, "What was I doing wrong? That was my first thought. What am I doing wrong?"

For many of those interviewed, it appears that those first feelings of guilt and self-blame are hard to let go, especially when they are often reinforced by the behaviors and statements of mental health professionals.

A mother who was diagnosed with major depressive disorder and generalized anxiety disorder before her daughter was born, and is still being treated for these disorders, feels that her daughter's mental disorder may have been caused by her own struggles with mental illness, both past and present. This particular parent and her daughter are living at the intersection of the nature/nurture debate. She says, "You can't help but think that you gave it to them. Then you wonder how much is inherited and how much is because of the way I am as a person suffering [from depression and anxiety]?" It appears that this parent continually questions how her role as a parent has contributed to her child's illness. Interestingly, this same parent reports that one of the main topics that she and her therapist discuss is the burden that her daughter's ongoing mental illness places upon her as a mother.

In one of the more extreme descriptions of personal guilt, one mother, whose youngest son had been diagnosed with ADHD and bipolar disorder, stated that she felt that having a son with mental illness was a form of punishment from God. She explained that her first husband, who was not the father of her children, had bipolar disorder and that his negative behaviors, which were often a result of his untreated mental illness, had ultimately led to their divorce. This parent interpreted her having a child with mental illness, and particularly with bipolar disorder, was punishment from God for not being more accepting and understanding of her first husband's behaviors and his mental illness. According to this parent, "I think about it all the time. I can't help but think that God is punishing me by giving me this child." Because this parent's older daughter does not have a mental disorder, she believes that she cannot find any other explanation for why her son would have a mental illness. Clearly, such feelings of guilt and personal responsibility for her son's struggles have a profound effect on this mother's mental health and her role as a parent. One might wonder about the roots of such extreme guilt and how much of this sense of personal guilt is socially constructed and socially reinforced.

One final example of the way parents interpret their various encounters with blame and guilt comes from a mother who, with her husband, has been caring for a mentally ill child for over 12 years:

Initially you go through a period of "Oh my God, what did I do wrong?" Plus our neighbors, health care professionals, and others sometimes say it's our fault. They like to point fingers. You blame yourself until you finally realize it isn't your fault. You constantly think, "It must be something we're doing wrong." I've learned it's not what we're doing wrong. But it took us a long time to learn that.

It appears that in the course of being involved in the mental health system for a number of years, this parent has learned to come to terms with her experiences of guilt and blame. Among those parents I interviewed, however, this is a unique perspective and one whose foundations merit further investigation.

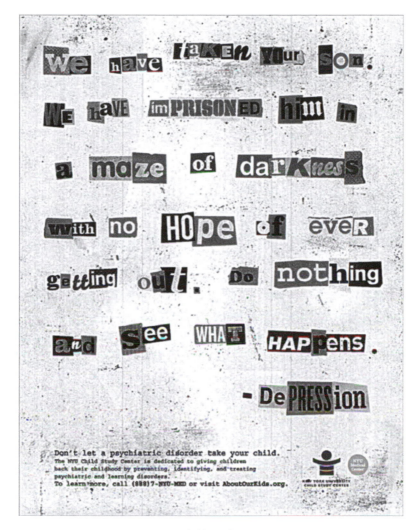

NYU Child Study Center

A MISGUIDED PUBLIC ADVERTISEMENT: PARENTS SPEAK OUT

The ad shown here does a good job of suggesting the difficulty of caring for mentally ill children, yet the ad campaign stepped over the line for many parents. The intent, according to the New York University Child Study Center, was to raise awareness of what was referred to as a silent public health epidemic of children's mental disorders. The well-intentioned ads, designed as ransom notes, were meant to get out the message that, if left untreated, a child's mental disorder can hold the child hostage. The umbrella ad is "12 million kids are held hostage by a psychiatric disorder. Help a child at AboutOurKids.org." Each ad addressed a specific disorder, including depression, ADHD, Asperger's syndrome, autism, bulimia, and obsessive–compulsive disorder. The tag line for all of the ads was the same: "Don't let a psychiatric disorder take your child." The "ransom notes" in the ads included the following text:

- We have your son. We will make sure he will no longer be able to care for himself or interact socially as long as he lives. This is only the beginning. —Autism.
- We are in possession of your son. We are making him squirm and fidget until he is a detriment to himself and those around him. Ignore this and your kid will pay. —ADHD
- We have your son. We are destroying his ability for social interaction and driving him into a life of complete isolation. It's up to you now. —Asperger's Syndrome
- We have your daughter. We are forcing her to throw up after every meal she eats. It's only going to get worse. —Bulimia
- We have taken your son. We have imprisoned him in a maze of darkness with no hope of ever getting out. Do nothing and see what happens. —Depression
- We have your daughter. We are making her wash her hands until they are raw, every day. This is only the beginning. —OCD

After a campaign by parents and professional organizations representing many of the disorders, the ads were stopped. In a twist of fate, these dramatic ads—which were designed to catch everyone's attention—ended up offending many of the parents they were attempting to reach. Parents reacted negatively to the ominous subtext of the message in these ads: "If you don't get your child help, then you have given him or her a death sentence and there is no getting out." As many of the quotes provided in this book illustrate, parents often feel imprisoned by their child's illness. However, parents want others to know that they can and do cope effectively, and many have made positive adjustments. What is missing from the ads is the reality that children's mental illness represents a continuum—some kids suffer a minor form of an illness, while others suffer a major form of the illness—so the ads don't fit everyone. A lot of the criticism was directed to concerns that the ads could generate stigma and even fear of kids who had mental illnesses. Increasingly empowered parents fought back because they did not like the stereotypes.

CHAPTER 4

Searching for Help: Expertise Is Hard to Find

Society is organized on the principle that any individual who possesses certain social characteristics has a moral right to expect that others will value and treat him in a correspondingly appropriate way . . . he automatically exerts a moral demand upon others, obliging them to value him.
—E. Goffman, *The Presentation of Self in Everyday Life*

In the last book I wrote, *The Call to Social Work: Life Stories*, I interviewed social workers about the work they do,[1] their life experiences, and what it means to be a social worker. A major theme of that book was that social work is a call to service—and it presented social workers in a positive light as they search for meaning in their work and offer help to those in need.

This book looks at help from the other side—how parents and families respond to the help they are being offered in the community by mental health workers, many of whom are social workers. As I listened to parents talk about their experiences, one thing stood out: Most did not believe they received very effective help. Too many mental health professionals have not been able to respond in a manner that helps parents manage and cope with their child's mental illness, or at least the responses have been lacking in many areas.

GENEROSITY: A FORGOTTEN NOTION

Arthur Frank has written extensively about illness, including how individuals can use narratives and stories to help themselves make sense of their experiences.

In his latest book, he tackles the concept of *generosity* and its role in helping those who are ill. His goal is to fundamentally change how medical doctors respond to those who become ill. I would like to see the same change occur for mental health professionals who are asked to help those with mental illnesses. Frank states his goal succinctly: "My conviction is that at the start of the twenty-first century, the foremost task of responding to illness and disability is not devising new treatments, though I'm grateful this work will proceed. Our challenge is to increase the generosity with which we offer the medical skill that has been attained."[2] It is shocking that anyone would make such an assertion, yet how we help those who are ill and how we help parents of mentally ill children can be dramatically improved. Frank's fitting thesis for the mental health community is that before we offer help, we should first offer the comfort of consolation: "Consolation may render loss more bearable by inviting some shift in belief about the point of living a life that includes suffering."[3]

Offering consolation is an act of generosity. Most parents I interviewed for this book did not see efforts to help them and their families from the mental health community as anything close to offering consolation on a level of generosity. The human gift of consolation has been neglected and deemed less valuable than treatment or the search for a cure. Yet, as we will see, offering consolation would expand the framework of helping from cure to lifelong coping—a paradigm shift that needs to happen if we are to truly help the parents of mentally ill children. A renewed focus on generosity would allow parents to feel less stigmatized and isolated.

As parents talked about their experiences, it became clear to me that no one—not friends, family, or professional helpers—was interested in listening to their pain and despair. This absence of interest in their experience leads to feelings that no one understands and cares about *them*. Some parents believe that honest expressions of how they are feeling are not welcome—that they represent what others do not want to hear. As a consequence, they shut down these feelings. The norms of support in clinics, in support groups, and on the Internet encourage hope and optimism. The message is that despair is not allowed.[4]

One parent described her experience as akin to being part of a secret society:

The first problem I see is isolation. When you have a child with a disorder, you feel like no one understands you. It's not something that you can talk about. I mean, when you go with a group of moms, they're talking about their four-year-old son writing their name—and you talk about your four-year-old son pooping his pants and painting with it on the wall. You're just not going do that. So you can't talk to—you're reluctant to talk to—other moms. You're reluctant to talk at all. It's like you're in this secret society. You're just hiding it. Your stories are totally different. You can't relate. A lot of parents will say, "Oh, every kid goes through that." I don't think so. And that makes you feel stupid, because then you're thinking, "Well, maybe I'm just too tough." So you ease up, and then somebody says, "If you're just more strict with that kid, he'd shape up." They have no clue. They have no clue what your home life is like, and you're not going to admit it to them. I mean, I feel like I understand what abused people go through now.

Hello? Somebody? We are out here. I'm not asking for handouts. Don't give me anything. But hear us speak if you're so interested in mental health awareness. Hear us speak. Hear my child speak firsthand.

Another parent, who is raising an extremely difficult son, spoke directly about his experience in sharing with people about his situation:

People really don't want to think and talk about all this stuff.

Many parents found the social services agencies completely unresponsive to their needs. Perhaps the biggest lament was that parents would call and not receive even a courtesy call back. One parent, a therapeutic foster parent, explains:

You'd leave weeks of messages, and then after about the fifth message, you start getting rude. I left messages for a week straight. He never called me. So then I start calling people under him to give him the message. I got a hold of his secretary a couple of times. I said, "What's up?" He needs to call me.

As this parent describes it, the social worker never did call her back but he did show up for a case planning meeting where the parent was a participant. In that meeting he told her, "You can call me any time you want." Her experience with this agency has a clear undertone of rage: *They are the most incompetent people.*

THE FALLACY OF POSITIVE THINKING

The notion that even health and mental health professionals do not want to hear what their clients are really feeling was addressed by Barbara Ehrenreich in her book, *Bright Sided: How the Relentless Promotion of Positive Thinking Has Undermined America.* After being diagnosed with breast cancer, she found herself surrounded by an obsessive culture of positivity that didn't fit—a place where anger, fear, and depression, all of which are reasonable reactions to a fatal disease, were looked at as both compromising her chances of survival and representing missed opportunities for spiritual growth. She challenges the zeal of positive psychology, noting that both science and the practice of optimism may have their limitations.[5] Certainly, within social work and psychology, there is an increasing emphasis on "being positive" without an understanding of how that may fit for people in different circumstances.

Ehrenreich is brilliant at bringing forth the unintended consequences of this perspective. If you can't say, "In most ways my life is close to ideal" (an item on the *Satisfaction with Life Scale*), then you have only yourself to blame. Never mind that your only child has a serious mental illness, that you cannot find insurance to cover the needed medical treatment, that you are completely isolated and alone in attempting to cope with this issue. The danger is that practicing mental health practitioners will fall in love with positive psychology because it places a focus on the practitioner, and the result will be a push toward developing positive attitudes in parents while ignoring what the parents are really feeling—and thereby failing to respond in an authentic manner to them. Ehrenreich believes the widespread use of positive thinking is "beginning to be an obligation imposed on all American adults."[6] In reality, parents can better understand the value of "staying positive" when others acknowledge the uphill battle that this effort entails for them.[7]

A recent newspaper article addressed this issue in a different, but poignant way. The article, titled "When Thumbs Up Is No Comfort," addressed the very public, very positive image presented by Senator Ted Kennedy when he was dying of cancer.[8] Some lamented that Kennedy gave others a glimmer of unjustified hope, while others worried the result of his being positive could lead other patients to feel guilty for not being as upbeat as Kennedy appeared, and even angry that Kennedy's reality was being misrepresented. Rachel Schneider, a social worker at the Sloan-Kettering Cancer Center, summed it up: "Hopefulness is real, but patients say, 'I have to be positive, I can't cry, I can't let myself fall apart,' and that is a burden." Recognizing that different people's responses will vary is part of the process of helping that too often gets buried in psychobabble.[9] There is no master blueprint for how to successfully move forward from misfortune, but being realistic and discussing where parents' emotional reactions have taken them is a start.

Dr. Joseph Finns, an expert on medical ethics, comments on helping those with terminal cancer, "If we fail to meet patients where their grief has taken them, we have sequestered them off."[10] Much of the recent emphasis on positive psychology can lead to poor causal explanations for the difficulties we are sometimes saddled with. Didn't exercise enough? No wonder you have heart disease. Don't eat enough vegetables? No wonder you have cancer. Don't parent effectively? No wonder your child has a mental illness. Because of this prevalent attitude that we are the authors of our own misfortune, some parents see their frustrations with the mental health system as more of a burden than their own efforts to help their child:

> There are a lot of changes to be done that have to start somewhere. Maybe it is the parent advocating and saying, "We should try this" or "Have you heard of this program?" Maybe even the mental health professionals need to stand up and say, "We're harming, not helping, these children."

> I explained to the CPS worker yesterday at this meeting I was at that she goes home at the end of her day. She does not go home to my children. On Saturdays, Sundays, and holidays, the children are there. They give you the [line], "You made your choice to have a child." Yes, I did.

> Jeffrey, when he turned 18, left home, didn't go back to school, didn't have the support, decided the mental health system was useless. To this day, he thinks it's useless and it's manipulative. Well, it is in its very nature.

I assume it's the TV shows, when you go to a psychiatrist, you talk to your psychiatrist, not to a case manager. It's like playing "telephone," by the time it gets to the psychiatrist, it's gone. The emphasis that you wanted to put on certain words doesn't quite come out the same way. I've got into the habit now of not leaving my messages, but faxing messages. At least I can get my words, [though] not necessarily the emphasis of what I want to say, down on paper and fax it.

A parent also needs a lot of nurturing. Sometimes the parent is in as much trouble as the kid, because of their lack of ability to have privacy, to own anything, to get a good night's sleep, knowing you bought a week's worth of groceries and came home and your kid ate it all for snacks. Now I can afford it, but when I used to have envelopes that said this is rent, this is utilities, if your utility bill was any higher, you couldn't borrow from Peter to pay Paul. That was living in New York on welfare—[the cost of living was] much higher than where I live now. Welfare says you can't collect it unless you're working. It's a vicious cycle. It takes a village to raise a child; you have to find more villages. You have to break down the walls of confidentiality. Let parents know that we're not alone. Some of us don't know how to walk over to that other parent.

IN DEFENSE OF CARING

The role of caring for those less fortunate in society is deeply embedded in history, and comprises more than simply administering treatments. The lost emphasis on *caring* as well as curing and treating needs to be resurrected in the helping professions. Reframing the concept of "caring" and its role in the mental health field might be a new starting point in helping mental health agencies as well as practitioners. What is missing in the mental health agencies that service children with mental illnesses is an overall perspective about how and why such agencies should promote "caring." All too often, mental health agencies position themselves as neutral entities with no responsibilities for caring above and beyond the provision of individual counseling.

If agencies did perceive themselves as social structures that provide lifelong caring for families who suffer with mental illness, their role would be to build connections and structures that go beyond just individual work. This collective caring would look much different than the 50-minute therapy session clinics provide—often to children, and not to parents. How can agencies that purport to help these families organize themselves into structures that are caring institutions? Little work has been done at this level of caring. However, in some communities parents have been able to organize themselves into effective caring organizations.

As one parent put it:

The agencies I notice are okay with breaching confidentiality from parent to parent. I had suggested for years, including yesterday at this meeting I was at, explaining that when parents are mentors to each other, we find a way to deal with crisis, to have instant support, to have respite options, and [to do] the things that the system is not currently able to do. Keeping children in an environment that they're familiar with, as opposed to sending them to a shelter where they will outstay their welcome very quickly. Maybe instilling in the child that it's okay to ask to go to the neighbor's house for the night, because they're feeling the stuff working out. Empowering the children to make some of these decisions, as opposed to the parents. Even though I may want to send my child to a shelter in a mental health crisis, it doesn't mean (a) the shelter's going to have a bed or (b) my kid's going to say yes. He's truly in control. Let's give him the control on something he can control.

That book, It Takes a Village to Raise a Child*—our systems aren't working to create that village that includes the parents and the family, and extended family.*

Diana Rauner presents a framework for thinking about caring with four levels:

1. The face-to-face interactions
2. The actions of professionals
3. The structure of organizations
4. Societal policies that represent caring[11]

In addressing levels 1 and 2, I realized as I talked with parents that *some* were deeply helped by the one-to-one interactions they had with professionals or other caring individuals. In looking across the field of children's mental health, on both national and state levels, it is clear that some professionals are committed to making the "system" work better to meet the needs of parents.

Looking at levels 3 and 4—the structure of organizations and societal policies—it is clear that organizations that provide clinical services and that are designed in a manner that also promotes broad-scale caring are less common.[12] For years, many advocates have promoted the need for better social policies, such as allowing financial resources to provide a level of family care that is now often not available.

For example, sociologists examining how services are provided to children immediately see the demise of *mediating structures*—associations of neighbors, friends, churches or communities that can help provide care in an organized and facilitated manner.[13] These structures are not meant as a replacement for parental responsibilities, but rather represent an asset that can be used by parents in meeting their needs to best nurture and parent their children.

The level of isolation for parents of mentally ill children can be severe. Many are naturally reclusive, with little support. The mentally ill child is often shunned by other children, which isolates the parents further. One of the most compelling notions in sociology is our need for social integration and social connection. Weak ties to social life are often seen as a factor in people's stability, health, and happiness. Long ago, Durkheim pointed to a link between social connection and suicide—so the significance of this need for social interaction is well established.[14]

Indeed, people's overall mental health is deeply connected to the manner in which they are connected to their communities. Society itself functions best when the community of people within it feels interconnected. This point was made popular again in Robert Putnam's 2000 book, *Bowling Alone: America's Declining Social Capital*. In it, Putnam points out the serious reduction in our social interactions, the cornerstone of civic engagement and democracy. Increasingly people live in social isolation—and parents with uncontrollable children face the prospect of even greater isolation than the typical American. Underlying modern society is an individuation that pushes each person to make do on his or her own. Robert Bellah states it succinctly: "The freedom to be left alone is a freedom that implies being alone."[15]

As Putnam notes, when people associate with one another in different capacities, they become mutual assets, people who can sometimes be relied upon when needed. The more relationships, the greater the accumulation of assets and the larger bank of what sociologists call "social capital." Conversely, if even similarly situated individuals are not feeling socially connected, imagine what it feels like to be a parent of a mentally ill child: isolated and completely unconnected to others, with no real social capital to manage the most difficult job in our society—parenting. Because parents of mentally ill children often describe deep feelings of isolation, helping parents create a sense of social support is a worthwhile goal.

As one beleaguered parent put it:

Society has changed. We don't send our kids to school in our neighborhoods sometimes. We don't necessarily go to a neighborhood church or synagogue. We don't go to church or synagogue at all, and we don't know our neighbors. Grandmother doesn't live around the corner. You don't have family. You emulate family, extended family. Times have changed, but it's not helping our children, whether they're mentally ill or not.

We could probably create a respite naturally if an environment were created to bring us all together, maybe in the quiet times. That's sometimes the benefit of having group therapy, because as parents, you get to sit in the waiting room, and I notice that we all look at each other. If someone comes out as the catalyst to start a conversation, you might be surprised that, without breaching confidentiality, you can get to your goal. Peer support, like AA, 12-step groups, peer support services—to me, this is natural.

That's what they did in New York; the community came together [after the 9/11 terrorist attacks;] the rest of the country said we need to deal with this crisis. Children are in crisis. Some of them can hold it together enough to stay in school, in special ed, or whatever. Many of them can't. Even the schools don't particularly [encourage] peer support. There's a lot of peer tutoring, and they do it in the school.

SUPPORT GROUPS

Many parents talked about the help they received from various support groups they participated in. Most communities offer support groups ranging from those that address mental illness to support groups for specific mental disorders like ADHD or bipolar disorder. Social support is offered through self-help or mutual-aid group processes. These groups seek to provide mutual aid through the exchange that occurs when parents share a common problem. Such exchanges may have strong biological and social roots. People are often drawn to small groups, perhaps because of the evolutionary benefit of being members of such groups; groups provide emotional and physical security. After all, human evolution took place in the context of small groups, which provided security from predators. In a similar sense, small groups provide protection in contemporary life, where we experience urbanized mass society as stressful. In self-help groups, people join together to help one another cope more effectively with shared problems.

Support groups or mutual-aid groups can be classified into two basic types: social-change groups and personal-coping groups. Social-change groups typically focus on changing public laws or attitudes; the best example would be the National Alliance on Mental Illness (NAMI). These groups are often involved in awareness campaigns and efforts to ensure that group members receive the kind of services and treatment to which they are entitled. By comparison, personal-coping groups focus on getting help for individual members that will influence their behavior or personal growth. The best example is Alcoholics Anonymous, the oldest self-help organization of its kind. In both types of groups, members retain control over the group's resources and are actively involved in helping programs built on their own experience.

Personal-coping support groups are best understood as performing three functions: (1) exchanging information on how to cope, (2) offering material help when necessary, and (3) encouraging members to feel cared about and supported. The helper and the beneficiary become peers, if only in the sense that they share a common problem. As they discover that what seemed unusual is common to others in a similar situation, they no longer feel alone with their problems. Their emotions and experiences are legitimized, and a framework is provided for coping with the situation. They receive specific guidance on how to implement change, thus expanding their repertoire of appropriate coping strategies.

The relationship between self-help groups and professional organizations has not always been cooperative. Indeed, self-help groups may be reluctant to associate with professionals, fearing their autonomy may be compromised. Furthermore, many people who use self-help groups may have had poor experiences with formal helping systems. Many professionals have attempted to intervene with self-help groups in an effort to impose their professional knowledge. As a result, tension sometimes arises between professionals and self-help organizations.

The number of self-help organizations has grown so rapidly that many people now refer to "self-help" as a movement. One can only assume that the rapid expansion of self-help reflects the readiness of people in all segments of society to solve their own problems in concert with others like themselves. Libraries, grocery stores, and community organizations list information about self-help groups. Computer access through the Internet has greatly increased people's ability to find others with like problems and to join self-help groups electronically.

Why has the self-help movement gained such popularity? Part of the answer to this question lies in the evolutionary benefit achieved by such groups. In addition, the growth may reflect dissatisfaction with the increasing depersonalization of the professional care being offered.[16] Perhaps the rapid changes taking place in society are limiting opportunities for people to obtain needed social support through traditional channels. The growth of self-help also parallels the consumer movement, which advocates greater personal involvement in one's own care and less reliance on outside professionals. Silverman concluded that the growth in self-help indicates people want a different form of help that is simply not available in the existing service system.[17] People often seek help that can be made available to them only through association with others who share similar experiences.

One of the most commonly occurring suggestions to parents of a mentally ill child is to "find a support group." E. Fuller Torrey, a well-known expert on mental illness and the author of Surviving Schizophrenia, stated early on that families should find support for help in dealing with mental illness by reaching out to other families who have experience in this area.[18] This suggestion is, sadly, a very good one because, on the one hand, the truth is that too often mental health professionals do not have enough expertise and understanding to help families. On the other hand, parents—an enormous resource—have been undervalued until the recent, growing trend toward adoption of a consumer mental health model.

Here are the comments of one parent who joined a parent consumer and support group:

> I was very lucky to have found Project Match. Project Match was one of the greatest things I ever did. They are very parent based. Parents have a voice. Parents are recognized, and they listen to you. Because the parents are the ones sitting home with these children. The other people, like the therapist, only see the child for an hour every week or two. Even if you have in-home therapy, they're never going to see what a parent sees.

In discussing mental illness, Elizabeth Swados, in her book The Four of Us: A Family Memoir, notes that it is "an extremely guilt-provoking disease. It often strikes promising, gentle, bright young people, and the rapid changes into incoherency and vicious rejections are almost impossible to understand. The acceptance that it is a disease is the only positive first step."[19] That acceptance often comes only after parents have found one another in efforts to better understand their experience. The value of coming together as a group can be enormous and empowering. The well-established Al-Anon group for family members dealing with alcoholic husbands, wives, or children frequently starts with a coping mantra referred to as the three C's: "I didn't cause it. I can't cure it. I can't control it."[20] Parents of mentally ill children would be wise to also repeat this mantra when they come together for support.

Few professionals have considered the parent's perspective in examining the implication of helping families. As one group of researchers noted, "Unfortunately, most research examining children's mental health systems has failed to incorporate input from parents of disturbed children, even though parents have information that cannot be obtained from professionals. Parents are uniquely qualified to describe the progression of a child's problems, the kinds of services sought, and the barriers to service delivery that might be overlooked by provider-experts. They alone know about informal assistance and social support or the impact of a child's disturbance on the rest of the family."[21]

The support group was really a group. The first thing they taught us is "You're not alone. It's not your fault. It's just nature. There's nothing you could have done to prevent it. It's just one of those things that happens." It made it a lot easier. But because you're a parent, you blame yourself. It's like, What could I have done different? What should I have done?

There's an online support group called Hope for AD Kids that, unlike [some other groups], is real hopeful about the prognosis for attachment-disordered kids. And someone in that support group has experienced every one of the rotten behaviors they can exhibit, every one of them—and they have some really humorous ways of dealing with it. You can vent on there, too. That's one of the precepts, you know, not to be mean or anything, but you can say, you know, "I don't know what to do"—and it's okay. The other online support group I belong to is for parents of children adopted from Eastern Europe who have a special set of issues. That's been real helpful. They're not quite as blunt as the other one, but you can get some information on what this behavior might mean and how to deal with the school.

That was probably the biggest step I ever made, going to a support group. I thought I was the only person in the world with this monster child, especially with Baxter, who tried to kill me and stab me and kept my household in turmoil. I went to a support group and thought, "Wow, it's not just me. I'm not losing my mind. There are other kids out there who do this." I was able to take a more global look at my family. Parents just need to be made more aware of support groups and other things that can help them. There need to be more mentors and pairing of parents. Parents who have been there, done that, with parents who haven't. If we [are matched] together, we can teach each other.

For some parents, support groups did not work or were not accessible. Many parents, however, found support from other individuals, friends, or professionals that made a difference in how they were able to function as parents.

I think that everybody who has a child like this needs to find somebody that they can have that kind of connection with. These kids are not easy. You cannot do it by yourself. Family's great, but family doesn't always understand. It's too close. You need to find someone else who has the same things going on as you. Make that connection. Even as I work mentoring and talking to parents, telling them where to go, every person I talk to, I learn something from them. The more people you talk to, the more people who learn, [the more you can] help others help their own kids. [It's a] wonderful spider web that gets bigger and bigger.

It seems like they have groups for everything, but they don't say, "Let's get a group of parents together and talk about what we're dealing with daily." They don't seem to have that. I think so many people are scared of admitting the truth of what's wrong.

I need a parent to talk to who's going through what I'm going through. But I haven't found that support.

AN AFTERNOON WITH A THERAPIST

The 60-year celebration of the School of Social Welfare at the University of California at Berkeley included a hosted picnic on homecoming day with alumni at the school. I had the good fortune of bumping into a fellow who is a mental health practitioner in a county nearby. After some general chatting about this and that, he asked me what my role was at Berkeley. I explained that I was at Berkeley as the Visiting Zellerbach Professor, doing a study on parents who have mentally ill children. "Oh, really?" was his reply, with an intriguing glance. I quickly ascertained that he was a child and family mental health practitioner who worked with parents, the mental health system, the school district, and other child welfare agencies. He was, in many ways, an ideal "informant" about children's mental health issues. An Asian American man in his forties, he had returned to school for a second career. He was quickly insightful, and not too entrenched in his work so that he could be more objective, perhaps more critical, in describing issues in delivering mental health services to families. After this conversation, I realized that I did need to talk directly with mental health practitioners and incorporate their perspectives into my analysis of how parents interact with professionals and the "system" of care that is provided to them.

This colleague was quick to offer critical comments about how the "system"—in this case, the county system—did or did not deliver appropriate services. "Off the record," he said, "I sometimes have to tell parents, 'You can call an IEP [individual educational plan] meeting.' " (In an IEP meeting, the child's plan of care is discussed by the school and other participating agencies, and it can be critical when parents believe there are missing services that need to be provided.) "I also tell the parents, 'Don't let anyone know I told you this, but you should contact an attorney who can get the school and county to provide the services your child needs.' " This suggestion, he explained, has to be off the record because such an action can end up costing the county additional money—and if county authorities found out he was costing them more money, he might lose his job.

This mental health practitioner also explained to me that he sees a big differ-ence in how parents of middle and high income deal with the system compared to parents who are of low income. "The middle-class parents come to meetings with entitlement," he said. " 'If you don't do this for my child, I'll ... ,' whereas the low-income parents are simply appreciative: 'Thank you for providing this care to my son or daughter.' The low-income parents don't know that other ser-vices and expenditures could be garnered with some advocacy on their part."

An example of the difference that can be achieved with advocacy is clearly demonstrated by one of the lower-income mothers I interviewed:

> I'm so excited, because of this component of it. It is advocacy, and learning how to advocate for your child. And that's what I feel has been my biggest weakness, for my kids. If I had known how to do it, I might have been able to find support for Andie sooner. I certainly might have been able to get her into some special education services at the school. In fact, right now she had her neurology appoint-ment, and the recommendation is that she have complete special education assess-ments, particularly for ADD. And that's something the school is supposed to do, but because they talked me out of it last year, I can't say they refused to do it, because they're not allowed to refuse to do it. But, I mean, it was obvious. . . .
> I mean you go to these child study meetings, and there're 10 professionals who are all telling you that your child is not that bad. "She's doing well. She's great. We love having her in the classroom." I don't know what's good or not.

Wraparound services have been provided in my colleague's county for several years. Because many states, such as Arizona, have focused on a wraparound approach as the way to address the poor quality of care that was provided for chil-dren needing mental health services, I wanted to get his opinion on this model. Again, my Berkeley colleague's approach was particularly revealing about the potential promise of this model of care. "Wraparound is not that great," he told me. "Too much sugar" and "patronizing too many parents" were expressions he used. "I believe in the strengths model," he said. "I was trained in it but it is too much." He gave me an example of a case conference the previous week in which parents were asked how things had gone in the preceding month: " 'Fine,' the parent said. 'How has it been going in the past month?' Pretty good,' was the reply. 'How about the last six months?' 'No real problems.' The practitioners were not connected with this parent, and the parent wasn't interested in hearing about their 'strengths.' They know what they are doing well; they know where things need to go." My colleague and I discussed this further and concluded that strengths can be a very helpful perspective for practitioners to adopt, but many practitioners do not understand how to use the model in an appropriate manner.

In my interviews, a few parents talked about wraparound services, and their experiences with this approach varied. One parent had not had success:

> I wrote the guy that presented the wraparound training. I said, "What you showed me, knowing government as well as I do, this is a smokescreen." The

thing is, it's not going to work until it's a requirement of the people at the top lev-els of the agencies, and it's in their evaluation, and it's a major portion of their evaluation. If you leave it to the people in the field, they can't make it work. They don't have the wherewithal to make those kinds of decisions.

This mother's main frustration is that the wraparound concept involves ser-vices, and she was not able to obtain the services she needed despite participating in the wraparound approach. Later in the interview, she spoke of not being able to obtain any respite services, noting that in six years she had received only two days of respite care for her child. This lack of available services made the wrap-around strategy seem more rhetoric than reality. She summarizes her frustration with wraparound services:

In the meantime, nobody's getting the services. Nobody's getting equipment, counseling, therapy. The ones who are in the system aren't getting as much as they should, and there's a lot of them who aren't getting into the system that ought to be there.

My colleague's last criticism dealt with the use of parent aid; in this regard, he made an interesting point worth pondering. In his county, other parents provide sup-port for the family. While it is clearly recognized that support is needed, often the support from these parent aids can be counterproductive. For example, the parents may receive advice that doesn't represent current knowledge about how to inter-vene. Thus, while the concept of parent aid makes sense and seems like a good idea, the implementation of such aid in ways that are most helpful has yet to be realized.

The wraparound approach isn't really anything new, as the importance of pro-viding services and supporting families has been a long-established notion in social work. However, what it has brought is some new services, such as shadows, in which a practitioner follows the child closely for several days to make a more informed assessment. Another innovation is in-home training for parents who are struggling with a complex behavior problem that doesn't seem to be getting any better.

Unfortunately, even these newer approaches can have their drawbacks. For example, one parent explained how she got into a power struggle with the thera-pists at the local agency: "They were mad at me because I was refusing one thera-pist." In this case, the parent believed the child had obsessive–compulsive disorder, but the therapist did not agree. This situation left the parent with no options and no say in how the treatment progressed. When I talked with the parent, it was clear from the tone of her voice that she just didn't feel that the therapists were interested in her opinion. This conflict revealed how therapists sometimes exercise significant power and authority over parents in limiting or restricting the services the child receives.

Additional emphasis on the importance of parental involvement in children's mental health treatment comes from Delaney and Engels-Scianna, who state that "Although parents are uniquely qualified to describe their child's problem and the type of services their child needs, most research on child psychiatric treatment fails to incorporate parents' perceptions."[22] According to Nevas and Farber, "Little attention has been paid in the child therapy literature to parental feelings, reactions, or responses to the child's therapist and therapy. This is true despite the fact that parents usually make the decision to initiate therapy for their child, are essential for both the continuation of treatment and the maintenance of gains following termination, and surely affect the nature of their child's symptoms."[23]

The parents I interviewed sometimes received help for their mentally ill child in the process of obtaining recommended medication. Nevertheless, these parents consistently talked about how therapists and psychiatrists would assist them in medicating their child, yet rarely reached out to them to determine their other needs.

When considered in light of projections of attrition rates in mental health counseling, this situation underscores the importance of the relationship that parents have with both professionals and the greater mental health system. As Vitanza and Cohen note, researchers have found that such families perceive services to be less than optimal. They do not view professionals as supportive of families, and they encounter a variety of obstacles to care, including being required to relinquish custody of their child to obtain services.[24]

It does appear that gradually the gravity of the parent's perspective is being recognized on a national level. It is encouraging to see that this attention appears to be generating changes in the field in terms of the relationships forged among professionals, consumers, and their families.

Typical for successful outpatient therapy would be the situation described by Paul Raeburn about his son's therapist's description of what he did: "This is a place where he can say what he wants, and act the way he wants, and feel safe."[25]

In reaction to his son's acting-out behavior at school, Raeburn confronted the school's inability to provide any real help: "The school officials said they were unwilling to apply their regular disciplinary code to Alex. They wanted Liz and me to solve the problem. But we weren't with Alex at school. We didn't see what was happening, and, as I kept saying, it wasn't up to us to set classroom rules for him. We did what we could at home, and they had to handle the chore at school."[26]

PROFESSIONAL HELP: A CRITIQUE

While for the most part psychologists and social workers are committed to helping parents and children who suffer from mental illness, it is worth mentioning that this assumption is not always held to be true. In a serious critique of the social work profession, Leslie Margolin, in *Under the Cover of Kindness: The Invention of Social Work*, explains how social work developed essentially as a profession to justify itself and its actions.[27]

Similar criticism has been documented through in-depth examinations of how social workers function in the context of their jobs. In *The Professional*

Altruist, Roy Lubove wrote that inherent conflicts exist between the efforts of social workers to do good and the sometimes overly bureaucratic agencies for which they work. Social advocate and lawyer Joel Handler examined social workers who worked for the child welfare system and found clear examples of the misuse of power. It is interesting to reflect on how the mental health professionals who work in the field of children's mental health try to justify the need for their actions. This sociological analysis helps explain, in part, the "need" for therapists to truly care for the children whom parents have not been able to properly manage. Hence, there may be a rather unaware level of blame placed on the parents by therapists, as this practice justifies their existence.

In fact, several exposés have been written on the power bestowed on psychiatric institutions that care for children. Most alarming is Louise Armstrong's *And They Call It Help: The Psychiatric Policing of America's Children*.[28] Most of Armstrong's case against psychiatric institutions is overstated, but she rightly points out that abuse of power does exist in the field of children's mental health, and she clearly documents the history of the growth in reimbursement-driven hospitalizations. The book provides the good dose of skepticism needed in reviewing how we attempt to provide help to children who have mental health issues. The labeling and interactions that occur when a person is defined as "psychiatric" can sometimes be harmful, as described by this young person who read *Psychiatric Policing* and wrote a response:

> As a creative and depressed young adult struggling to understand myself and the world around me, I was sucked into the psychiatric complex and spent three years in and out of for-profit psychiatric hospitals, on and off heavy psychiatric drugs. The experience crushed my faith in myself and snipped threads of hope that linked me to the future.
>
> After my insurance ceased to pay for treatment, the treatment ceased as well, and I was able to shakily resume the process of growing up. Reading And They Call It Help gave me a socio-political and outside narrative background for why "psychiatric policing" occurs and why its natural effects in patients are a sense of disempowerment and helplessness.
>
> Put simply, this book changed my life. It helped me move on after my own run-in with the mind police. If parents considering inpatient psychiatric treatment for their children and others who work with children and young adults could read this book, the trauma caused by common psychiatric abuse and manipulation could be minimized and alternatives to expensive and spirit-killing treatments would be better explored and practiced.[29]

Newer models of care (e.g., wraparound services) often put together "teams" of professionals, including parents, to make good decisions for the child. These models are moving in the right direction because they address, on some level, the fragmentation of services and the need for greater coordination. However, while the parents may be an integral part of the team, all too often they occupy a very powerless position.

We're told we're an integral part of the team, but it's the parent, the child . . . and you have a case manager and a psychiatrist and team leader. You've got four of them, and one of you. Majority rules on all this stuff. You don't have majority.

When I was in MIKID, I went in and said someone needs to be a traffic cop and say stop! Mom has something she'd really like to say in here. I needed that as a mom. You sit there listening to these people talking about all this stuff and using acronyms. They know what they're talking about; you know your kid. You come in with that expertise. You know if your kid has taken the medication they want to put him on and had adverse reactions. They don't always want to hear it.

Day one, it was difficult. I have a background in education psychology and I have worked in a school district. I know what the law says. Day one, it was "We do things our way, regardless of what he needs. We have these few programs, and this is the way it will be." I wish I had taped it now, I really do. Regardless of what your doctor says or [what] you say as his mother, we make the team decision, and we will decide.

MEDICATION: A MAZE OF CONFUSION

Medication has important implications for the treatment of mentally ill children. Psychiatry is focused only on the person's internal functioning, and as such it offers little in helping us understand how *society* influences the decisions of individuals. We have increasingly become a medicalized society who looks to science and medicine for curing most ailments. Just as Peter D. Kramer, the author of *Listening to Prozac*, raised questions about the future of medication in the daily lives of adults, similar concerns can be raised for children. *Listening to Prozac* was a critique of cosmetic psychopharmacology. A similar concern can be termed "cosmetic parenting." I will never forget the title of an article I read when I first got into the business of helping children, because it exemplifies society's compulsion to manage children: "Current Behavior Modification in the Classroom: Be Quiet, Be Still, Be Docile."[30] Teachers, who refer thousands of kids for medication, naturally prefer a classroom that is easier to manage. But is that really the primary goal of education? Should we medicate children to achieve this result?

Overall, I take a positive stance toward the potential role that medication can play in mentally ill children's lives. At the same time, I believe that the research needed to fully investigate the bottom line for a child who takes such medication is meager, is often misguided, and merely scratches the surface. Much information has come out in the last several years about drug companies' and less objective researchers' proclivity for hyping medication research results.

One parent recounted how 28 different psychiatric drugs were prescribed over a three-year period for her child.[31] There is increased concern not only with the number of psychiatric drugs being taken by children, but also with the extensive combinations of drugs being taken. In one study of psychiatric drug use in children, 1.6 million children were given a combination of two drugs, 500,000 were given three psychiatric drugs, and more than 160,000 were given four medications.[32] While psychiatrists might argue that multiple-drug regimens are necessary, the bad news is that little evidence supports the use of medications in this manner. A former director of the National Institute of Mental Health notes, "There are not good scientific data to support the widespread use of these medications in children."[33] Parents are left at the crossroads, trying to decide if medicating their children is right or wrong and if treating their mental illness in this way might compromise their physical health because of certain medications' known side effects.

As one example of the dilemma faced by parents, a recent study found that the effectiveness of drug treatment for ADHD is likely to dissipate after 14 months of treatment. At three, six, and eight years of treatment, when assessed across 30 measures of behavior and academics, children still being given medication "fared no better than their non-medicated counterparts, despite a 41% increase in average daily dose, failing to support continued medication treatment." Furthermore, the researchers found that such drugs can stunt physical growth.[34] Predictably, their findings became a very controversial piece of research, but the study clearly points to the fact that we just don't know as much about the impact of medications as we have been led to believe by psychiatry and "Big Pharma."

Drug testing is admittedly difficult with children. Parents and providers don't want to adhere to the practice of random assignment to experimental groups, which means that some children will not receive medication. For this and many other reasons, very few psychiatric drugs have been approved specifically for children—although medications approved for adults are often prescribed "off label" for children with mental illness (i.e., without being explicitly approved for this use).

Psychiatry typically focuses exclusively on medication administration. After a very short visit and interview, the psychiatrist will prescribe medication, in part because insurance companies aren't interested in paying a high rate for a psychiatrist to manage the child's long-term therapy, when a psychologist or social worker can do it for far less. The result is an uncoordinated system of care—a psychiatrist giving the medication and a therapist to help the family (in most cases, just the child) to understand and cope with the child's illness. Surprisingly, the psychiatrist and the therapist rarely talk together about the individual case, so neither is fully informed in a manner that would lead to the best outcomes for the child.

As Raeburn noted regarding the experience with his children, who were quickly given the drugs and sent home, "I was never told to watch for a change in mood, an obvious precaution that all parents should take. No doctor or psychiatrist ever offered to call regularly during the first few weeks my children were on antidepressants. I was never told to check in. And yet a simple program of regular calls and visits during those first few weeks could probably eliminate almost all of the suicides that occur following the use of antidepressants."[35]

The parents I talked with expressed a consistent theme of confusion regarding how the medication was determined, which procedures they should follow, and how to make sure they were getting the best medical treatment.

[With] older kids, if you tell them, "I'm giving you something that's going to help you" [and tell them] not to be so afraid—immediately the next day, [my son] wasn't afraid. It's a magic pill. We could have given him sugar pills. He knew what it was, what it was supposed to do. It's very hard to get [children] to explain to the psychiatrist what it is they're feeling. I went in, I had some experience, I told the psychiatrist that Adam's having racing thoughts. "No, I'm not!" "Okay, so tell her what it is you're having." So he explained it to her, and she says, "By the way, Adam, that's called racing thoughts." I don't know how, when the kids are taking cocktails of medication, they have any idea what anything's supposed to do and whether something is working. How is the doctor going to figure out that this is the particular medication that's doing that? . . . Adam takes four or five different medications. I don't know how the doctor can ever figure out exactly what it is that works, that's creating the sleepless nights, or this or that.

The importance of taking the medication is another thing that I don't think the children, or many times the parents, have any idea about—the consistency of taking your meds, what to do when the child doesn't take it, what to do if a child skips a dose. If he skipped a week, now we have another story. It's not so much educational, but assumptions, and, of course, good advice from all the fronts.

You don't get much in a 10-minute doctor's appointment. If your child is prescribed medication, they tell you this, they'll write it down, but you're overwhelmed. You're taking this kid on a bus, who's just screaming in the bus, yelling, "I want an ice cream"; you bought him the ice cream, and it's not good enough; and then they're giving you all these instructions verbally, and you're supposed to take this. You get to the pharmacy, and of course, they've got [label warnings] like "Do not operate heavy equipment while you're on this medication" for your six-year-old. "Take with milk"—but you can't get your kid to drink milk. "Take with food"— when it's not appropriate to do so. It's almost impossible to follow through sometimes. What to do? You call the case manager; you don't get a call back.

Ritalin is a drug generally used for attention-deficit/hyperactivity disorder. My daughter's been on that drug for three years. Why? Shouldn't there be some type of specific drug that deals with her moods, her emotions, her spectrum of problems? She's taken Ritalin, Ziprexa, Trazodone—a lot of different drugs. Ritalin is the one they tend to stick with. Although she may have some hyperactivity/attention-deficit disorder problems, I feel that they're way underscored by the bipolar.

She was diagnosed with oppositional defiance, Tourette syndrome, obsessive–compulsive disorder, and hyperactivity. When she was diagnosed, they put her on Prozac. The doctor kept saying it was her behavior and kept raising the Prozac [dose], and she kept getting worse and worse. Three days before we started restraining her, she tried to smother herself by putting plastic bags over her head. The Prozac was agitating her and making her worse.

Another parent had a similar horrifying experience with the child's medication:

They started him on medication, and he ended up on Zoloft and Adderall. Then he couldn't stay stable. He was getting in more and more trouble. He busted out all the walls in my home in his room. He put knife holes in the doors, and he'd never been in any trouble legally at all, and he ended up—no, he tried to commit suicide. After he got out of the hospital, everything happened. He tried to commit suicide.

A consistent theme that can compound the confusion is the sheer number of medications that are prescribed. Many parents are prescribed a different drug every time the child sees a different psychiatrist. For example, Paul Raeburn, in *Acquainted with the Night*, carefully tracked the medications prescribed for his child and listed the following drugs:

- Mellaril, originally used to treat schizophrenia
- Zoloft
- Tegretol
- Ritalin, added Ativan
- Lithium
- Risperdal
- Celexa
- Depakote

And this was over a fairly short period of time!

For many children, however, the medication process works well and is perceived as exactly what the child needs:

He gave us extended-release meds. It's just been huge. I didn't even realize that John had outgrown his former dose. It's dramatic. It's night and day. The dosage is right.

What happens when children get older and have to manage their medication as they go to school and carry out life with their friends? Medication management from the adolescent's perspective hasn't been addressed much in the professional or practice literature. Research studies on adults have found that consistent adherence to medication is a serious issue, with the consequences of non-adherence including relapse, leading to rehospitalization, and suicide. As children grow older, the skills of medication management will be critical. Unfortunately, psychiatrists tend to issue the prescriptions and therapists tend to focus on behavior; left unaddressed is the implementation of a long-term medication adherence strategy. This gap exists despite the fact that it makes sense that how teens manage medication, school, and peers can be critical to successful coping.

David Karp has extensively studied how individuals respond to medication for depression.[36] While many mental health professionals assume medication adherence is a simple process, Karp points out that individuals go through different reactions as they adjust to taking medication. While Karp carried out his studies in adults, it is seems clear that as adolescents get older, their response to medication is likely to eventually follow the adult pattern. For many adults, following a medication regimen begins with a struggle and a resistance stage where having to consistently take medications is rejected altogether. At some point, many individuals hit bottom and become more willing to follow the medical advice they have been given. At this point, they begin a trial commitment, in which they agree to experiment with medication for a limited time. If the medication has a positive impact, they are more likely to accept a biological or biochemical explanation for their illness and more likely to see medication as a reasonable response to their difficulties. Even so, many—including some who believe the medication was critical to their stability—become disenchanted (many relapse into depression) and eventually want to get off the medication and see if they can do without it. Karp's recent book, *Is It Me or My Meds?*, extends his discussion to the impact of taking psychiatric medication and its influence on one's identity.[37]

Taking medication, even for children, begins a process of socially labeling the child as someone with a major difficulty. Many parents recalled a period of time when the child developed a keen sense of awareness about their difficulty.

I remember him telling me one time, he was upset about something and crying, saying, "What's wrong with me? There's something wrong with me." That broke my heart.

He's upset to this day he'll never be anything. He says, "All I am is schizophrenia. All people see me as is my illness."

Erik Parens and Josephine Johnston discuss this dilemma in their article about medication and children's mental health:

Both pharmacological and nonpharmacological treatments can reduce the severity of the symptoms of emotional and behavioral disturbances in children and improve their overall functioning in life, but there are differences in which treatment people value. Medication enthusiasts note that the effects achieved by drugs and psychosocial interventions are similar and that, therefore, it makes no moral difference which kind of intervention is used. After all, in the best cases, drugs and psychotherapy both produce long-term changes in the brain. Gerald Klerman, a psychiatrist who studied depression, long ago suggested that a knee-jerk preference for psychotherapy over drugs was a symptom of "pharmacological Calvinism," an unexamined gut feeling about the wrongness of using drugs to treat emotional and behavioral disturbances.[38]

They further note:

Critics, however, argue that the treatment we choose does matter morally insofar as different treatments can reflect and reinforce different values.

If we increase the teacher–student ratio to help students focus better on their work, we may be emphasizing the value of engagement. If, instead, we give students stimulants to help them achieve the same goal, we may be emphasizing the value of efficiency. Engagement and efficiency are both important and compatible values, but they are different, and emphasizing one or the other can influence whether we choose pharmacological or non-pharmacological means to achieve the purpose of reducing emotional and behavioral disturbances.[39]

PARENTS AND MEDICATION

What is the impact of medication on parents? How does the decision to put their child on a psychiatric medication affect them? As I listened to parents, a consistent theme for many of them was that the prescription of medication was a turning point—a shift in their reality of what their child was experiencing and a shift in the realization that their child was significantly ill. To agree to medication represents a public declaration that your child is in serious need of help. For some parents, getting to this point was a relief—they were finally on a path to control the disorder. Other parents, however, never became comfortable with the notion that their child needed to be medicated to be helped.

Parents' experiences with medication often lead them to redefine themselves. Their public acknowledgment of the child's need for medication provides the groundwork for seeing themselves as not just a parent but also a caretaker of an ill child. This new sense of parenting emerges as they interact more with professionals who talk about medication and the ways medication can counteract the child's symptoms. By seeking or accepting medication, they create a new role focused on how to be a parent—a parent of a mentally ill child.

One parent described earlier, Christina, talked about an incident where her child came to terms with his mental illness after he started taking medication, and both parent and child realized they were on a life course together that wasn't going to be easy. In this example, the parent explains how she adopted a new role after recognizing the need for medication:

> We had him on medication for bipolar disorder, because that's what the doctor diagnosed him with. All the treatment my children have had was after I'd adopted them. As his mom, when we first put him on lithium, I was really bummed. I didn't want a child on lithium with bipolar [disorder]. The reality was, we had to deal with it.

One parent I interviewed refused Ritalin medication for her son, who was diagnosed with ADHD. She took an extremely anti-medication position, in part because she was a former drug addict and didn't want her child to take a drug that might lead him to further drug use in the future. In rejecting the medication, this parent encountered a lot of pressure and confrontation from professionals, who insisted she should medicate her child. She summarizes her opinion:

*I think that we need to stop preaching that in our society—that pills can make you
happy. That's how society ends up with people like me, addicts and alcoholics.*

Similarly, Mandy, who is just starting to address medication issues, has
reservations:

*I don't want to put him on any medication. I want to exhaust every other option
that I can find right now.*

   *Many people want me to put him on medication. I don't think it's fair to put a
four-year-old on drugs.*

Reservations about medication have only grown since concerns emerged
about whether some psychiatric drugs for depression lead to an increased risk of
suicide of depressed adolescents. Because of some troubling data on this front,
in 2004 the FDA issued a "black box" warning for selective serotonin reuptake
inhibitors (SSRIs) being used in children and adolescents. The prior year the
New York State Attorney General sued GlaxoSmithKline, which holds the pat-
ent on Paxil, for concealing evidence that the drug caused suicidal behavior in
young patients. The media reported many of the heart-rending stories that
parents told in Congressional hearings, recounting how their children committed suicide after starting the medication. The black box label, which highlights
the risk of suicidal behavior and thinking, led to a 25 percent drop in prescriptions written for SSRIs.
   The controversy around medication use for children and adolescents has at
least focused increased attention on the need for more research, and in particular
the need for research examining the use of psychiatric medications with children. Despite the lingering questions, some researchers now believe new data
and a reanalysis of existing data show that the risks of antidepressant therapy in
adolescents are exceeded by their benefits.[40]

CHAPTER 5

Finding Help: What Matters to Parents?

One sees clearly only with the heart. Anything essential is invisible to the eyes.

—*The Little Prince*

"We needed help from someone. But when we tried to find it, it wasn't there. We took the children to a series of psychiatrists who repeatedly misdiagnosed them and treated them incorrectly, sometimes making them worse. We talked to therapists who threw us off course again and again with faulty assessments. We took the children to hospitals that did not keep them long enough to help them, because our insurance company wouldn't pay for the care. We talked to school officials who must have seen dozens or hundreds of troubled kids, but who told us they'd never seen such problems before and had no idea what to do. We spent tens of thousands of dollars, some of the money wasted on inappropriate care, to try to fill the vast gaps in our insurance plan. Sometimes these efforts helped, sometimes they didn't. What we found was a splintered, chaotic mental health care system that seemed to do more harm than good."[1]

This description of parents' perceptions of how they and their children are treated within the larger mental health system addresses some significant barriers to families receiving the services that they need. A number of more specific examples of such barriers can be found in the literature. In a refreshingly straightforward and enlightening article that appeared in *Social Work*, entitled "Parent–Professional Relationships in the Treatment of Seriously Emotionally Disturbed Children and Adolescents," the authors explain that "a review of the literature on the parent–professional relationship reveals little research on how parents and professionals actually interact."[2] They go on to report that the literature on this topic that does exist, combined with anecdotal evidence, reveals that "parents have complained that the only time they are involved in treatment is when the etiologies of their children's disorders are discussed, that they are not given access to their children's records, that they are asked to release information about their children from one professional or agency to another but are not allowed to read it, and that they are responsible for monitoring their children's progress through a fragmented system—yet are assumed by professionals to be incapable of understanding either the system or their children's problems. Parents have reported their anger at seeking help and receiving too little and at being asked to provide information but not to participate actively in making decisions."[3]

In a critique of the public mental health system for children, John Lyons notes that few professionals recognize the difficulties parents experience because they are not privy to complete information about their child's condition.[4] Such unequal information can often put professionals and parents at odds. Parents don't understand the treatment options, the types of therapy available, the way in which psychiatric medications work—yet all of this information is needed for the parents to feel comfortable and be true team players with the mental health professional.

Furthermore, major obstacles to family involvement and improved care, such as a lack of supportive family services (for example, respite care) and numerous problematic policies, regulations, and practices, have been noted in studies. From the viewpoint of the parent, professional attitudes and behaviors need to change. All of these factors lead Collins and Collins to reach the following conclusion: "The traditional orientation of mental health professions is toward pathology and the weaknesses or inadequacies of parents, usually mothers. The professional–client relationship traditionally has been conceptualized in ways that emphasize the power and expertise of the professional over that of the client. The resultant hierarchical relationship, as reflected in the professional attitude and language, is then coupled with the professional focus on parents' deficiencies. The types of experiences many parents have critically described seem to be an inevitable outcome."[5] Young supports this contention, noting that "parents may be considered at least partially responsible for their children's disturbances and therefore not useful or valid evaluators of a service."[6] In light of these statements, one can see how challenging it is to overcome many of these barriers to service when parents' views and opinions are not valued.

Upon querying a group of parents about barriers to service, in addition to other topics, one study found that often, even when parents were asked to participate in treatment, they felt that their input was treated as secondary to that of professionals—that is, given lesser weight. For example, parents reported being asked to review a treatment plan that had already been formulated by the professionals involved. Faced with the official, typewritten opinions of professionals, some parents did not feel free to dissent.[7] This study also found poor coordination between agencies, a lack of consistency in treatment plans from provider to provider, and a paucity of referrals. Parents reported being met with incredulity and skepticism when they talked about their children's emotional and behavioral problems, which were routinely attributed to poor parenting procedures. Parents who already felt guilty for their children's problems sometimes withdrew from treatment after feeling further blamed by mental health professionals.

In this study, the lack of validation some parents received from professionals for their perception of their children's problems became a stressor in its own right. Regarding the subjects' unmet needs as parents, the most significant desire reported was for more open communication with providers about such topics as other available resources, and more active involvement in treatment planning. The authors explain that while these desires are modest in scope, they heavily influence the perceived quality of care for the family of a disturbed child, thereby greatly affecting overall satisfaction and attrition rates. As this study shows, specific evidence supports the important role that parental perceptions play in treatment, and this topic merits further attention.

The parents I interviewed reinforced the desire parents have for a good professional–parent relationship:

> Counselors have to go on about their lives, and I understand that. [They want] a better-paying job—great. But at least have the integrity to have closure with your clients. Not even a notice. I just heard about it [the counselor leaving the program].

> We've been through the whole psychiatry thing. We had a really good psychiatrist, and then our insurance didn't want to pay for it anymore—and we didn't want to start over with a new one. You get really tired of having to do that: each new therapist, each new psychiatrist. You've got to go through the whole background, and it gets so frustrating.

> I don't think he got really good care. The caseworker was really not the best. She didn't come to the team meetings, would only show up once a year. The person prescribing Malcolm's medication at the time was a physician's assistant and had him on all kinds of different cocktails. He'd blown up like a balloon. He was bumped into four or five different residential settings. Some were horrible. The system out there was awful. We had a very hard time finding him a home.

The search for an answer, for the cure, can be all-consuming for some parents. They can be driven and obsessed with a search for the right medication, the right treatment, the right person to help. Parents will take their children to expert after expert, from town to town, and sometimes, if financial resources are available, across the country in the search for help. With children's mental illness, such a search can be a tricky endeavor, although quality expertise and advice can be found and can be helpful. Yet a cure—a permanent end to the difficulty—is not likely to happen and even less likely to be attributable to some specific drug or special treatment procedure. The community of "experts" offers a bewildering array of choices that parents must sort through. Some are ready to empty the purse of the concerned but low-income mother; others, at no expense but out of humane caring, become heroes who take the precious time to answer questions, provide critical advice, and help the parent accept what must be.

THE SERVICE DELIVERY SYSTEM THAT WASN'T

Mike and his wife spent years trying to manage an extremely difficult autistic child. Like most parents, they confronted a shortage of services. They describe the point where they didn't see any viable options after having seen numerous doctors, traveled to other states, and tried experimental treatments—doing everything they possible could:

> Raymond was always a threat to wander off; he almost never slept more than a few hours at a time. His outbursts continued, and he required attention 24 hours a day. He attended special education classes and an after-school program and, on occasion, there was respite care.

For the most part this family was completely on their own, and they found it almost impossible to find anyone capable or willing to take care of Raymond for even an hour or two. Their situation led mental health professionals to suggest a group home for their son. Initially they were defensive about such a suggestion, but eventually they saw it as their only "salvation." Reluctantly, they placed their son in the home and found it worked well for their family. Raymond still comes home to his parents on a weekly basis.

Again and again the literature, the conceptual models, the experts, and the proposed service options all talk about the need for a continuum of care. Raymond's parents were lucky to find a group home—but far too many parents are left with no options. In talking to parents, I was not able to find a continuum of care, but rather a jumble of disconnected experiences. Instead, parents talked about visits to a therapist and occasional visits to a psychiatrist or trips to the hospital for emergency purposes. In many cases parents had to rely on the police for help with their child.

Since the establishment of the President's New Freedom Commission on Mental Health, much focus in the adult mental health field has been on recovery and resilience.[8] In contrast, the children's mental health field has largely revolved around the *system of care* model. The concept of recovery emerged from the observation that people with severe mental illness could develop positive outcomes, which contradicted the more negative and pessimistic perspective that was traditionally put forth. However, recovery implies a medical perspective that seems inconsistent with mental health. Redefinitions such as "recovery and resilience" often provide a fresh way of thinking about this issue. The notions of resilience, hope, and optimism are what resonate with most people.[9] Nonetheless, the system of care concept aptly describes what I observed as critical for the proper care and treatment of children.

A system of care is defined as "a comprehensive spectrum of mental health and other necessary services which are organized into a coordinated network to meet the multiple and changing needs of severely emotionally disturbed children and adolescents."[10] Most experts in children's mental health have advocated for a "systems" perspective to manage the multiple services needed by their young clients.[11] This model became popular because children's mental health services were well known as an example of "failure by fragmentation." Experts in the field began to recognize this basic problem and have attempted to move to a broader systems focus in thinking about the delivery of services for children. We know that many of our children need a range of services tied together in an integrated manner, but making these connections is often complicated because policies and fiscal constraints do not support the system of care approach. Even today, some experts who have studied how the children's mental health system works lament the ongoing failure to coordinate services to these youths. One such expert, John Lyons, notes that "despite the widespread acceptance of the basic tenets of the systems-of-care philosophy, the progress toward the implementation of this philosophy has been slow; in some cases, no progress has been observable."[12]

The system of care model includes 3 overriding core values and 10 guiding principles. The core values are as follows:

1. The system of care should be child centered and family focused, with the needs of the child and family dictating the types and mix of services provided.
2. The system of care should be community based, with a locus of services as well as management and decision-making responsibility resting at the community level.
3. The system of care should be culturally competent, with agencies, programs, and services that are responsive to the cultural, racial, and ethnic differences of the population they serve.

The guiding principles include some basic notions that children's mental health services should adhere to—such guidelines as "comprehensive services," "individualized services" for the child, "integrated services," "case management," and a "smooth transition to adult services."[13]

In a rare but insightful analysis of what parents want from a "system of care," Richard Donner and others identified the following attitudes that parents seek in case managers: providing hope and vision to the future, promoting children and families being together, respecting families as experts on their needs, and being nonjudgmental.[14] The parents whom I interviewed made it clear that what they commonly experienced was a failure to meet this need—that is, no "system of care":

> My experience with a mental health agency was horrible. After my son turned 18, I had to wait almost a year for him to get any kind of therapeutic intervention. He was on a waiting list. He would get his meds; his case manager would never call me back. I would try to make an appointment to see her. Jacob would

get psychotic or in trouble, and he would end up going into the hospital. We'd have these little emergency meetings and then he would get back into the real world and I would say, "Don't you think you have some kind of therapy that could help him cope? At least give him a place to check in every week."

We got into a huge fight. It was physical; she was biting me, kicking me. I called the mental health agency and left a message but no one called me back. I said I needed someone at my house right away, but they didn't even try to call. When I finally got to speak with someone, I was angry and mad. The person from the hospital told me that I was the one who needed to be in a psychiatric hospital, not my daughter. I took her to the hospital the next day and they still wouldn't accept her. And the third day she takes a broom, whacks it across my face, and breaks my glasses. I called the police, and the police officer came and hauled her to the hospital.

They finally learned at the behavioral health agency that I don't call unless it's really bad. I call and say, "Tessa's acting really weird. We need to change her meds." But before they wouldn't listen. Now they've realized I'm not going to call unless it's something that I'm really noticing. They have to learn you. You have to learn them. But it's hard at first. Initially they were a lot more resistant. But you have to keep calling, yelling. It can be frustrating.

While this book is primarily about parenting, I found a very compelling first-person account from a young adult who described her experience "surviving the system":

My name is Angela Nelson, and this is the story of my survival. I grew up in the child welfare system in Illinois, spending most of 11 years in psychiatric institutions and group homes. I can honestly say that the system did not help me recover from any of the problems I came in with; in fact, it created additional difficulty. The system focused on controlling my behavior with little regard to the issues that brought me into the system in the first place. In particular, I received very little education and there was no effort to keep my family unit together. Despite the lack of regard for my future, I still maintain hope and I am living independently today. I know reaching my goals will be difficult, especially since there are few resources and little support available to me now.[15]

Although what I found in my interviews with regard to mental health services for families paints a very pessimistic picture in general about how we can help children with mental disorders, the different states vary in the design, organization, and accessibility of such services provided to families. For example, an enormous resource for learning about children's mental health services from a national perspective is the Portland Research and Training Center.[16] From the start, this center has been in the forefront of promoting a model that will transform mental health care for children and families by recognizing the value and strengths in families, being family driven and youth guided, promoting cultural competence, and emphasizing programs with evidence of effectiveness.

One inspiring story described in the Portland Center's newsletter, *Focal Point*, is about a boy named Jason from Louisiana.[17] Jason has autism and suffered from a number of problems, and his aggressive behaviors made his situation especially difficult. After an extended stay in a psychiatric hospital, he was ready to return to his community, but there was no place for him to go. For Jason to receive the support he needed in the community, his parents would need to give up custody and allow him to become a ward of the state. Jason's parents, like many parents in their situation, were not interested in this option. The parents came to realize that no community treatment, hospital, or residential program could substitute for his own home, but the question remained, "Can Jason live at home?"

In an extraordinary example of coordination and commitment, a network of agencies, the parents, the state mental health office, and many others got together to attempt a plan to keep Jason at home. It worked. Jason's father agreed to stay at home with Jason as his "personal care attendant," and funding from multiple sources paid the father for his efforts. The ultimate plan was a "wrap-around" of coordinated services that included such elements as a transitional plan to teach the parents behavior management strategies; crisis management and physical management strategies; a fence around the family's yard to protect Jason; social skills and treatment integration therapy for Jason; medication management; respite care for one day a month; and a public school aide as part of his individual education plan (IEP) when he returned to public school. In the end, the answer to the question, "Can Jason live at home?" was yes, but it remains difficult and challenging.

Jason's mother sums up what it meant to be able to work out a solution to finding the proper services for her child:

> Home life with Jason remains a challenge. My husband has become a full-time handyman as he strives to keep the damage under control. Our life does not have the freedoms found in most families. We are not able to get up and go; Jason is always a major consideration. We do not take vacations; we have never had a Christmas tree—but both of our sons live at home. All of the services, the time and the money, have given us a complete family. Autism placed a hole in our heart that can never be mended. When Jason came to live at the hospital, another hole was made. This hole was repaired when Jason came home.[18]

Even when families do find services, ongoing engagement with treatment can often be an issue. Researchers have addressed this problem by examining "intensive engagement interventions,"[19] which boil down to reminder calls. The underlying issue, however, is about respect. Parents accept phone calls as respectful actions of caring and, therefore, are motivated by them. If practitioners are to better serve parents, they could develop an "enhanced respectfulness" intervention to great impact. In which ways are parents most influenced by the actions of service providers? How can respectfulness be increased? There's much to gain from a more complete analysis of actions that parents perceive as respectful.

Mary Mckay has developed a protocol for more effectively engaging families and children, and while not noted as such, it represents an approach based on *listening* and *respect*. According to this protocol, the tasks of the therapy are as follows:

- Clarify the roles of the worker, agency, intake process, and service options.
- Set the stage for a collaborative work relationship.
- Identify concrete practical issues that can be addressed immediately.
- Develop a plan to overcome barriers to ongoing involvement with the agency.

A research study that examined this approach found the trained practitioners lost only 5 cases from the first to the third session with clients, whereas the untrained group lost 35 families during the same time. Clearly, this intervention had a large impact, perhaps because it delineated a respectful approach toward working with families.

WHAT CHOICES DO I HAVE?

While the theory of a system of care model sounds great, many parents seeking to manage and find the proper treatment for their child face a single choice: hospitalization or residential care. Yet hospitalization might not be necessary if "wraparound services" (a new description for the system of care model) were more widely available. These services would include intensive home and community-based services, case management, parent management training, respite care, and day treatment.

Recent work on developing effective models of family involvement in community-based intervention has been tested with some positive results.[20] In some states, the wraparound approach has emerged as a true model of community-based service delivery. Wraparound Milwaukee has more than 80 services that it can use with families. The mobile unit alone responded to 1,500 calls in one year. But the reality is very different in other states. A core principle in the wraparound model is this: *What does the child need to be successful?* Unfortunately, that is a moot question across a lot of the country because services are so seriously restricted.

As many newspaper headlines have documented, to get needed treatment some parents have had to resort to giving up custody of their children. Indeed, the reality is that to get a child into a residential facility, relinquishment of custody is required. Often these children cannot be managed at home, and there is little community support to help the parents keep the child at home. Without needed community programs and additional services, the family believes the only treatment option is residential, and as a result they are forced to give up guardianship.

In one year the parents of 241 mentally ill Texas children relinquished their parental rights after telling judges that they had no other alternative.[21] What would it feel like to be a parent who has to completely give up your authority and guardianship to get your child into some form of treatment you believe the child desperately needs? Usually, these parents do not retain any control as to when and under which circumstances they can regain guardianship.

The recently published *Handbook of Child and Adolescent Systems of Care* presents the new paradigm of "community psychiatry,"[22] although traditionally psychiatry is the profession furthest from understanding the realities of community-based care. Perhaps psychiatrists with caseloads from wealthy patients can address this issue more effectively, but all of the parents I interviewed were concerned about their psychiatrist's lack of follow-up and limited involvement. The psychiatrists themselves are often frustrated, too. As one psychiatry resident noted, "I find I am being trained to perpetuate the problem of over- or misdiagnosing. We are forced to categorize patients into neat clear-cut packages to manage their treatment. Once this is done, it often precludes us from taking a broader view of the situation, where we could encounter other factors or behavioral nuances. In my experience it is the approach of medical training that needs restructuring, so we will stop putting square pegs into round holes and admit that psychiatric diagnoses are not one dimensional."[23]

Parents recognize that psychiatric diagnosis is a critical factor in how their child is helped—or not helped. As one parent put it, "It is a shame that our kids have turned into a bunch of labels and experiments in the medical world and it is us parents who were the gullible bunch who let them. We need to take a stand about what we know is right and demand psychiatrists to get to know our kids better before they make up their minds about a diagnosis that may change a life forever."[24] Despite this critique, the movement toward understanding community-based solutions among psychiatrists is reassuring.

Unfortunately, the current reality remains a long way off from this view. Almost all of the parents I interviewed complained about the lack of services available to meet the needs of their children:

We tried getting her into the hospital. They wouldn't keep her. They said nothing was wrong with her. Then finally we got hooked up with another agency. They said it was going to be 3 days before we could get her into that treatment setting. Then my husband and I had to restrain her for 28 straight hours. She only went to sleep about two or three times.

Raymond needs 24-hour one-on-one attention. We tried to get him into a therapeutic group home or a therapeutic foster home. There was nobody out there who could do that—no services available. Foster homes were all full. They couldn't get him into anything, and that's why he ended up back in our house.

I've gone through every agency I can think of—every single one. There is nothing, nothing. Childhood schizophrenia—nothing. There's no caseworker.

Nothing we can do, no social skills. There are no real support meetings for him. There are a few for me, but I guess most children don't have this diagnosis. There's no one to really talk about it to. There is no one to discuss the agony.

He keeps getting worse. But I'm not going to lock him up in the hospital with strangers for seven weeks and let him descend back into pure terror. It's not going to happen. I know what he's got. There's no doubt; I don't need you to tell me. I know he's suicidal. The doctor in the hospital, of course, is never the doctor who knows the kid. Where can we find the help we need for this family?

There has always been a lack of service and continuum of care. Always and still is. We had to fight for every service. We actually went to a state-level hearing once with the judge, and we won.

Many parents spoke of the need for relief—some respite care where another caretaker will come in and relieve them of their 24-hour parenting responsibilities. Although these services are supposed to be available, only a few parents were ever able to access them:

Then we asked for respite care. After almost six years, we've only had two days. And those two days we were in the seminar on attachment disorder. Everything is "No, we can't do that."

Oh, respite care—that's the other issue. Because there isn't any. But it's really stressful on the whole family. Everybody.

PSYCHIATRY: A VANISHING FIELD

One crucial factor in service delivery is having access to a qualified psychiatrist. The lack of child psychiatrists is a huge issue for parents with mentally ill children. Many parents are desperate for a psychiatric consultation, but are unable to find one. While identification of children's mental illness has steadily increased, the number of child psychiatrists has remained far below the level of need. One mother whose daughter began cutting herself and talking of suicide compared her situation to having a child get a concussion with pain and vomiting and not being able to find any medical help. There are currently 7,418 child psychiatrists in the United States, and the demand for services is expected to grow—one estimate is that the nation needs 30,000 child and adolescent psychiatrists.[25] Only about 300 new child psychiatrists complete their training each year. How can we meet the mental health needs of these children with so few psychiatrists?

One parent describes her experience with psychiatrists she worked with from private and public systems:

You asked me about differences between private and public systems. I can go to the private psychiatrist at 5:30 at night. I don't have to take the boys out of school. I can call and get forms filled out, prescriptions filled, within 24 hours, not 72. Sometimes you need them within 24 hours. I can call and get a med change quickly. I probably have direct access to other services—hospitalization, triage. There's no case management to mess with, no contact person. Consistency is better. You can usually follow [doctors] if they left the place. Or they will try to work you in with somebody whom they feel would work well with your kid. It's not just the next person who's going to come in and fit into this hole.

CAN ANYONE HELP WITH THIS CRISIS?

Many of these parents live in a world of chaos and crisis, and it is most certainly a world where they have lost control. Without control, there is no sense of resolution. The parents' lack of control over their child's symptoms is complemented by the mental health system's inability to control the symptoms as well. For many mental health professionals, there is a denial of the limits of the extent to which their work can affect the child. It borders on a breach of ethics, because no one helps the parent confront the awful truth about the likely prognosis for his or her child or the difficulty inherent in obtaining a reduction in behavior symptoms. When there is a pretense of successful treatment, there is denial of the suffering for which there is no treatment.[26]

I will never forget how one parent, Christina, talked about the utter lack of control in her life. She finally figured out for herself that to get any sleep, she had to unplug the phone and simply not worry about her child (now old enough to be "independent") until the next morning when, after a full night's sleep, she could address whatever presented itself to her. Prior to adopting this strategy, she had cried herself to sleep too many nights.

One study of parents' perceptions notes how "The child's illness seemed to tear at the very fabric of the family when parents were forced to use extraordinary means to control the child. Parents talked sadly about holding down the child, restraining them, and sometimes, in frustration, hitting the child."[27] It was clear that parents deeply regretted having to use these extreme measures.

The parents' descriptions of crises were overwhelming. Many parents whom I interviewed faced intolerable situations with very little help or support. One dramatic example came from a parent who faced many situations where she had absolutely no control over her child's behaviors. You can hear her resentment and anger at this situation:

She got me down on the ground, on top of me, and tries to put her finger through my clothing into my vagina to rape me. This was two years ago. I just called the crisis team a little before this happened, because I could see it coming on. I wanted somebody there. Nobody answered. She poured a whole pitcher of tea into my fax telephone. She completely busted my other phone. My cellular phone battery was charging. I was furious. No phone. All my neighbors were used to her high-screech screaming, because that's part of her Tourette's disorder. I'm trying to yell for help. Nobody's hearing me. I'm black and blue all over. She bit me, she kicked, hit me, raped me.

Other parents talked about how the mental health system and professionals were unprepared to address the number of crises families confront:

One of my biggest gripes right now is children's crises. Children have many crises—we have many more crises than the system is capable of handling. When a child goes into crisis, the family is in crisis. I think both the clinicians and the law enforcement and the family members agree—I've served on committees in the community—that a child's crisis becomes the family's crisis. We have a system that says if the parents are in crisis, we don't deal with the parent; we deal with the child. Child care is family focused, but somehow or other, the needs of the family doesn't necessarily get met.

There's no help in a crisis. There is not a crisis place anymore. We've been to the local psychiatric hospital and they are not good for crisis because they deal with older teenagers and adults.

An interesting concept relevant to addressing a crisis is Arlie Hochschild's notion of "emotion work."[28] Hochschild has focused our attention on "feeling rules" and "emotion management" in times of difficulty. This line of thinking leads her to question how we manage our feelings over moments in time. As David Karp points out in his analysis of families with mentally ill members, "breaches of social order generate exceptionally strong negative emotions; the case of mental illness allows us to examine how caregivers reconcile love for a family member with such emotions as fear, bewilderment, frustration, resentment, anger, and even hate."[29] Parenting mentally ill children leads to many situations where one confronts "emotion work." A crisis where the parent cannot control the child presents a thorny question: How should a parent respond? What is an appropriate way to feel about the crisis? The parents I interviewed confronted many of these situations that demanded emotion work in the aftermath of a crisis.

From this perspective, parents can benefit from help with the emotion work required to manage their presentation of themselves in the social world in which they live. Such emotion work is not often addressed as an explicit skill, yet most people will agree we perform this work often as part of our daily lives. As cognitive psychologists know well, how you label or frame a situation can change how you feel about that situation. If a parent attempts to deal with a public crisis from the perspective of "I must be in control of my child at all times," he or she will likely feel a lot of guilt and distress about not managing the crisis. In contrast, if the parent approaches the crisis from a perspective of "I have a special child who is difficult to manage," he or she may be better able to release feelings of guilt and notions that the parent has to control the outcome of every situation. As I listened to parents, one of the most difficult experiences they described to me was trying to deal with their child in a crisis situation—and almost none of the parents felt they had ever received any help from mental health professionals on how to deal directly with the crisis *and* how to deal with their residual emotions following the crisis.

The current mental health delivery system is slowly recognizing that services must move from a focus on "curing" mental illness (especially serious mental illness) to providing long-term supportive services that facilitate the opportunity for each individual with mental illness to lead a safe and quality life in the community.[30] The point of this book is not to write a treatment manual on how to help parents with mentally ill children, but it is clear that parents need certain things to help them manage effectively while parenting their child. They need access to detailed information so they can understand, assess, and respond to their child's needs. Some parents can access this information on the web, others read books, and still others talk to parents with similar challenges. All of these things can be "packaged" for the parents by professionals, although this is rarely done. Parents need help in managing the most difficult times—the crises—that they too frequently have to deal with. They need skills to calm the situation down and alternatives to try when things get out of control. They need respite care to help them manage *over the long term*, and they need access to therapists who will make home visits and who will fully understand their family context.

It is clear that parents can be helped with support and counseling—for their own issues and also to help them maintain a good level of stability. While agencies sometimes offer "therapy," what parents need most are skills—basic parenting skills, skills to manage their child, crisis skills, communication skills, home organization/management skills. The parents would like their children to receive *practical* therapy—anger management skills, coping skills, self-soothing skills, organizational skills, learning skills, friendship skills, and so forth.

The Criminalization of Mental Illness

As the sun rises, hundreds of children and adolescents will wake up having spent the night in juvenile detention centers, juvenile jails, and adult prisons. A 15-year-old with schizo-affective disorder, bipolar disorder, and depression spent two months in a juvenile detention center in Pennsylvania.[31] No residential placement would accept him, even though his assault was not serious enough to keep him in prison. A 16-year-old with bipolar disorder and substance abuse also ended up in the juvenile detention center. He had a delinquency charge for burglary at age 14, but the identified issue was "failure to adjust," which means he wasn't following established rules. Often these children are apprehended by police and hauled off in police cars, some even handcuffed.

One of the main issues that leads to the criminalization of mental illness in children is aggression. The psychiatric hospitals, the group homes, foster parents—none of them wants to contend with a child who is "out of control." One of the few hospitals in Anchorage, Alaska, has an informal policy to refuse service to mentally ill children with aggressive tendencies.[32]

In a recently reported case, mental health workers were desperate to find space for a teenage girl who was seriously ill. When they called the only available psychiatric hospital, they were told to call back in the morning. Frustrated and convinced that the girl needed to find a safe haven, they took her to a local hospital, where an ER doctor made a referral from the hospital. With the referral from the hospital, they knew she would not be turned away. This scenario is repeated in many places across the country.

The detention center in Idaho Falls, Idaho, reports keeping a 16-year-old boy in its facility for almost a year because the mental health agencies all complained they couldn't safely care for the youth—despite the fact that his violent attacks were all directly aimed toward himself. He was cutting, was banging his head, and even ripped his toenails out, but everybody was afraid to confront his serious problems. As this story demonstrates, mental health facilities will often refuse to provide services if they believe they can't "safely detain" the person. That leaves a lot of gaps in services for those individuals in high need.

This problem is widespread; a report from California found that more than half of all juvenile detention facilities held youths who were waiting for mental health services outside of the juvenile justice system. Many detention facilities were holding children as young as 8 to 12 years old. Some children had committed minor crimes, but many came into the system when parents who could not manage the children called the police. One director of a facility told reporters, "Our institutions are designed to help children involved in criminal activity. They are not psychiatric hospitals." Administrators in California are frustrated because the detention centers do not have the resources to respond to the mental health problems they are confronting.

At many of these detention centers, the average stay is short—one or two weeks—but for children with mental disorders it can be six months or longer. Recent studies have found that as many as 35 to 50 percent of the youths held in these facilities have mental disorders. Some 20 percent of the boys and 33 percent of the girls have reportedly considered suicide.[33] In some states, mental facilities for children have been shut down, with smaller residential treatment facilities being used for their care. Making matters even more complex is the fact that many of these facilities are privately owned and, therefore, can refuse the kids who are the most difficult to deal with.

Some state laws are very restrictive in the extent to which facilities can restrain an out-of-control child.[34] After many publicly reported abuses and even child deaths due to restraints, states have had to tighten up their oversight of these services. As a result, most residential treatment centers just don't want the complication of dealing with aggressive kids. Many parents and professionals see a dire need for more institutional placements, or at least the development of regulations that do not allow residential treatment centers to easily reject difficult children.

"Arrest My Kid: He Needs Mental Health," an article by Anne-Marie Cusac,[35] tells the story of Wanda Yanello, the mother of a child with bipolar disorder, who was trying to get her child into long-term inpatient care, as

recommended by the psychiatrist. Her insurance had lapsed, and she could not afford the treatment herself. Her child, Heather, was often out on the streets, unsupervised and in danger. She had already been raped and beaten up, had attempted suicide twice, and was taking drugs. When Heather took her mother's car for a spin, Wanda saw her opportunity to have Heather arrested. That arrest helped place Heather into the juvenile justice system, where she ultimately received a referral for residential treatment.

Wanda Yanello was not happy with the treatment Heather received, but she was cut off from any involvement in Heather's treatment. Like many parents, to get treatment within the juvenile justice system, she had to effectively give up custody of her daughter. Across the country, many parents are resorting to this same formula—get your child arrested in the hopes of obtaining mental health treatment. It is unclear how many parents are taking this tack, but many professionals believe the numbers are significant. In some instances, social workers or other mental health providers give parents a blunt piece of advice: "Nothing can be done unless your child gets arrested." Of course, arresting the child is nò panacea; often parents regret the decision and discover that the envisioned help is not there. But for too many parents, this option is their last resort.

A survey by the National Alliance for the Mentally Ill, entitled "Families on the Brink: The Impact of Ignoring Children with Serious Mental Illness," found that almost half of all parents with a mentally ill child were denied or received limited services for the child by their managed care plan, to the detriment of their child's health.[36] Even more dramatically, 36 percent reported that their child was placed in the juvenile justice system because they could not get the services they needed.

PEOPLE OF COLOR: IT ONLY GETS WORSE

The barriers facing parents of mentally ill children in obtaining quality care are tremendous. Now consider how much greater these barriers can be for minority parents, who are often marginalized by society. Many of the parents I interviewed were minority parents, who spoke mainly of their perspective as parents of mentally ill children, not minority parents of mentally ill children. However, their stories often differed from those of their white counterparts in several ways.

Some parents said they felt "overrun" by professionals, and never felt they could ask the questions they wanted to ask. As one minority parent told me, "They made me feel stupid and I was afraid to ask questions." Information and access to information can become a critical issue for some minority parents.[37] Many of the parents who were interviewed spoke only Spanish, and these parents were comfortable with verbal information but did not have access to any written information about their child's disorder. "Official" documents in Arizona are translated into Spanish, but when parents wanted to seek more advanced knowledge on their child's illness, they had nowhere to go. "I wanted to learn about my child's ADHD but I couldn't find anything written in Spanish," one parent explained.

Most in the mental health profession recognize the ongoing need to produce "culturally competent" workers who can work effectively with people from a wide range of cultures. A helpful way of thinking about what it means to deliver services that are culturally competent is to recognize that this competence is distributed along a continuum.[38] At one end are the professionals who represent "cultural destructiveness," a demeaning and often harmful perspective—one hopes that they are a very small group. Next on the continuum would be those who might be said to have "cultural incapacity," a lack of capacity and motivation to truly help others who are different from themselves. "Cultural blindness" represents the midpoint of the continuum; professionals here believe that cultural differences do not exist. The last two points on the continuum are "basic cultural competence" and "advanced cultural competence," which represent ideals in the mental health field. Professionals on this end of the continuum are engaged in attempting to create and promote a mental health system that avoids racism, eliminates disparities in services for those of different cultures, and seeks improved relations between cultures. As the following discussion demonstrates, achieving cultural competence is more difficult than it might seem.

If you didn't think cultural differences were relevant to how families obtain needed help, Ann Fadiman's *The Spirit Catches You and You Fall Down* will change your perspective. This amazing book tells the story of the clash of two cultures that come face-to-face but cannot see eye-to-eye. Lia Lee, the infant daughter of Hmong immigrants, arrives in the Merced, California, county hospital in a seizure. She is diagnosed with epilepsy, but her parents believe her trouble is caused by spirits. The doctors insist the seizures can be fixed with medication. Because of the family's belief system, they try to cure the child's illness not with Western medication but using their own Hmong methods.

Fadiman's book demonstrates the profound misunderstanding between the parents and the doctors. The Western doctors never understand that in Hmong culture, Lia's epilepsy, although considered potentially dangerous, makes Lia distinguished and indicates a possible future as a shaman. The family's challenge to the treatments suggested frustrates the doctors, who aren't used to having their authority questioned. Compounding the difficulties, the prescriptions are written in precise dosages to be given a certain number of times per day. But Lia's parents cannot speak or read English, so it is impossible for them to comprehend or follow the doctors' instructions. After their child experiences several recurring seizures, they come to believe that the medicines are doing more harm to Lia than good. They prefer their own Hmong healing methods to those of the American doctors.

As the impasse continued, the Lees were accused of child neglect, and Lia was taken away from them by Child Protective Services and put in foster care for one year. She was allowed to rejoin her family when the Lees promised to give her the medication prescribed by the American doctors.

On November 25, 1986, Lia had the worst seizure she had ever had. It took the doctors more than two hours to fully revive her. By this time, the damage had been done: Lia had suffered such severe trauma to her brain that she was effectively brain dead and the American doctors thought that she would surely

die. The Lees made preparations to take Lia home so she could die with her family, but she didn't die. Thanks to her parents' love and care, she survived, although in an unresponsive state.

INSURANCE: IT DOESN'T COUNT FOR MUCH

The most significant barrier to obtaining proper mental health care for children is cost. When the National Survey on Drug Use and Health examined a sample of almost 6 million people with serious mental illness who did not seek treatment, researchers found almost half of respondents identified cost and insurance problems as a major reason for not seeking help.[39] Interestingly, a large portion of the sample identified stigma as a reason for their failure to seek treatment (22%), and another 7 percent noted fear of being forced to take medication as the underlying reason.

When you listen to parents and learn of their experiences with local agencies in obtaining help, it is easy to understand why a consumer-driven system of mental health care has become increasingly popular. The Surgeon General's report on mental health identified consumers as "the critical stakeholders and valued resources in the policy process."[40] Many parents have been looking forward to a managed care model, hoping that its adoption would lead to more consumer choice and greater accountability by providers of services. As described by one activist, this approach would be "less expensive and less offensive to us."[41] In a provocative article entitled "Recovering Consumers and a Broken Mental Health System in the United States: Ongoing Challenges for Consumers/Survivors and the New Freedom Commission on Mental Health," Athena McLean contrasts the consumer model and the managed care model. She notes some fundamental differences in their approaches, leading her to wonder, "Why is the mental health system so unresponsive in comparison to the medical system?"[42]

Consumers of mental health care have made significant gains in the form of improved mental health delivery, and one hopes that they will continue to do so under the health care reform currently taking place in the United States. But whatever the health care system, finding care looks to remain a serious problem for parents. As reported in the *Albuquerque Journal*, as many as one third of the psychiatrists in New Mexico have left because of difficulties with the state's managed care policy. The paper reports that only 46 psychiatrists are left in the state, which is half the national average per capita. In addition to the dilemma of finding care, parents are faced with inferior or inappropriate care. The insurance companies have also played a role in this issue.

Many parents end up like Linda Groden, whose daughter Erika suffers from anorexia (which can be a life-threatening disorder) and who is now facing serious debt.[43] At 13, Erika weighed just 85 pounds and had been hospitalized with a feeding tube when the insurance company stopped paying for her care. Frantic to find the proper treatment, her mother spent her life savings and her children's $50,000 college fund to send Erika to residential treatment. Eventually Linda resorted to using a low-interest credit card to pay for treatment and ran up $9,500 per month in charges. Erika was sent to three different centers; each time, she would put on weight but then come home and throw up as many as 25 times per day, quickly losing the weight she had gained. Eventually, her parents brought her home, but they are now trying to sell the house to pay off the $23,000 owed to creditors. Erika remains very sick and without proper care.

In Minnesota, Mike Hatch filed a lawsuit against Blue Cross Blue Shield of Minnesota, charging that the company was "engaging in a pattern of misconduct in denying medically necessary health care treatment recommended by Physicians for Minnesota children and young adults suffering from mental illness, eating disorders, and chemical dependency."[44] Hatch explained that the insurance companies were blatant in recommending that mentally ill children be taken to juvenile court. One plaintiff in the suit was a chronic runaway who had been diagnosed with major depression. A psychologist had determined that she was a threat to her safety and needed inpatient treatment at a residential facility. The insurance company refused treatment, claiming that the girl should be treated through the juvenile justice system. This outcome was very upsetting to the father, who stated, "This was incredibly difficult for us, because the juvenile justice system was exactly what my wife and I were trying to avoid by seeking appropriate mental health treatment."[45]

The parents in my study weighed in on the insurance system and had plenty to say about their own difficulties:

Without the insurance I'd be going in Mexico once a month, and I'd be afraid of the medications he'd be taking. I would be afraid of the quality.

Our insurance company could not understand that a two-hour therapy session every other week didn't cost any more money than an hour every week. And they did not want to pay for that second hour every other week. But the therapy had to be done in longer blocks.

The insurance is totally inconsistent. Even when they start covering something, sometimes they stop. I'd estimate that for every time we get a new referral to a specialist, it takes at least two hours just for the initial consult to two hours of me calling the insurance companies to get everything straight.

My husband's insurance company has changed the benefits for psychiatric health. It's ridiculous. We can't get the help he needs. If we continue services, we might have to borrow from inpatient hospital care. We are worried inpatient [care won't] be available. I scrape to get the money together right now to pay the co-pay costs. If I divorced my husband and I lived on welfare and let the government pay for everything, my son might get some help.

We have to be able to find a way to flex that money, because my kid needs therapy a lot more than they need a new couch. My kid is broken and needs to be fixed. I can only do so much. I needed some professional assistance in this. If you can't give it to me, I need you to tell me where I can get it.

I feel very fortunate, because the psychiatrist whom we take the children to now— the three teenagers—was a medical director. I've got the best of both worlds, because she's aware not only of what we're eligible for through our insurance, but what we should be asking the system for. She's played both roles. When I brought her my determination papers after mine ran out the other day, she didn't have to say, "What is this?" She just signed. She can make her own decisions. She can say, "Come and see me in a month," whereas you know for most people in the public system it is probably every three months.

PARENTS AS ADVOCATES

One aspect of the system of care model calls for adhering to a family-driven philosophy, which requires cultivating and promoting parents as advocates.[46] In this framework parents are often employed as providers, support staff, and advocates for other families who have mentally ill children. These positions are sometimes labeled "community liaisons," "veteran parents," or "parent-to-peer counselors," and the parents are said to be part of a "parent empowerment framework."[47] Recently, the family support literature has recognized a need for "patient navigators"—individuals, often parents, who are experienced in navigating a complex array of services and barriers to services that are faced by many parents. Across the country, a growing number of communities are utilizing parents to promote peer advocacy and help promote support systems for parents.

This new field of parent support is increasingly being reviewed; one expert claimed that the approach is helpful but the field needs to better understand the underlying mechanisms of effective peer support.[48] The approach does appear to be promising, however. For example, one study found that peer support helped parents return to the workforce after they gained new coping skills and confidence.[49]

Some of the parents whom I interviewed discussed the value of functioning as resources for each other:

Twelve years ago, I was the person who ran MIKID [a parent support organization], for about five years alongside other parents. . . . We weren't as much educational to the community as we were supportive to each other. We truly mentored each other and traveled with each other. I'm not sure what MIKID does today, because I pretty much dropped out of that. It takes a lot of energy to do case management when you're not a case manager. That's what parents truly need to do for each other.

One of the greatest assets to the Department of Developmental Disabilities is the use of parents and family members in the case management, in the overall delivery of services. Somehow mental health has lost that. There needs to be a network, an opportunity for people to come together, to share skills. When I was on welfare, we lived in welfare apartments, and you kind of shared food with your neighbors. It was like a natural community built with like-minded people in similar situations.

It was a lifestyle. I'm not in that lifestyle anymore, but there was a time where my door was open and I would be willing to watch the neighbor's kid while she went somewhere. Or I had a car, and I could take people. You shared resources. Somehow or other in mental health, these big walls of confidentiality are up, and perhaps [there is] fear on the part of the system of parents truly gaining strength.

It was unclear to me in my conversations with parents whether and to what extent they were recruited as parent advocates as part of a "model implementation." Also, while this model has great merit, it is likely that only a small number of parents can function in this capacity. However, parents did speak to me about their personal need and desire to be self-advocates:

You have to be aggressive; you have to advocate; you have to be loud and persistent.

You have to be straight to the point and aggressive and loud. You can't make any jokes. You can't be relaxed. You have to be blunt and to the point. That's how we've gotten as far as we have.

I've been receiving services for a month and half now. It was very hard to get in there. It was a lot of fighting. I had to call the district. I went to five meetings. I called these meetings. I did everything but go for a hearing. I threatened them with the hearing, and then they reevaluated the situation.

I couldn't get an appointment with a director of the school, so I literally barged into her office, and I said, "My son needs to get enrolled in school."

I still have to fight with a mental health thing, because I want more services for him. The school is finally pushing for him to get DD [developmental disabilities] services. He's going to get occupational therapy, physical therapy, adaptive physical education. He's going to get more one-to-one help. Things are starting to pull together for him, but it's been a fight.

He does have the services now, but it took two years and several hard meetings. The hearings are not done at the school. They are done downtown in the state building. We had to go for two or three days, all day long. But it was a good feeling to know that you were right, to win something, whether it be the school district or mental health. But it's exhausting to have to do that.

I know there are a lot of families out there who could avail themselves of more services. They are not as aggressive as I am. For these people, the first rebuff they get, they go away and suffer. Somebody says, "There's nothing we can do for you," and they go away.

You have to literally go out and pound on the desks. As a juvenile court judge told me, if you want to get it, you got to piss somebody off. It shouldn't be that way.

There has to be a way. They found ways to respond to the AIDS disease. If they can do that for AIDS, they can do it for mentally ill children. I think that we're not pushing hard enough.

Bart has very serious social deficits, and I tried to work with the school district. They were very difficult to work with. "Well, we don't care what you say," your doctors say. "We decide when he needs to be with people or when he doesn't." And I went, "I'm sorry, but you don't even know this child. Who are you to come in without any kind of medical background, except for educational psychology? You're not an expert in mental illnesses." Eventually the doctor and I realized we had to sue the school district. Would that be a benefit to Bart? No. Because this is so important we have to do it.

One study found that parent involvement and advocacy was one of the best predictors for whether children received services funded by the school district.[50] Those parents who have the means and resources to advocate are obtaining needed special education services, but parents who are less fortunate are not.

I've taken a break from writing this book—I'm in London with my family for 10 days. It's difficult to leave book writing when you are in the flow and making progress. But now, away from the book, the same issues I've been thinking about confront me head on. Sipping my "long coffee" in London, I'm sitting next to two women and can't help but overhear their conversation: "The family needs help; they aren't getting the services the school should be providing." The child they are talking about has developmental and mental difficulties, and one woman appears to be a legal advocate. The gist of the conversation has been repeated to me so many times—not enough proper services for the children who need them. I'm not certain how the United States compares to other countries in developing needed services and assisting families with mentally ill children, but this conversation reminds me that helping parents find the help they need is urgent, and probably not just in America.

A useful document for parents who want to be advocates is the Bill of Rights for Children with Mental Health Disorders and Their Families. This bill, which was created by a coalition of the American Academy of Child and Adolescent Psychiatry (AACAP), the Autism Society of America (ASA), the Child and Adolescent Bipolar Foundation (CABF), Children and Adults with Attention-Deficit Hyperactivity Disorder (CHADD), the Federation of Families for Children's Mental Health (FFCMH), Mental Health America (MHA), and the National Alliance on Mental Illness (NAMI), is described on the American Academy of Child and Adolescent Psychiatry website. It includes such rights as "Treatment must be family driven and child focused," "Parents and children are entitled to as much information as possible about the risks and benefits of all treatment options," and "Children and families should have access to a comprehensive continuum of care."[51] These rights are a long way from being fully realized by many parents.

BAD THERAPY/GOOD THERAPY: NOT AN EVEN MATCH

In my job as a professor at Arizona State University in the School of Social Work, I'm privileged to teach my favorite class, "Social Work Practice with Children and Adolescents." Approximately 25 to 30 students show up each spring for this class. They often come excitedly up to me after my first class to explain how they are really interested in "play therapy" or "attachment therapy." I immediately cringe upon hearing such statements. I explain to them my fundamental philosophy: Good therapy with children and families isn't about what *you* want to learn; it's about what you provide to others that will help *them* the most. I try to convince the students that one of the most important things they can do is make decisions about what most helps families—and to cast aside their preconceived notions about what they themselves want.

Christina, a bright and energetic woman in her late twenties, is a good example. She came into the class wanting to learn about psychodynamic play therapy. I immediately disappointed her by explaining that other treatments were probably more beneficial to the families she would be trying to help.[52] Alan Kazdin, a noted expert in child therapy, lists more than 230 therapies that are used to provide psychological treatment to children and adolescents.[53] Clearly, selecting the best treatment is something mental health practitioners need to focus on.[54] Perhaps the advent of "evidence-based treatment," which endeavors to find and promote the treatments that most likely to produce the intended effects, will move us closer to truly helping parents who are searching for the best services possible for their children.[55]

While I cringed when my student Christina mentioned treatments I didn't believe were best suited for helping children and adolescents, I am equally dismayed to hear parents speak so often about their negative experiences with therapy. The following statements provide an overview of many of the issues present in doing "good therapy":

The first year of the therapy was a complete waste of time. It was really bad. There was no interest in really and truly helping him. And then I said, "Enough is enough. I want somebody else." It took a couple of months, and we got somebody from the same organization. He was a little more familiar with the disorder. He was a little bit better prepared, and he communicated with my son.

I let the professionals tell me how it should be. I learned with Dylan, no, the professionals are not always right.

One of the problems that he has is difficulty getting along in groups. I'd like to see him in a small play group where you can observe his therapy. To me, that's play therapy. Play therapy is not sitting with a grown-up and drawing, or sitting with a grown-up and getting your hands into sand and making stick figures. To me, I would like to observe a child play. They don't get it.

So we have no therapy, because the therapist has really never built a rapport with this child. We have him in somewhat of a therapeutic environment that is helping him to learn the skills with other children, which is my hope and desire.

I call it the "doc of the month" club, or the "clinician of the month." "You have an appointment in room B." That is not good therapy.

One therapist whom we had insisted that in between sessions we have a family meeting. It acts as therapy sometimes. I'm tired of doing therapy in my own home. We discuss what's on everybody's mind: How can we work this out? What would be a feasible solution? Are we all going to participate? It's therapy. That's about all we have. Family therapy to me was basically learning to communicate within the family. We don't. The decibel level in my house is very high. In spite of the fact that we have family meetings, the decibel level is high. We've gotten used to yelling. We have selective listening, and we live in a three-story house.

So he ended up at [a residential treatment agency], spending a lot of time in their day-treatment program and their after-school program. He would come home black and blue all the time from being restrained. They would restrain him so tight that his clothes had line marks on them. Finally one day I went in and this guy was restraining him, and Dylan was screaming, "Just let me go, let me sit in the corner." "When you're in control, I'll let go." I threw open the door, and I said, "Your sorry ass better let go right now." He let go. Dylan went over in the corner. He sat in the corner. He got in control. He was just a child who as soon as you tried to contain him, he couldn't handle it. He couldn't handle it, so he would fight because it just didn't work for him.

By then, I'd gone back to school, gotten my ... certificate in social services, taken psych classes, done all this stuff to try to figure out how to help him, and I'm watching this lady, going, "You know, lady, you're doing everything in the world that the books tell you not to do." She would let them crawl underneath the table to do their work, crawl behind bookshelves, do stuff. There was no stability in the class. My child needs structure. At the time he really needed that definite structure. I said, "I want him out."

The biggest mistake we make as parents is [to think] the professional is always right. I've been to a few professionals who didn't have a clue. "You need to do this and this. You need to take everything away from him and make him sleep on the floor. That will make him straighten up." I have this bipolar child who doesn't understand why he can't sit in a regular classroom and function, and because he doesn't know how come his thinking is all garbled, I'm supposed to take his bed away from him? Let's get a clue here. So as parents, we need to learn that advice from professionals is wonderful, but do your own research. Figure out what's best for your child. What's best for your kid may not be best for Freddy's kid. If you talk, you might be able to figure out what works best for both of them.

The therapist would say, "Bart's got a lot of anger, so get some ice cubes and have him go throw them against the sidewalk." To me, you're just telling him it's okay be violent. I ended up with a brick through my truck window. What the hell. Throw ice cubes?

He finally got a therapist, and this guy had an MSW. I was thinking this is going to be good. My son would go in for 10 minutes and come out, and the guy said, "He doesn't feel like therapy today. We drew some pictures." My son has Asperger's syndrome. He needs direction, structure. You can't use this philosophy with this population. "Would you like to draw a picture? Is there anything else you'd like to say? Okay, you can go now!"

Sara Fritz, a newspaper writer, shared the tragic story of her son's suicide.[56] It is a gripping story that speaks to the seriousness with which "good therapy" is needed among mental health professionals. Sara found her 12-year-old son Daniel dangling by his neck from a chin-up bar where he had hung himself. Daniel had a history of difficulties, and by the sixth grade he was diagnosed with ADHD. After a summer vacation, Daniel's parents met with the therapist who was treating their son for ADHD. The parents informed the therapist that they thought Daniel was depressed. The therapist scoffed at this suggestion, saying, "What, you want more drugs?" Instead, the therapist said that Daniel needed a "good kick in the pants" and perhaps military school.

After Daniel's suicide, the parents obtained the therapist's case notes, which revealed that the therapist did not attempt to fully explore whether Daniel might be depressed. There was no evidence that the therapist explored whether Daniel might be suicidal. In retrospect, it seems clear that Daniel experienced many of the symptoms of depression as well as ADHD.

Daniel's mother talked about her grief: "Our grief is more painful than anything we had known. My whole body literally ached for nearly two years after Daniel died. I felt as bruised as if I had been run over by a car. And along with the pain, there were the inevitable questions." These parents are committed to sharing what they have learned from their tragedy and operate a website geared toward this issue (www.depressedchild.org). Daniel's mother concluded her story in this way: "If my husband and I learned one lesson from Daniel's death it is that parents of children with emotional problems cannot simply leave their treatment to the professionals."[57]

Emmy Werner conducted a landmark study that followed individuals from infancy to adulthood.[58] This study is well known for having identified the resilience factors that protect children who grow up in high-risk environments of poverty, divorce, low education, and parental psychopathology. In Werner's study, the impact of psychological treatment on these individuals was surprisingly small: Psychotherapy helped only 5 percent of the individuals. The majority of this group also received medication. When asked about the relative helpfulness received from various individuals, participants in the study ranked mental health professionals (psychiatrists, psychologists, and social workers) as less effective in terms of their advice and counseling than spouses, friends, extended family members, teachers, mentors, coworkers, members of church groups, or ministers. These low ratings were consistent in each survey of the respondents at their second, third, and fourth decades of life. According to the authors who summarized the study results, the youths who made "a successful adaptation in adulthood despite adversity relied on sources of support within their family and community that increased their competencies and self-efficacy, decreased the number of stressful life events they subsequently encountered, and opened up new opportunities for them." This sobering study does not reflect well on the long-term outcomes of mental health therapy, but it does say something about the community-based, family-centered models that are being increasingly implemented.

Another side to the therapy story was revealed in my own interviews—some parents spoke very favorably about the treatment they received. The following quotes, although not typical, represent the positive side of therapy:

> The clinician we have right now is so great. I cannot say enough about her. She in no way discriminates against Mandy. She will sit and listen to every word she says, even if Mandy's not making any sense. She will listen and respond to Mandy. She's made Mandy trust her. She gives her eye contact. She asks, "Mandy, how does that make you feel?" Mandy knows that she listens and cares. That makes a huge difference. Tammy cares what happens to her. She wants her to finish the program. That's what all the staff up there have done: They've proven to Mandy that they care. That's what you have to do with Mandy. If you prove that you care, she'll open up. That's where we're at now. I've shown her I care. I love her. She hugs me. She cries now. She never did that before.

> The best case managers and therapists are willing to share a little bit of themselves. Step out from behind that desk and become a human being, not a case manager. Those are the people who have helped me the most.

> One of the best counselors whom Jamar had, and Byran as well, started teaching him breathing techniques. And that's really helpful, especially when the kids are impulsive—to sort of detach for a moment from the situation.

> It went fine. He went with another teacher for fifth grade. Every time I think of this woman, I cry. I have never seen a teacher work so hard to make kids self-reliant. She took a kid who had absolutely no self-confidence. She took him from that to being "I can do anything I want if I set my mind to it. I can beat this ADHD thing. It is not in control of me. I'm going to be in control of it." They had him out doing [positive activities]; he had a job at the school working with the nurse. If it hadn't been for that teacher, I could have lost my child. She was just awesome.

> You do get frustrated. When we took Bart out of the house the first time, I cried for weeks. And I kept telling the therapist, "I feel like I failed." She said, "Pat, you

didn't fail. You did not fail. They're not even your children [Pat is a foster parent], and you blame yourself. They're kids. They've been through more than I've been through. Let's try and get some normalcy for them." That meant a lot to me.

NARRATIVE ETHICS

In his book *Illness Narratives*, the medical doctor Arthur Kleinman tells how a patient who had suffered loss and was seriously ill asked him, "Can you give me the courage I need?" This obviously has nothing to do with the proper course of treatment and everything to do with Kleinman's moral relationship with the patient.[59] His role as a *doctor* is not really relevant here. How many mental health professionals would recognize the idea that they may be called upon to have a moral commitment to help a parent? It is an interesting perspective, sometimes referred to as *narrative ethics*, that is perhaps considered more in medicine than in mental health, but the relevance remains the same.

For Arthur Frank, author of *The Wounded Storyteller*, the importance of narrative ethics lies in how one retells the patient's "story," or narrative. He points out that "the danger for ill people is that they are often taught how to be ill by professionals. Illness is not presented to the ill as a moral problem; patients are not asked, after the shock of diagnosis has dulled sufficiently, what do you wish to become in this experience? What story do you wish to tell to yourself? How will you shape your illness, and yourself, in the stories you tell of it?"[60] The practical implication is that there is value in helping parents construct and tell their story—a story they may end up telling many times. "Narrative ethics takes place in telling and listening."[61]

In the social work school where I teach, a large part of the curriculum concerns teaching students to have "empathy" for others. Frank takes this notion one level deeper, arguing that it is important for people to understand that each of us lacks something that only the other can fill. In this sense, empathy is not what a person *has* for another person, but what a person *is* with another person.

Most parents are left alone in their journey to find meaning in their experience. What can therapists, doctors, or policy makers do to help the parent find meaning? An exclusive focus on change may lead in a direction that does not allow this outcome. The existential imperative is to find the meaning in the experience. From this perspective, a relevant question is, What can practitioners do to help parents live a good life while caring for a mentally ill child? When people find a sense of meaning, that realization often opens the window to better coping and management. We will explore this notion more fully in the next chapter.

CHAPTER 6

Managing and Coping with Everyday Life: Struggles and Tribulations

It happens that I am going through a period of great unhappiness and loss just now. All my life I've heard people speak of finding themselves in acute pain, bankrupt in spirit and body, but I've never understood what they meant. To lose. To have lost. I believed these visitations of darkness lasted only a few minutes or hours and that these saddened people, in between bouts, were occupied, as we all were, with the useful monotony of happiness. But happiness is not what I thought. Happiness is the lucky pane of glass you carry in your head. It takes all your cunning just to hang on to it, and once it's smashed you have to move into a different sort of life.[1]

—C. Sheilds, *Unless*

To fully describe the life of a parent of a mentally ill child, this chapter focuses on the everyday experience. What is the "burden of love" that parents struggle with as they care for their children on a daily basis? How do parents cope with their responsibilities and manage their emotions?

EVERYDAY LIFE: STRAIN AND BURDEN

What parents talked about when I attempted to learn about their everyday life is their daily strain and burden. Interestingly, throughout these interviews the words "burden" and "strain" were never directly used, but many of the interviews were indirectly built around these themes. Perhaps one of the most common elements that arose in the interviews was the limited amount of time that many parents had for themselves and their relationships with others because of their commitment to their mentally ill child. One mother explains:

> [My daughter] needs my attention 24 hours a day. She is very demanding. She drains you. She drains you physically, she drains you emotionally.

Another mother reiterates this sentiment when she explains that her job as a parent of a mentally ill child is different than with her other children:

> [Parenting a mentally ill child is] hard because it's something you have to deal with on a daily basis. . . . If your child was sick, had the flu or whatever, they're going to get over it. But this is daily. It's 24/7.

Another parent described how her 12-year-old son was still keeping her awake at night, which further contributed to her overall experience of burden:

> It was hard to get him to bed. When I put him to bed, he would lay there for two hours and not go to sleep. And, I'm thinking, "This isn't normal because he is getting up early. He's up in the middle of the night. He should be tired." And the doctors were saying, "Well, he just needs more sleep." And I'm saying, "I'm telling you, he's not sleeping."

Another mother explains that for her, the burden of raising a child with a mental illness affected her personal life every day, both inside and outside the home:

> I don't have a relationship [with a man] right now, and it's been a long time since I've been in an intimate relationship. Because I don't have the energy. And that's basically why I'm not in an intimate relationship right now. The timing's not right, but it's a lot more than that. I don't have the energy—the time or energy—to take a shower, to take five minutes for myself, much less do anything else in my life right now.

While undoubtedly all parents' schedules and personal lives are affected by their children's needs, those parents interviewed for the present study appear to be impacted by the ongoing needs and behaviors of their children, to a point where they become so frustrated that they are unsure how to handle their child's behavior or how to best care for themselves and the rest of their families. Another aspect of the daily burden that many parents experience has to do with the consistent unpredictability of their child's behavior. One caregiver who adopted her daughter's two children, one of whom has a history of post-traumatic stress disorder (PTSD) and ADHD, explains that in addition to the everyday coordination of appointments and meetings, her granddaughter's behavior is also greatly affected by her time in therapy. Oftentimes the fallout from these encounters occurs at home after the session. She explains:

> [Y]ou take child number one to this therapist, that therapist, and this neurologist, and this eye doctor and this dentist. And you take child number two to this dentist, this doctor, this speech therapist, this occupational therapist, and we'll have this person come into your home. That's every week. I just marked off 12 things. There's five working days in a week, but you do this, so you take them. And then you bring those children home, and child number one has come from play therapy. . . . you could live with child number one before she went to play therapy; you were having a good day, before you went to play therapy at 3 o'clock. You bring child number one home from play therapy, and [now] child number one hates you. Child number one is beating up child number two. Child number one has turned into Dr. Jekyll and Mr. Hyde. Child number one is having seizures that she hasn't had in months. Wait a minute. An hour ago, you were a semi-happy child. What in the hell happened here? What in the hell is wrong with you? What is wrong with you? And I am human. I'm not a machine. I am human. One, I have emotion and love for that child. Two, I'm tired. It's 5 o'clock. I still have to get dinner.

In this case, the addition of a child with a history of trauma into an already hectic family milieu greatly increases the level of burden and strain that this grandmother experiences on a daily basis.

Another mother whose child has been diagnosed with bipolar disorder echoes some of these sentiments and often finds herself similarly confused about the unpredictability of her child's behavior as well as the roots of such behavior. She explains:

> There are so many forms of mental illness, and bipolar [disorder] is the one that I think I misunderstand the most. It's like being on a roller-coaster ride. She gets up one morning and, "Oh, hi, Mom. I'm ready to go to school." She's all happy, fine. Then two hours later she's like Rosemary's baby. Grrrr. Wow! "What happened to change your day?" "I don't know—just stay away from me." You can't even look at her without causing an extreme fight. If you don't feed the fight, she'll do anything she can to keep pushing, until she can find someone to fight with.

While certainly a great many children are often moody, many of the parents interviewed for this study perceived the mood swings of their children to be well beyond the normal range. The extreme nature of these mood swings appears to have had a tremendous impact on the stress levels of the parents, who were often at the receiving end of such behaviors.

Another significant and particularly powerful aspect of the daily burden that many parents experience is having to witness their child's ongoing emotional pain and confusion, which is inherently linked to their mental disorder. One parent, whose son experiences auditory and visual hallucinations, explains that sometimes she feels that her son's behavior and experiences are both foreign to her and strangely familiar:

There are times, you know, when you almost get lost in this unrealistic world of "shadow people." You talk about shadow people like they're real. And you kind of get mixed in with the shadow people—the closet guy, the cops. The different senses he has. The way he sees lights differently and hears things we don't hear. Background noises. They're probably there, but I can't hear them. He hears the quiet. I can't. The quiet is so loud to him, it destroys his ability to think. There's no one for him to connect with like that.

This inability to fully understand what her son experiences as a result of his mental illness is a great source of emotional pain and angst for this particular mother. She goes on to explain that having to observe her son's ongoing isolation and confusion about his own mental health is hard to bear:

I recently realized for the first time that he is alone. His brother has a girlfriend. His sister has a boyfriend. I have a husband. He has nobody. There are days I'd rather be dead than watching him suffer. Gladly.

Clearly, being so close to her son's suffering has had a major impact on this mother's own mental health. As one who has struggled for years to comprehend the etiology and expression of her son's mental disorder, she exudes a profound sense of helplessness and exhaustion.

Another parent recalled a time when her six-year-old son was in the midst of a deep depression and expressed a significant amount of suicidal ideation:

He told me he wanted to die. And he was telling me how. You know, [he said,] "I just want to sit in front of a cross, and I just want to die, Mom." I was terrified. At six, that's a terrible feeling.

Another parent related a similar story about her five-year-old, who had recently been diagnosed with ADHD and depression. She explains that her son had already started taking medication; because of that, he knew there was something wrong with him. Like the previous parent, this mother described a time when her child expressed his belief that things would be better if he were dead.

It would be difficult to measure the effects that such experiences have upon a parent. One can safely say that such experiences and statements by their children would underscore for parents the gravity of the situation and cause them to consider their role in such a dynamic. Another parent, reflecting upon how difficult her child's behavior was at times, states:

[It] just got to be so overwhelming at times that . . . I felt like I hate my own child. And then you feel guilty—because I hate my kid. And there were days when he was just kind of mean for no reason. . . . I just felt like, "I'm going to crack."

It became more apparent throughout the interviews that a number of parents struggled with the "love–hate" relationships that they often had with their children—where they cared so much about their children, yet became so frustrated with their ongoing negative behaviors. Such daily frustrations and burdens led a few of the parents who were interviewed to seek out counseling for their own mental health. One mother explains:

> I've had a lot of counseling. The counseling that I get personally for myself, she [the therapist] still tells me to this day, "It's your daughter. Your daughter seems to be causing the issues and problems that you're having." Well, what am I supposed to do, dump my child? That's the only thing I cannot do.

This same mother, whose child's mental illness has led to her involvement with the juvenile justice system, finds that she is in constant internal conflict over how to best handle her daughter's behaviors, for both her child's well-being and her own:

> She steals. There's nothing safe unless it's nailed down. I have to have a lock box for my husband's and her medications, because she'll sell them. Life is not in any way normal. But she's still my child and I still love her. It makes it really difficult.

For many parents, this burden of responsibility seems to be the driving force behind their commitment to care for their mentally ill child. While this dedication to their children is obvious, what is less clear is the impact that such an ongoing struggle has upon their own health, relationships, and general well-being.

The concept of fear also emerged as a common response to the experience of raising a child with mental illness, and this undoubtedly contributes to parental burden. One mother explains:

> It's scary thinking that there's something wrong with your kid. More than anything, we want our kids to fit in and be like other people. Be normal, average, happy, and have a good life. When you get news when they're two and three [years old] that they aren't doing things the way other kids do them, not in a good way, it's scary and frustrating.

For many parents, these fears for the future can go beyond "scary and frustrating." This same mother explains that when she and her husband first started to notice that "something was wrong" with their child, they began to think about any number of negative consequences and outcomes:

> We would talk to him about his behavior, but he was only three and four. Even though his vocabulary was good, he just didn't get the concept. It was almost like he didn't understand that hitting other children with metal trucks was wrong. That was one of our biggest concerns. That he was going to turn out to be some antisocial homicidal maniac who had no clue.

Throughout the interview phase of this study, it became more and more evident that this uncertainty about the future and the loss of expectations resulted in a high level of expressed emotion for the parents. Indeed, the impact such emotions have on these individuals' overall experiences of burden not can be overstated. The examples of expressed emotion in the data appear very similar to Marsh and Lefley's conclusions about the role that grief and the grieving process play in the amount of subjective burden that a parent experiences.[2] As some of the earlier quotes show, some of the parents whom I interviewed felt that they were in the midst of a grieving process. While the grief that parents of mentally ill children experience originates from many sources, the present data suggest that the loss of expectations and the chronic nature of the mental illness are the main contributors. It is these feelings that appear to be among the more constant sources of burden that parents experienced.

ROLE THEORY AND DAILY STRAIN

Role theory can help us understand the daily strain that many parents of mentally ill children experience. The role of "parent" carries some clear social expectations. To what extent do the parents suffer from a perceived inability to fulfill their role as a parent? Beyond perceptions and social expectations, which kinds of role strain are present?

One factor that is commonly overlooked by professionals is the challenge that parents who have family and work commitments must negotiate. Often parents must balance caregiving and employment responsibilities without a lot of support. As a consequence, parents often limit themselves to employment that will offer some flexibility in scheduling. Furthermore, they must arrange for proper child care, provide transportation for their children, and deal with school crises as needed.[3] Because of the stigma they may experience, many parents are not comfortable sharing with employers their unique demands, which merely adds to their daily strain. Parents who suffered from role strain shared the following:

> When you have to go to sleep at night and lock up your knives, the thing that kills me is that I have to put my purse in my room, and I have a deadbolt lock on my front door and take the key with me, because I don't want my kid to leave. It's an awful system. You don't rest. You pray that the kid sleeps late, because then for 20 minutes you can actually do something.

> Living in welfare, in that poverty state, I didn't know that there was a whole different life. It's very easy to get into this place in your life. It's harder to come out of it. You still think you're in it. For a period of time when I went back to work for the university, I was still getting my Social Security checks. I thought I was truly rich. I was still living this welfare lifestyle with this welfare mentality. You get the check; you better spend it now, because you'll lose it before the end of the month. You put all your money in envelopes. I had to buy a car, and I had to continue to take the bus.

> I never knew who was going to call me. I never looked forward to those calls. Now I have learned how to answer them. Now they call and say, "You have to

come here", and I say, "I will call you back in five minutes. I need to process this." . . . I learned that the threat was really a veiled threat: "We're going to call the police". Well, you know, I'm going to call you back in five minutes, because I need to process this. Also, I work right across the street . . . so I didn't need that extra five minutes to get there. Sometimes I just show up in five minutes, but I need to allow myself not to get angry in my office, slam the door, maybe have an accident on the way, and become an idiot.

CHRONICITY: WHEN THERE IS NO END IN SIGHT

The material for writing this book is a series of transcribed interviews. When doing the "coding for categories" stage of data analysis, I noticed that the general category into which the most quotations fell was the "Daily Stress and Burden" category. Unfortunately, there is little literature that addresses this specific aspect of caring for a child with a mental illness. There is a significant literature revolving around the daily burden experienced by caregivers of adults with mental illness.[4] There is also a rather substantial literature that addresses the daily burden and strain experienced by those who care for their aging parents, whether or not the parents have mental illness.[5] While these various literatures can shed some light on the topic at hand, there still exist some significant differences between the burdens of caring for adults and for children.

It is my hope that a more specific literature will be developed around the concept of daily stress and burden experienced by parents such as those interviewed for this book. This lack of current research is particularly revealing when one considers the frequency with which these issues arose in the interviews conducted for this study.

For many parents, the daily stress of dealing with a mentally ill child led to their emotional depletion because of the chronicity of the problem. While many—maybe even most—mental health practitioners do not address the chronic nature of these parents' difficulties, it is becoming increasingly recognized in some circles as significant. The first recommendation of the American Academy of Pediatrics in the treatment of ADHD is for "primary clinicians to establish a treatment program that recognizes ADHD as a chronic condition. Conduct disorders tend to persist into adolescence and adult life through substance abuse, antisocial behavior, relationship problems, employment problems, and poor physical health."[6] Likewise, adolescent onset of depressive disorder has been found to continue into adulthood and to be associated with high rates of suicide and suicide attempts, increased psychiatric hospitalizations, and lower educational achievement.[7] As one last example of the chronicity effect of mental illness, almost one fourth of college females with eating disorders met the diagnostic criteria for these disorders when assessed 10 years later.[8] Clinicians should continually educate parents, children, and teachers about the mental illness condition, and establish a monitoring system to track the effects of treatment and developmental changes in behavior, while recognizing that for many children their disorder may persist a long time.[9]

Many parents spoke to their feelings about the likely chronic nature of their child's illness:

The truth of the matter is, even though my daughter's 14, it won't ever stop. She'll have these issues the rest of her life. That's what I'm trying so hard now to tell her after all the years of my own ignorance of trying to save her; instead, I just hurt her by not allowing her to have to stand up to the consequences of her actions.

How will my child manage when I am not around, when I am too old?

He's not going to change. This is probably your life. And I can't fix it. And there's no answer.

No one's ever helped me to discover the chronic nature of his illness. Because of who I am, a researcher myself, I try to understand as much as I can. I began to read about what Asperger's was. No one ever tried to help me understand. They basically told me you have six months to get him enrolled in the division of developmental disabilities. Otherwise, he's probably going to be left out in the cold without any services whatsoever. Why is that important? He's going to need care for the rest of his life? Wow! Care for the rest of his life.

When he was diagnosed, my head was spinning. I had no idea how severe bipolar [disorder] could be. The closest thing I could say would be like being in a mental whirlpool. We'd seen James's rages. I was afraid of him hurting someone or himself. He was taking antipsychotics, which help him with the rages, and he's only five to six years old. Before he turned seven years old, he was started on Risperdal. It made a dramatic difference in a good way. I had this feeling, though: "If you take medication for an earache, how soon until we can stop giving him these meds and he'll be better?" It was so hard for me to get used to the idea that this is lifelong. This isn't "10 days, twice a day, and then see how you are." It was a struggle. It bothered me for a long time. I hated the medications he was taking. I just couldn't get over the idea of taking the medication every day for the rest of your life. We couldn't make him better. All we could do is control the symptoms.

For many parents, the chronic nature of the problem led to a deeply felt level of exhaustion. When one considers all the various stressors that parents of mentally ill children and adolescents must face, as evidenced in their testimonies, it is hard to imagine their lives being anything except utterly exhausting. Such ongoing exhaustion likely affects many other aspects of parents' daily lives and long-term sense of well-being. It comes as no great surprise that the presence of any of these core factors, as presented by Lefley and Gravitz, can lead to a fair amount of perceived burden and strain on caregivers. What *is* surprising is that a similar framework has not been developed for the population that is the focus of this discussion. The creation of such a framework would undoubtedly serve to better inform research, practice, and policy in the area of children's mental health. After all, it seems clear that the amount of burden and strain that parents experience can have a profound impact on treatment outcomes for their children with a mental illness. By familiarizing themselves with a framework that acknowledges the various elements of burden, researchers, practitioners, and policy makers would be better prepared to meet the needs of those parents who are experiencing high levels of burden, and consequently help their children.

SELF-CARE

Over time, parents get to a point where they understand there is equilibrium to be found between what they can do for their child and what the child needs. In my interviews, however, I observed this understanding only in parents who had struggled with their child's mental illness for many years. Some of the coping strategies that parents end up using emerge because they understand this equilibrium. When parents talk about unplugging the phone so they can get a complete night of sleep or calling 911 to stop an out-of-control episode, they have found new ways of coping. The term "workable level of responsibility" has been used to describe the way in which parents of mentally ill adults come to terms with this process.[10]

The following parents address the need for self-care in the face of their ongoing struggles:

> Crucial coping strategies at our house and in the families I've met include a sense of humor, a tolerance for eccentricity, flexibility, and support from other parents. We call our angelic-looking little girl with blond hair and big brown eyes "Mountain Goat," for her facility at scaling the kitchen cupboards, and send her to a summer camp that offers climbing lessons where she can safely indulge her need for risk taking.

> Our kids often blame us for their rages, emotional hijackings in which their hair-trigger limbic systems perceive even the gentlest parental guidance as nuclear attack and react accordingly. So we dub ourselves "honorary lifetime members of the Mean Moms Club," but when the dust has settled, [we] take our kids on our laps and point out the difference between thoughts, feelings, and actions, and teach ways they can make choices about those things.

> It was a way for me to take care of me. It's taken a number of years for me to learn to take care of me first. If I do go in looking like this crazy mother, it's not helping my kid.

With the completion of each interview, I became more keenly aware of the enormous variety of ways in which each parent handled the impact of daily burden and stress. Whereas some parents appeared to be completely overwhelmed, others explained that they ran their house much like a "drill sergeant" and that this rigid structure served to diminish some of the occasions for trauma and stress. The majority of those interviewed fell somewhere in between these two extremes. Some reported that they were relatively comfortable with the amount of day-to-day stress in their lives, but the majority expressed concerns about their perceived lack of ability to handle some situations and their ongoing uncertainty about the effectiveness of their coping strategies. While it is unlikely that there is one "right" way to handle the ongoing strain of caring for a child with a mental illness, parents, practitioners, and policy makers could undoubtedly all learn a great deal from a comparative analysis of various techniques and strategies.

STIGMA AND EVERYDAY BURDEN

Chapter 2 introduced some aspects of stigma associated with mental illness. Its influence is so pervasive, however, that this section describes in more detail how stigma can affect the everyday lives of parents. In *Stigma: Notes on the Management of a Spoiled Identity*, Erving Goffman, the well-known sociologist, documents how society demands a level of control over its members.[11] Any loss of control or loss of control over one's child is stigmatizing. Especially critical is Goffman's observation that such stigma is embarrassing; in our case, it is embarrassing to be out of control of your child where control is expected. This chance of embarrassment often leads parents to avoid any brush with situations that might reinforce the stigma.[12]

Patrick Corrigan has written about how clinical diagnosis can exacerbate the stigma of mental illness.[13] He uses the following quote as an example: "Autistic children never play normally with other children. They often do not respond normally to their mothers' affections or to any tenderness."[14] As Corrigan points out, using diagnostic terms in this manner can worsen the stigma of mental illness by strengthening the stereotypes that lead to stigma.

Corrigan describes three ways that stigma can harm people with mental illness: label avoidance, blocked opportunities, and self-stigma. Label avoidance occurs when individuals decide to avoid seeking treatment because they do not want to be labeled, or have their child labeled, as "mentally disordered." Blocked opportunities arise when people with mental illness are perceived as less capable because of their illness. Such prejudice comes from teachers and employers in the case of young adults. Self-stigma occurs when one's identity is influenced by the stigmatizing ideas imposed by society. If individuals are stereotyped as less valuable because of their illness, self-stigma can emerge as individuals internalize this message. To counter these negative results from stigma, Corrigan emphasizes the need to understand diagnosis as a continuum; to increase contact with the individual, which can lead to changes in how mentally ill people are perceived; and to replace assumptions of poor prognosis with models of recovery.[15]

Let me tell you a story from my own life about everyday stigma. For my son's ninth birthday, we went to Legoland in California. While waiting for a popular ride, we witnessed a parent–child conflict. The child quickly became "out of control," and the parent appeared ashamed and embarrassed by both her child and her own efforts to control the child. At first, both my wife and I judged the mother as incompetent and lacking in parenting skills and, after observing her quickly hit the child, unfit to be a parent. However, after more extended observation, it became clear to us that this child had a "mental disorder" or "behavioral difficulties" and was difficult for the parent to manage. I share this story with humiliation, because we subjected this mother to a serious degree of stigma. Had I not been thinking about the issues faced by parents with children who have such behavioral difficulties, my only conclusion would have been a negative opinion of this mother and old-fashioned "mother blaming."

Goffman was also astute to observe that we must often present ourselves in different ways depending on the circumstances. For example, parents of difficult children quickly learn—must learn—to put aside their true feelings and act as if things are better than they truly are. Especially during the early period of acceptance, parents often put aside their true selves and become another self—an interested, informed, and even light-hearted self. Goffman wrote about the need for the "presentation of the self in everyday life." However, when these parents return to their own independent day-to-day life, tears and sadness come easy and fast. Their "two worlds" are difficult to reconcile. They feel good when leaving behind their difficulties and presenting themselves as unscarred, even if at a surface level, to others, perhaps as a means of escape. Yet, underlying this facade is sadness at not being able to be their true selves, at not being able to share the real and deep aspects of their lives. As time moves forward and as they begin to reconcile and accept their two worlds, they do slowly merge into a more coherent whole.

Many parents reach a point where they have accepted what is, and are comfortable sharing their feelings and their stories with others, resulting in more meaningful relationships. An important caveat here is that this phenomenon occurs only if they can find others with whom to develop such relationships. Far too many parents whom I interviewed described their complete isolation from others, living only "with themselves" and lacking any real companionship and support.

Another aspect of stigma that is rarely addressed by therapists is the need to help adolescents cope with the stigma of mental health problems and the stigma of being on medications. Because medications are now so widely used in mental illness, it seems surprising that coping with the stigma of medications is neglected as a topic of therapy. Perhaps this neglect occurs because a child's mental illness is often managed in stages and across different sets of crisis points. What parents and children need is a *long-term view* of the mental illness that suggests various courses of intervention at different times. As the child gets older, he or she must learn skills that directly relate both to the mental illness and the stigma associated with it and with taking medications. One recent study[16] examined the likely stigma experienced by adolescents with mental disorders through in-depth interviews:

"Kind of weird. . . . Can't really mention it at school because I'll get made fun of, and can't really mention it anywhere 'cause I'll get made fun of. . . . I've heard people refer to other people as it who are really not bipolar. . . . Like when you're acting really weird, people go like, 'You're bipolar!' . . . Yeah, at school and it's just not fun." (Fourteen-year-old male, Caucasian, bipolar spectrum disorder, antipsychotic medications)

"Nobody can understand it, because you're not laughing at the jokes in the corner with the rest of the kids. You're not doing any of that. You're by yourself. You're the kid that's by themselves, and everybody's like, 'Why are you just sitting there and why are you, you know? What's up with your appearance? You don't seem like you're paying that close of attention. Why are you wearing sweats again?' You know, stuff like that." (Seventeen-year-old female, African American, major depressive disorder, antipsychotic medications)

These authors call for "stigma reduction interventions" designed as psychoeducational interventions. Such measures include understanding how stigma affects individuals, developing narratives that "tell their stories," and educating patients about mental illness in ways that do not support existing stereotypes.

FEELING AND BEING ALONE: SOCIAL ISOLATION

While undoubtedly all parents who are actively raising children in the home do experience some level of social isolation, the parents and caregivers who were interviewed for this study described levels of social isolation that appear to be well out of the ordinary. These experiences of isolation, while often taken for granted by parents and professionals alike, profoundly influence the parents' day-to-day experiences and ongoing mental health.

Perhaps one of the most common phrases that I heard over the course of the interviews was that when you are caring for a child with a mental illness, "you feel like a prisoner in your own home." Many parents related how their lives had drastically changed since their child's first changes in behavior. Often, they did not feel comfortable leaving their child in the care of another individual for fear of what the child might do while they were gone, and of what negative behaviors the child might exhibit. One parent explains:

> With special needs kids, you can't call the teenage girl across the street and say, "Could you watch them? Could you baby sit so I can go to the beauty salon, or so I can meet Susie for lunch, or so I can go to a doctor's appointment?" You can't do that with special needs kids. Your daily routines are gone, totally disrupted.

Compounding this dilemma for many parents is that even when they are away from their children, they are constantly worrying about their well-being and behaviors. Even for many parents who have school-age children, the disruption of daily routine continues because the school often calls to ask the parent to come and pick up the child because of behavior problems in the classroom. Often further complicating this situation is the presence of other children in the home, who also require a fair amount of attention and time, causing many parents to have to choose which child gets their full attention and which goes without.

A number of the parents interviewed expressed a great deal of frustration and emotional pain resulting from their loss of a social network and close friends because of their caring for a child with a mental illness. Much of this loss of social contact occurs simply because the parents do not have enough time in the week to maintain such friendships. One parent states:

> You're limited in your life; you're limited at your work. You eliminate your friends. They disappear. I used to be part of the "Let's do lunch next Wednesday" crowd. I can't do lunch next Wednesday—unless you want to meet at McDonald's.

This same parent, whose children are adopted, explained that her loss of friends has come about as a result of both their not understanding what she is going through and perhaps their not making the time to do so:

> Your social circle thinks that you're doing a wonderful thing. They think you're God. They tell you, "Oh, you're such a wonderful person." But that's as far as it goes. It kind of disintegrates. They kind of disappear. Meaning or not meaning to, they're always busy. They're doing their own thing, and I don't fit into that thing anymore. I don't fit into that Wednesday lunch thing anymore.

It is this loss of independence and flexibility that this parent feels is at the heart of her feelings of isolation.

It is apparent that the sense of isolation that many parents feel goes beyond simply not being able to get out at as much as they did in the past. In addition to feeling like prisoners in their own homes, many parents do not perceive that their day-to-day experiences with their mentally ill child are even remotely understood by friends, family, and the greater society. Such misunderstanding further contributes to their ongoing sense of isolation, in part because of fears of sharing their experiences with others. As one mother of two children with mental disorders explains:

> The first problem I see is isolation. When you have a child with a disorder, you feel like no one understands you, because it's not something that you talk about. When I go with a group of moms, and they're talking about their four-year-old son writing their name, am I supposed to talk about my four-year-old son pooping his pants and painting with it on the wall? You're just not going to do that. So, you're reluctant to even talk to other moms. It's like you're in this secret society. You're just hiding it. . . . Your stories are totally different. You can't relate. A lot of parents will say, "Oh, every kid goes through that." I don't think so. And that makes you feel stupid, because then you're thinking, "Well, okay, maybe I'm just too tough." So you ease up, and then somebody says, "If you'd just be more strict with that kid, he'd shape up." Because everybody who warns you is parenting pretty typical kids, but you're not. . . . they can't understand, they have no clue. They have no clue what your home life is like—and you're not going to admit it to them. I mean, I feel like I understand what abused people go through now.

This concept of a "secret society" is particularly poignant. Not every parent interviewed articulated their experiences of isolation in such a way, but they all conveyed through their testimonies how few people in their lives, if any, truly understood what it was like to raise a child with a mental disorder. While some of the parents admitted that some people in their lives tried to empathize and support them verbally, they still hoped for more concrete support and understanding. One mother, whose son experienced auditory and visual hallucinations, explained:

> [My son is so] lonely and desperate, so hopeless. And I don't have any answers, and I feel bad . . . and there's nobody to talk to about it really.

This pain caused by lack of support has no clear termination point, further contributing to parents' feelings of hopelessness and ongoing burden. It appears that in many cases it is not so much validation that they desire, but rather understanding and tangible assistance from laypeople and professionals.

A very few parents in the study saw the loss of friends and subsequent social isolation in very straightforward terms and did not appear to be terribly affected by the loss. One such parent matter-of-factly states:

> I've lost friends over my daughter. I'm only going to explain myself once, explain the situation. If they're going to be my friend, they're going to be my friend. Through thick and thin, no matter that my daughter's acting like this or that. "I don't want to be around you." Well, you knew that from the gate, so why now? Even my [other] children have seen that a lot. Their friends haven't been able to come to our home because of the other parents who have seen Melissa's behavior.

Despite her matter-of-fact attitude, in this case it appears that not only has the parent's social life been affected, but so have the social lives of her other children.

Another parent also sees this issue in a very straightforward way:

> Friends will come over and ask why she's doing this or that. That's Nancy [her daughter]. I've lost a lot of friends over this. That's okay. If they were really friends, they would be more tolerant. If not, it's a good thing they went on their way.

Of all subjects interviewed, these were the only two who did not express any clear sense of burden as a result of their social isolation.

Why, given that the majority of parents caring for mentally ill children seem to suffer from a sense of social isolation, has this emotional burden—as opposed to, say, blame—been virtually ignored in the literature? Part of the reason for this discrepancy is that for many people, blame is a more tangible concept in that we have all both blamed others and felt blamed for various viewpoints and behaviors. Social isolation, by comparison, is a bit more abstract. Given the numerous forms of social isolation that exist, it is inevitably more challenging to explicate this concept. Moreover, although researchers, mental health professionals, and laypeople alike have all had some contact with blaming behavior, far fewer of us have ever lived with or raised a child with a significant mental illness; thus it is more difficult for us to relate to these experiences of social isolation and subsequently to study them.

It is nevertheless clear from this study that the experience of social isolation and of "being a prisoner in your own home" has profound effects on the overall mental health and well-being of parents. People who were once trusted and caring friends have disappeared. There is little time to cultivate new relationships. These events are just a few of the isolating situations that parents of mentally ill children must face. This leads them to penetrating questions that are always unanswered: "What should I do?", "How can I live?", and eventually "But isn't my child a person, a human being, someone to be loved unconditionally?"

The experience of social isolation can also greatly affect internal family relationships. A few of the parents interviewed related how, because of their child's mental illness, they often felt less of a connection with their spouses and other children within the family. This lack of connection was in part attributable to the fact that everyone in the family handled the impact of the mental illness differently. It appears, then, that many parents experience social isolation on a number of levels, any one of which can greatly affect their overall mental health. Given that so many of the parents whom I interviewed emphasized the negative effects of social isolation, this area of study clearly warrants further research and investigation. Such investigation will not only draw more attention to this important issue, but also help both parents and professionals to more fully appreciate the consequences of social isolation, and lead to identification of ways to combat its negative effects.

EXPECTATIONS/FUTURE ORIENTATION

How do parents consider their lives in terms of the future? What concerns do they have about their child as he or she grows older? The parents in this study expressed many deep feelings about what the future held for their children. One mother, whose son had been diagnosed with ADHD and oppositional defiant disorder, expressed a common sentiment—that her child's mental illness has taken away both her own and her son's expectations and hope for the future. She explains that parents are socialized to expect that

> [T]he world should be his oyster, . . . not only has my child been robbed of his own childhood, but as a parent I have been robbed by not having the typical parenting experience—the gratifications and the rewards . . . everything has been a fight . . . and that's a real loss.

This same mother, who is a parent advocate, relates a story about a time when she was giving a speech regarding her experiences with her son for a group of professionals. Noting that she's a "pretty tough cookie," she describes getting to the part about her son's social life and talking about how he's never been invited to a birthday party and never had a best friend. At that point she broke down and started to cry in the presentation. It just "broke my heart," she said, as she continued describing the loss of friendships and opportunities her son had to experience because of his mental illness.

This consistent feeling of loss, either well articulated or merely implied, permeated nearly all of the interviews. Considering that it is often hopes and expectations that help parents and families to navigate through difficult times, one cannot help but wonder where parents who have lost such hopes and expectations find the strength to persist and persevere.

Some of the parents who were interviewed clearly had no idea what to expect from the future for their child, and this uncertainty created a significant amount of angst and confusion for them. One mother, whose son has Klinefelter's syndrome, ADHD, and oppositional defiant disorder, explains:

> I like to look at it like he's going to grow up and go away, go to school, get married, have kids. He's not going to have kids. That's sad. He talks about it. He doesn't know that it's going to be me and him. It's really frustrating when I think about it. He wants to be a racecar driver. He wants to be a pizza delivery man. He wants to be a janitor. I'm right there with him. I don't know, when the time comes, who's going to be more devastated, him or me. He may be able to live in an assisted living home on his own, if there's somebody checking on him. I don't see it, because I don't see his mental abilities getting that high. I don't want to hold him back. I want him to go but I keep wondering, what does the world hold for him?

Other parents realized, as they were talking to me, that the relationship with their child is long term—the caring is likely never to end:

> To be brutally honest, I would say that Manndy's going to be around, in my life, most of the rest of my life. I have a number of things that I fear. Because of the history with her father—he has a real history of being incarcerated. I'm real afraid that she'll end up incarcerated. Another one is that I'll end up having to help, support her, do whatever I have to. It's hard because there's this mom part that says, "She's my daughter, and I'll do anything for her." Then there's that reality part that goes, "You're only human. You can only do so much."

> I have a lady I work with: She's 74 years old, and she's still working. She has a daughter who lives with her that's similar to Manndy. She has her daughter and her daughter's son living with her. The daughter's not working; she's supporting her. She can hardly walk, but she's still working to support her daughter. I see that and think I would never do that. But then I think, I would do the same thing. It's your daughter.

> In the beginning, there were those years where I didn't have any hope. I thought I had this really bad child, period. Behavior-wise. I don't think it really

dawned on me that we have an issue of "I don't know what she's going to do when she's an adult." I didn't think about that. She's still reading at a fifth-grade level. Her math is not very good. Her writing is terrible, and she misspells words all the time. It finally dawned on me that if I don't do something, now that she's 13, we've got only a few years. We're on that road. The next step is getting her ready to teach her some life skills so she can work. If we can do that, we'll make it.

Another parent's internal conflict about what will be best for her son in the coming years is an ongoing struggle for her, with no apparent end in sight. She expressed apprehensions about her child's future and appears particularly concerned about her own role in this pending transition. She states that she and her adolescent son:

have a relationship that I'm very concerned about because it's so close. And I worry how he'll survive without me. He doesn't know how to talk to anybody else. There's nobody in my family who gets it [his mental illness]. If something happens to me, I'm sure he'd go to a group home. There's just no one else for him.

It appears, then, that many parents find themselves both trying to manage their ongoing fears about their child's current well-being and hesitantly speculating about how their child will fare without their parental guidance and support. For some parents, this sense of fear regarding the future appears to go beyond uncertainty and transforms into a sense of desperation. One mother states:

I wish there was something that could show me that in the end, there would be some peace. I know a 32-year-old male who is bipolar who's not slowed down a minute. That thought really scares me to death.

Finally, I often heard sorrow as I listened to parents talk about the future. Such "inevitable sorrow" is not easily dealt with by parents. Yes, the parent is focused on the child, as are the mental health practitioners, but there seems to be no help for the parents' feelings. Many parents cannot easily see a bright side to their struggles; pride of parenthood is difficult. For these parents, there is a sense of being cut off from the child in some fashion. And what hope is there for future generations? *"Will my child simply pass this affliction on if he or she marries and has his or her own child?"* A few parents spoke of death as a preferable alternative, something final to deal with, knowing that concerns about the child's future and safety are now resolved. These feelings are deep, often conflicted, and difficult to accept.

It is this common struggle—this constant uncertainty and fear—that plagues so many of the parents whom I interviewed. What they perceive is a burden with no limits, extending far into the future, with little hope of resolution or even an extended period of peace and serenity for either themselves or their children.

Throughout the data-gathering process, it became increasingly more apparent to me that it would be a long and arduous task to quantify and discuss all of the different experiences of burden that these parents encounter on a daily basis. While the subject area certainly deserves such a comprehensive examination, it is beyond the scope of this study to do so. However, by grouping the gathered data into specific categories that capture the most frequently expressed forms of burden, we can at least begin both to consider the gravity of these experiences and to contemplate the countless other forms of burden with which these parents struggle. Thus, while the results presented here are not absolute, they do provide the reader with a significant window into the lives of parents who are raising a child with a mental illness.

CHAPTER 7

Faithful Acts of Caring: Lessons on a More Meaningful Life

> No matter what we encounter in life, it is faith that enables us to try
> again, to trust again, to love again. Even in times of immense suffering,
> it is faith that enables us to relate to the present moment in such a way
> that we can go on, we can move forward, instead of becoming lost in res-
> ignation or despair
>
> —S. Salzberg, *Faith: Trusting Your Own Deepest Experience*

Parent after parent has presented their story—a "story house" built, brick by
brick, out of numerous "faithful acts of caring." All of these stories have a theme
that describes untold suffering by the parent. Yet, these parents wake up every
morning to make breakfast for their child. They are on a journey of faithful caring. No matter what they encounter that day, they will call on faith to keep trying, to trust that things can get better, and to continue to live in the present.
Faith is fidelity to one's promises, loyalty to a person, something that is done
without question. The word *faith* comes from *fidem*, which in Latin means "trust."
C. S. Lewis described faith as a virtue that helps us hold to our reasoned ideas,
despite situations and moods to the contrary.[1] Sharon Salzberg talks about how
faith "reminds us of the ever-changing flow of life, with all its movement and possibility. Faith is the capacity of the heart that allows us to draw close to the
present and find there the underlying thread connecting the moment's experience to the fabric of all life."[2]

One of the greatest challenges to faith is the suffering of one's child. When
you are suffering personally, you have some emotional control, some ability to

---

Mia Zamora contributed significantly to this chapter and is considered a co-author.

cope, comprehend, and rationalize what is occurring on a more existential level. While you may not be in control of any of the events occurring outside your body, your internal reactions are your own. When their child is sick, whether it is with a physical or mental illness, parents have a primal drive to do everything in their power to take away that suffering. They can temper some of the fear, anxiety, and confusion that a child experiences when dealing with a serious illness, but they cannot take it away for the child. At times a mentally ill child is unaware of the risks he or she may be taking and may not, in fact, be suffering all of the time. It is as if he or she is wandering through a battlefield without even being aware of the war. In these cases, parents suffer *for* their child; they fight with doctors, the behavioral health system, the school system, and often their own child to get what is best for the child.

Michael Greenberg chronicles his teenage daughter Sally's sudden plunge into psychosis in his memoir *Hurry Down Sunshine*.[3] It began when his daughter had an epiphany about her own genius, and the hidden genius of everyone around her. Sally began approaching strangers in New York City to enlighten them about their unrecognized potential. At first Greenberg believed that this behavior was a result of her years of being described as learning disabled and perhaps some potent hallucinogenic drugs. He saw her new light and passion as her having "returned to her idealized instant of existence, before diagnostic tests and 'special needs,' before 'processing deficits' . . . before the word 'average' came to denote a pinnacle beyond attainment." Even after Sally's drug screening came back clean, it felt cruel to him to take his deliriously happy and energetic daughter, who was flushed with her own psychotic wisdom, and lock her in a psychiatric hospital and ply her with medication that virtually rendered her comatose. When he finally took that step, he still had to justify that decision to Sally's mother, Helen: " 'But she's suffering,' I say, and then immediately wonder if this is true or if it is *our* plight to suffer, while Sally barrels ahead without feeling, like a runaway train. Helen catches up to Sally as she enters the dayroom. 'Tell your father you're not suffering.' Sally replies: 'The truth comes disguised as suffering. My father has been destroyed by fear.' "[4] Sally's response, easily written off as the verbosity of madness, contains undeniable wisdom. For the mentally ill child, it is often the parent's job to be afraid for the child when he or she is incapable of such fear.

In many ways, illness is an intensification of every agony of parenting. Sending your child out into the world, a world that you know can be a harsh and dangerous place, is both your job and your greatest fear. When that world is complicated by illness, your ability to protect your child is even more compromised. Every parent reaches a point when he or she recognizes that there is nothing more the parent can do to make life more bearable. That is the point at which Christina, always fearful of what late-night call she would get, unplugged her phone at night to get a good night's rest. Peter Early describes his discovered "truth" after years of dealing with his son's mental illness in this way: "Mental illness is a cruel disease. No one knows whom it might strike or why. There is no known cure. It lasts forever. My son Mike has it. And because he is sick, he will always be dancing on the edge of a cliff. I cannot keep him from falling. I cannot protect him from its viciousness. All I can do is stand next to him on that cliff, always ready to extend my hand. All I can do is to promise that I will never abandon him."[5]

In one of the most difficult interviews I conducted, a parent provided the starkest example of the competition between her desire to protect her son and her need to ensure that she was doing what was best for the child. This mother described an exquisitely sensitive and loving child for whom the pain of living is almost too much to bear. He suffers from debilitating depression, hears terrifying voices that torment him, and is so anxiety ridden that he cannot lead a functional existence. After relaying her story she reflects on his multiple suicide attempts and wonders aloud how she can in good conscience continue to try to stop him from ending his own life. Why does she get to decide that his life should go on, when all he desires is a relief from the pain?

In part, her answer comes from her understanding that her child has precious contributions to the world:

> I wouldn't be the person I am if I didn't have a son such as Barry. I've met courage face to face. He's so forlorn and so depressed, and so hopeless, but yet he's not dead. He keeps waking up to this hideous terror, never in peace. . . . he's a human spirit that goes through this torture that he's living. . . . There really is no real silver lining for me. . . . I need to keep him alive. That's my job. I love him.

She is his mother. Her job is to keep him alive, to nurture her faith so she can develop hope when he has none left.

NARRATIVES OF SUFFERING

Much of this book is a narrative perspective about being a parent of a mentally ill child. After interviewing parents and hearing their stories, I began to read widely in the field of sorrow and grief. Eventually I found my way to Arthur Frank's book *The Wounded Storyteller*, which I have quoted from many times. This book focuses on how people with physical illness need to construct meaningful narratives as a way of creating a new map for their life.[6] David Karp, in his book on how the mental illness of one person affects family members, introduces the term *wounded listeners* to describe these individuals.[7]

My book is about *wounded parents*, who also can benefit from understanding that their story or personal narrative is a way to help bring understanding, self-compassion, and order from the suffering and chaos that characterize the process of parenting mentally ill children. What results from this process is a narratively understood self. Hope and meaning emerge from understanding that one's life has a story. And the development of this self does not occur in isolation: "The self that is narratively constructed is not an individual achievement but a self constructed in a community."[8] The parents of mentally ill children are engaged in narrative work that transcends telling stories about their experience. What is evident is that the parents who have derived the most meaning from their experience have created their *transformative life story*. This life story, in turn, cultivates hope. Hope involves "the creation of stories about personal transformation required in order to continue to hope, and to revise one's hopes, no matter how desperate the circumstances or how bleak the prospects."[9]

Perhaps Nietzsche sums it up best: "What does not destroy me, makes me stronger."

These narratives serve a purpose to both the storyteller and the audience. When parents believe they are the only ones to experience life as they do, they feel alone, isolated, and often at wit's end. A universal force in coping with the child's mental illness is hearing or reading about other parents' experiences. This reduces the parent's sense of feeling crazy or of being entirely to blame for the child's illness, as well as the feeling on aloneness. Recounting one's own story also gives the storyteller a more distant perspective, and an opportunity to begin to view the journey in its entirety.

Valerie Paradiz's memoir *Elijah's Cup* represents a compelling example of a parent's narrative. In the beginning, she is exclusively focused on understanding her son, who is on the autism spectrum. She reveals her endless questioning and guilt as she describes her reactions to his condition. Eventually, her quest moves beyond blame and cause-seeking to a level of appreciation of her son's "autistic culture." With pensive insight, Paradiz then begins to reveal the role autism has played in her family. Eventually she recognizes her own autistic tendencies. In her book Paradiz describes a personal journey that evolves over time; thus her story is an example of a "transformative" narrative.

Parents of mentally ill children must not only fight on a daily basis to maintain some form of equilibrium at home, but must also try to make sense of the unending struggle. Many of the parents interviewed for this book are living in crisis mode—caught up in battles with the behavioral health networks, with the school system, and, most painfully, with their own children. These narratives are chaos stories, in which parents live life from appointment to appointment, from crisis to crisis. Many of these parents have not had the time or achieved the distance at which they might find a greater meaning in their family's suffering. James Joyce, whose daughter was institutionalized for much of her life, eloquently described the day-to-day struggle as follows: "I can see nothing but a dark wall in front of me . . . a dark wall or a precipice if you prefer, physically, morally, materially."[10]

Nevertheless, some parents have been able to gain enough distance to make sense of their lives and the pain they have experienced. This understanding does not make their daily existence any less difficult, but these parents do demonstrate a greater sense of peace, of understanding the reason for the journey and not just seeing the steps in front of them. Although parents are not often conscious of it, a tremendous amount of the wisdom needed to overcome adversity lies within them. The warrior path of the parent is to take the path with a heart. In turn, a critical question is, "Does this path have a heart?"[11]

Part of my goal in interviewing parents of children with mental illnesses was to explore their spiritual and emotional journey—to identify what meaning parents ascribed to their pain, and to elucidate how they attained that meaning. There are rarely opportunities for parents to tell their stories. As discussed in Chapter 1, it is clear that behavioral health assessments do not generally focus on the family's narrative, but rather address functional and symptomatic problems and concerns. There are two reasons these narratives are so important. First, the parent's perspective is vital to understanding how to improve service delivery and address the ecological needs of the family. Second, telling their story from the beginning forces parents to take a step back from their daily struggles, to look at their journey from a distance. The process of conceptualizing their child's life in narrative form requires parents to begin to ask the questions that naturally arise in a narrative: What is the purpose? What greater meaning can I find from this tale?

The value of facing life's difficulties—of suffering—has been addressed through the centuries. Rumi, a thirteenth-century mystic noted, "Pain is a treasure, for it contains mercies."[12] Many have written how pain and suffering lead to strength and enlightenment. Buddhism considers pain to be one of its central tenants: "Life is suffering." This simple truth brings awareness of the universal truth that all of us experience a form of suffering. Listening to parents who have shared deep accounts of suffering points to some essential truths in life. One is that we all suffer and seek the strength to find wisdom in this experience, and that the resulting wisdom brings a hard-won understanding of a larger sense of meaningfulness.

Viktor Frankl, a psychiatrist who was held in a Nazi concentration camp during World War II, noted that "emotion, which is suffering, ceases to be suffering as soon as we form a clear and precise picture of it"; in that precise picture lies every individual's belief about the meaning of his or her pain.[13] This clear picture of suffering, as described by Frankl, seems to bring peace to parents when they are able to see it. Perhaps the most difficult thing about despair, beyond the daily pain and the uncertainty of ever reaching a resolution, is suffering without understanding the reason, without being able to grasp onto a larger meaning, leaving you trapped in every moment of sorrow. Pain without meaning leads to larger existential questions that haunt you on a daily basis; it leads people back to the basic question, "Why do I have to experience this pain?" Helping professionals need to investigate how and if parents come to their own understanding of this answer, and how we can help them to reach a resolution.

SUFFERING: EACH PERSON IS DIFFERENT

Carl Jung described a state of irrational suffering as an inability to find the meaning in one's pain.[14] Parents of mentally ill children experience a deeply felt despair. While some grow from their experience, others are left bitter and unable to rebound from the tragedy that befell them. Suffering alone will not create the conditions of growth and self-awareness that lead to a more meaningful understanding of the world. Anne Morrow Lindbergh wisely said, "If suffering alone talked, all the world would be wise, since everyone suffers."[15] Some parents grow in positive ways despite their fate; others become stuck unable to move forward.

Sadly, my mother was one of the latter people. My father was diagnosed with early-onset Alzheimer's disease. It was a family tragedy that came with plenty of pain and suffering. My mother was never able to move beyond her suffering. While other friends I talked with expressed both pain and meaning associated with a family member's Alzheimer's disease, my mother could only recount her losses. It was her sense of self-pity that limited her ability to find meaning beyond suffering. Yet, for many other individuals, a brush with such experiences launches a newfound interest and search for a more meaningful life. The serious illness jolts many people into a mindset ripe for discovery about what is most important in life and what one really wants from life. Even after my father's death, my mother could not turn her life around. But why? How do some people become energized to snatch more from the gift of life, whereas others dwell endlessly on sorrow? What can we learn from parents of mentally ill children who do find a window to a more meaningful life despite their sorrow?

James Joyce desperately searched for a reason behind his daughter's illness, blaming everything from his own novel *Ulysses* to a hormonal imbalance, and spent most of his money trying to cure her and keep her happy. In the end, however, he could find neither a cure nor a reason for her suffering: "I feel like an animal who has received four thunderous mallet strokes on the top of the skull. There are moments and hours when I have nothing in my heart but rage and despair, a blind man's rage and despair."[16]

Dealing with a child with a mental illness also means accepting that no matter how many interventions are applied, which parenting techniques are used, or how traumas are processed in therapy, there may never be a "cure." The battle to cope with the symptoms and behaviors of the child's mental illness is, for most, everlasting, and parents must face the reality that instead of being full-time parents for 18 years, they will be responsible for their children for the rest of their lives. Lorraine, whose son Warren has a chromosomal disorder called Klinefelter's syndrome that causes severe behavioral issues and learning disabilities, describes her anticipatory dread for the time when Warren realizes that he is not going to achieve the goals he is dreaming about:

> He wants to be a racecar driver. He wants to be a pizza man delivery. He wants to be a janitor. I'm right there with him. I don't know, when the time comes, who's going to be more devastated—him or me. He may be able to live in an assisted home or on his own, if there's somebody checking on him.

Imagine the pain of having to face the possibility of tempering your child's dreams instead of being able to wholeheartedly encourage them. Lorraine already fights:

> [feeling] guilty just because [of] the helplessness. Like watching him struggle when he has asthma. You're helpless. You can't do nothing. You can't fix it. This thing

that he has—[you] can't drain his blood and give him new blood. It's not going make it go away. It's going be there.

Perhaps it is how parents live their experiences—rather than the experiences themselves—that makes their lives tolerable and, for some, meaningful. Frankl describes the importance of finding the meaning within life experiences as follows: "a man who becomes conscious of the responsibility he bears toward a human being who affectionately waits for him . . . will never be able to throw away his life. He knows the 'why' for his existence, and will be able to bear almost any 'how.' "

Sometimes living a courageous life means waking up every morning. We wake up; we take one breath, and then another. As another parent described the journey:

You put your hiking boots on and you keep on walking. And as you fall down, you get back up.

Parents have to find a way to rise above the helplessness and despair inherent in facing a seemingly endless and impossible task. Helping professionals must find a way to help parents in their journey to discovering their whys and learning how to live that experience in a meaningful fashion. Arthur Frank contrasts the idea of *useless suffering*, which does not help people, but merely keeps them stuck in a position of suffering, with a transformative process. Clearly, some people are stuck with useless suffering, yet these experiences can typically be transformed into a more meaningful perspective. Mental health workers and parent advocates may be able to open up new opportunities for parents to view their experiences as a transformative process as opposed to a destructive force.

FINDING MEANING

Part of the suffering of a parent of a child with a mental illness involves the loss of control over one's understanding of oneself, or the loss of a part of oneself. This loss of individuality, of the ability to live a life not consumed with the care of another human being, means that parents must discover a new sense of themselves.

David Karp talks about how family members eventually confront the fact that the family member's mental illness will remain and in so doing reach an "identity turning point."[17] Michael Greenberg's ex-wife felt the loss of identity as an invasion by her daughter's vivid spirit: "She gets inside me. She always has. Being with her, I sometimes feel as if I'm going to break apart myself."[18] For Pete Early, the suffering comes from an inability to control his son's symptoms, or the outside world's reactions to his son's behavior. He describes his sense of acceptance in this way: "I cannot keep him from falling. I cannot protect him from its viciousness. All I can do is stand next to him on that cliff, always ready to extend my hand. All I can do is promise that I will never abandon him."[19] In some ways, this is the same struggle that every parent goes through—the realization that you are powerless to prevent your child's suffering. However, when your child is particularly vulnerable, the pain of being incapable of protecting him or her is especially acute.

Parents are often locked into a cycle of anticipatory dread in which they try valiantly to prevent crises from occurring. They must be vigilant about potential changes in mood or behavior, and keep track of dozens of upcoming appointments, all the while keeping a series of constant questions in the back of their head: "Where is my child going to end up in life? Is he or she going to be safe? Is something terrible going to happen?" Parents are too often trapped by worries of the future. This anxiety pulls them away from the small moments that often are what makes life treasured and meaningful.

In thinking about this day-to-day intensity, I am reminded of Thich Nhat Hanh, who discusses the importance of mindfulness in everyday life. This line of thinking leads me to wonder, Could this perspective help parents become centered in their own lives, to rediscover their identity as individuals and not just parents?[20] Hanh explains that, unless we are mindful during the most mundane tasks, such as washing dishes, "we are incapable of realizing the miracle of life while standing at the sink. If we can't wash the dishes, then chances are we won't be able to drink our tea either. While drinking the cup of tea, we will only be thinking of other things, barely aware of the cup in our hands. Thus we are sucked away into the future—and we are incapable of actually living one minute of life."[21]

Parents who can find the tiniest bit of time to themselves can bring greater balance to their lives. When I have the responsibility of walking our dog in the morning, that bit of time can help me experience my life in a different manner. If I can *listen* as the birds sing, *look* as the sun rises, and *smell* as the morning air lingers, then for that one small moment I know I have found a kind of peace within myself. While this prescription seems simple, it isn't: We have to find a time, seek the moment, and allow the awareness to emerge within us. In this moment it is possible to embrace our purpose and begin each day more hopeful.

Finding meaning is an important aspect of acceptance that is quite different from hoping for a cure. For many who have figured out how to survive, the most salient lesson has been to accept what has happened and to change how they respond to life's events. The success story—achieved by some parents of mentally ill children—is to turn their personal tragedy into a triumph of sorts. It is these parents who mourn their loss yet still find hope, who feel their pain yet remain strong, and who find purpose and meaning in life's cherished moments despite the difficulties they face as parents who confront a very long struggle with their children.

Parents often find that writing offers a great release for them as they try to cope with their everyday struggles. The following quote, taken from the National Alliance on Mental Illness (NAMI) website, is from a mother of a bipolar child:

In my stronger moments, I regard the challenge of parenting Rose as a gift: She blesses me with plenty of practice at staying present in the moment. Her days of irritability that begin with a barrage of angry words and end with slamming doors are sometimes endured only with help of the deep breathing techniques learned from childbirth. Her sunny moods, longer and more frequent since she began taking Depakote and Wellbutrin, are welcome oases of calm affection. On one of those precious days, she might wrap her arms around my neck and say, "I'm glad you're my mom, even though you don't always think so." Those days, I'm grateful for all the things she's taught me about patience, and love, and how much we take for granted in life.[22]

Former *Washington Post* reporter Pete Early turned his son's psychotic break in his twenties and subsequent arrest for breaking into his neighbor's house into an opportunity to research the role of the criminal justice system in the lives of the chronically mentally ill. He documented his findings in the landmark book *Crazy* and continues to advocate for reform related to mental health care. As part of his journey to understand the vast systems of public mental health and criminal justice, Early was also able to obtain a deeper understanding of his role in his son's tribulations. In reading his memoir you can sense how this pursuit represented a survival strategy for the author.

Parents have used their personal experiences in battling for services for their own children to become advocates for others. Pete Early interviewed a woman whom he met through the National Alliance on Mental Illness named Judy Robinson. Robinson served as a lifelong advocate for her son, Jeff, who began experiencing symptoms of a mood disorder when he was 12. Early found that Robinson drew much of her strength from her advocacy both for her own child and for other parents with children diagnosed with serious mental illnesses. Robinson finds purpose and meaning within the act of the daily battle: "All you can do is fight it, every day. You can't lose your patience with it, and most of all, you must *never* give up. You can sit around and complain, or you can empower yourself and tell yourself, 'Okay, life isn't fair—so what! What can I do to make this situation better?' That's the path I've chosen, and I will continue taking it until the day I die."[23]

As discussed earlier in this book, many parents experience an uncertain grief, and failure to address that grief is likely to make coping more difficult for them. A step in moving forward is climbing out of that uncertain grief and beginning to find hope. The human spirit is remarkable for its ability to find hope in tragedy. Many times such hope turns into advocacy and action. Parents rally to start new support groups, create new social networks, produce useful blogs, advocate for healthy policy changes, and help one another. If fully exploited, this as yet largely untapped resource could positively transform the broken mental health system. Advocacy is a strength born from caring. Many psychologists have asked the question, "What brings people happiness?" An emphasis on the "good life" and personal gratification leads to only short-lived pleasure; instead, when it comes to long-term happiness, caring actions far outweigh any emphasis on pleasurable activities.[24] For many parents who do find hope, that outcome emerges from their efforts geared toward reaching out and focusing on caring actions—it becomes a personal strength. It is difficult, but when parents do focus on being in the service of something larger than themselves, they may find their lives become more meaningful.

PARENTS AND PROFESSIONALS: SHIPS PASSING IN THE NIGHT

Community mental health clinics do not help parents find meaning in their child's suffering; sometimes they don't even acknowledge the pain that a parent of a child with a mental illness experiences. This disregard for their own pain can cause parents to feel that they are alone in their grief and despair. Ann describes her guilt and sense of isolation in the following way:

> It's hard as a parent. You're real torn. Most of her life I thought, "I love her; she's my child—but she's so difficult that I don't want to deal with it sometimes." That's a hard thing to admit. But it's okay to know that. Sometimes I can't and don't want to deal with her. I've had enough. So it is hard.

Without the support and validation of mental health professionals, parents may come to view their complex emotional responses to their children's symptoms as abnormal—something, as Ann said, that is "hard to admit." How is a person supposed to find meaning in his or her struggle if the universality of the individual's pain goes unacknowledged? Surrounded by an opaque silence—no one speaking openly or acknowledging the difficulties, or the feelings of anger, loss, and grief that well up inside the parent—those unacknowledged feelings can cripple the parent.

To adequately cope with a mentally ill child, parents need resources and support to find meaning in their experiences. Parents most often find this support in the form of support groups and community organizations, but clinicians are generally either the gatekeepers for information on these groups or the only form of support that a family has within the local community. Because mental health clinicians and social workers focus on symptom and behavior management, the needs of the parent are often overlooked—not even necessarily in terms of the burden of multiple appointments, but rather in terms of the psychic energy it takes to deal with these issues on a daily basis. The recognition of the immense impact a child's mental illness has on the life of the parent must be a part of the helper's perspective of the parent as a human being. All too often in the past, mental health professionals have missed the *long view* of parents who were asking, "How do I live and survive this experience?"

Clinical practitioners are taught about empathy and compassion. Yet, in the course of the interviews that I conducted with parents of mentally ill children, it became painfully apparent that few of these helpers are able to truly connect in a compassionate manner with parents. Compassion literally means "to suffer with," and the parents interviewed for this book rarely felt that their therapists and case managers were experiencing even a fraction of the pain they experienced. They point to the huge disparity between seeing a child once a week, sometimes once every other week, for an hour in an office environment and spending all day, every day, with a child in their home. The Latin root of the word *suffering* itself means "to allow" or "to experience." How can the clinician truly empathize with the parent, when he or she never "experiences" what the parent goes through?

American culture is not a culture that allows for suffering. We have pushed the bounds of science, medicine, pop psychology, and technology to fix, or at least conceal, anything less than perfection.[25] We have antidepressants to elevate our mood, Botox to remove our wrinkles, and innumerable technological devices to distract us from the reality that surrounds us. This pressure to construct our own, more perfect reality does not allow for the fact that at times, as Buddha says, "life is suffering." Americans want to believe that there is a way to fix whatever might be wrong, and this stubborn belief flies in the face of every parent who has a mentally ill child who has been on countless medications and participated in treatment after treatment with no "cure" in sight. As parents slowly come to the realization that no one combination of psychotropic medications and therapy will "fix" their child, they begin having to reach within themselves and beyond the limits of societal understanding for an answer. In this moment they can only "be" and experience the pain that has been thrust upon them. A developing sense of sorrow will overtake them, and that sorrow has greater depth and dimensions than anything else they may have experienced. In a culture that denies suffering, one is bound to feel alone in experiencing pain or loss.

FAITHFUL CARING AND MEANING

Parents of mentally ill children experience this suffering, the chronic sorrow that either causes them to sink into the depths of existential despair or forges a resilient and powerful belief in a larger meaning. The world is filled with stories of unimaginable cruelty, suffering, and injustice. While many people have some abstract and intellectualized explanation for the grim atrocities that occur every day around the world, when a person is confronted directly with suffering, the hard-and-fast realities begin to conflict with any soft notions of faith they may have previously had. Harold Kushner's book *When Bad Things Happen to Good People* deftly describes this rabbi's own search to find solace when facing his own child's fatal illness. This book is popular simply because Kushner's search for meaning, in the face of immense suffering, represents a dominant passion that is familiar to many people.

There is no universally agreed-upon answer, but every major religion must tackle the question of suffering in some form for its followers to find solace in its teachings. Many religions believe suffering as a path to wisdom and salvation—that one's faith must arise from deeply felt wounds. In the Buddhist religion, suffering is considered the proximate cause of faith; it is the door that opens one to faith. Nonreligious individuals are not exempt from this quest, the searching and contemplating how to find more meaning in life—a testimony to the universality of this journey.[26]

It was in the greatest depths of suffering in a World War II concentration camp that Viktor Frankl found the greatest strength: "A thought transfixed me:

For the first time in my life I saw the truth as it is set into song by so many poets, proclaimed as the final wisdom by so many thinkers. The truth—that love is the ultimate and the highest goal to which man can aspire. I grasped the meaning of the greatest secret that human poetry and human thought and belief have to impart: The salvation of man is through love and in love."[27]

The pain that binds a parent to his or her child is one of love—biological and unceasing. One unnamed participant in my own study, after reviewing her son's long history of suicide attempts, psychiatric hospitalizations, and social rejection, reflected: "He's a human spirit that goes through this torture that he's living. . . . There really is no real silver lining for me . . . I need to keep him alive. That's my job. I love him. I'd die if I lost one of my children. But in that kind of misery, how can I possibly force him?" In the face of her child's tortured existence, her maternal instincts began conflicting with her desire to see her child's pain end. This is a side of love rarely brought to light, and it illustrates the enormous moral complexities that accompany the process of raising a child with a mental illness.

Kathleen Brehony uses the metaphor of "life as a wheel," reminding us that everyone ends up at different places on the wheel of life—cycling through happiness, sadness, pain, sorrow, joy, and hope.[28] Even so, every day must be pursued with a sense of meaning to make the most sense out of what, too often, seems like a senseless life. Other cultures have emphasized the process of ongoing change: "It can be helpful to remember that even in the midst of our anguish, the wheel continues to turn."[29] In the worst moment we can reflect that time waits for no one—things will change, life will emerge different than before. Some parents seem to thrive and blossom under the same adverse circumstances that cause other parents to fold in on themselves in despair. What causes some parents to rise to the challenge of raising a difficult child, and how can we use them as examples to guide those parents for whom the task ahead of them appears hopeless?

Some of the people whom I interviewed were supported by a strong spiritual foundation, one that gave them support even when they were alone. One mother, Christina, uses prayer as an outlet when everything becomes overwhelming: "I just talk to Him all the time, tell Him when I'm pissed off, what's going on with me. Verbally releasing the hurt inside, out there somewhere. I just have to talk." Parents with faith, however that is defined for them, have something they can turn to for support at any time, but also believe that they were placed in this difficult situation for a reason, one that may be beyond their understanding. Phyllis is one such parent: "I just feel, all right, there's another plan. There's a divine theme to life. And just because this child needs to learn in a different way, [it] doesn't mean that we won't seek it out and find it." Her belief typifies the parents who responded to their mentally ill child as an opportunity to grow and learn and be blessed. Others, not so fortunate, see only darkness and live completely in that darkness.

In interviewing parents, it became clear that if they could have the kind of transformative experience described by Phyllis, it would make a huge difference in their quality of life. Do we do enough to help parents of mentally ill children to reach for this resilience? Do we support parents in confronting adversity and grow psychologically and spiritually, or do we allow them to resign themselves to a world filled with adversity and remain closed, angry, and hopeless? These pathways are dramatically different, yet both have lifelong consequences for how one lives—for the quality of one's life.

Parents do come to recognize the value of the child in the context of all this sorrow and difficulty. Children offer great potential to the human species. Indeed, what these parents have taught me is that we can learn as much from burden as from promise, as much from illness as from health, as much from despair as from optimism. "As many spiritual leaders know, out of suffering is born faith, and out of faith is born meaning, and with meaning life can be full and rewarding. Whatever we encounter in life, it is faith that enables us to try again, to trust again, to love again."[30] When the burden of caring suffocates parents, it is a sense of faith that lets them breathe again—that brings them back into the present moment so they can continue forward.

Children with mental illness—and indeed, all children—have a right to happiness and a full life. In spite of obstacles, their parents can learn to accept the child, mental illness and all, as a whole and complete person. Parents need to learn to be proud of their child as they "take on" those who fail to understand and appreciate the beauty of all children. All children, no matter who they are or what their condition, have meaning for their parents, their brothers and sisters, their families, their schools, their neighborhoods—for the world.

Kierkegaard talks about how "hope becomes faith through love." It is through one's love that the process of letting go can occur. With love, we can come to realize we cannot control outcomes; we can only have faith.[31]

The experience of parenting a mentally ill child is a reminder of the mystery in life we all face. Once parents climb over the hope/fear wall, their capacity for love deepens, or at least widens.

Faith is being open to the truth of what is happening so that one can experience life as the mystery that it is and obtain the big picture—that is, look down on the universe. With grief and despair comes a separateness from others, an aloneness that often moves us further from any meaningful connections. Because circumstances seem unlikely to change, a sense of hopelessness may arise.

Sharon Salzberg, in addressing the concept of faith, talks about the children's picture book, *Zoom*. With this book, you look at one page and see an image of what is being conveyed; you then turn to the next page, only to find that the previous image was simply part of the picture's reality; you then turn to the next page, only to find that the previous image was simply part of the picture's reality; and so forth. Salzberg interprets this metaphor as follows: "There is a far bigger picture to life than what we are facing in any particular moment. To see beyond the one small part in front of us and not think that's all there is, we have to look past our ready conclusions." It is faith that opens us up, helps us encounter the unknown, gives us courage, and provides a bigger picture of life. Accompanying that bigger picture is the ability to move forward. Many parents with mentally ill children have developed a resounding faith in which they have learned to "let go" but also to "begin again." They describe experiences of painful failure, but then begin again; they lose hope, but then begin again. To develop this sense of possibility requires something, which in this context can be called "faith."

In the Buddhist doctrine, faith means "saddha" or "to place the heart upon." Salzberg summarizes the Buddhist perspective: "To have faith is to offer one's heart or give over one's heart."[32] Parents of mentally ill children have to keep moving forward, even though they are trapped in the darkness of their experience. Eventually, most of them begin to perceive ruptures between the moments of suffering. In these circumstances, parents cannot get lost hoping for the future, and dwelling on the past does not make anything better; instead, parents need to live in the present, and faith helps them do that. "We must arrive at an inner faith not dependent on externals, some thing we can carry with us, that isn't born only of the compelling mirror held up by another, or the vibrations of a sacred place, or a wonderful feeling of possibility."[33] In my interviews, some parents, in explaining the pain they have experienced in raising a mentally ill child, described how this experience also marked the birth of a bigger outlook on life.

Chris, who was first introduced in Chapter 1, described her efforts to reach out to a faith community for support and guidance during her struggles with Jonathan. She was raised with a close connection to her church and had always felt that "church . . . was supposed to be a faith—a warm, kind place that you could go." Unfortunately, she quickly discovered that the same stigma she faced in schools, in grocery stores, and with friends because of Jonathan's behavioral problems carried over to church as well: "Now we were dealing with Sunday school classes, where there are [expected] behaviors. When [we went] over to dinner for couples, there were a lot of problems. So the invitations began to fade." Chris's story illustrates the complete isolation that parents of children with behavioral problems experience all too often. Even places that are supposed to provide solace and strengthen faith can withdraw their support from parents in need, either because they ascribe the child's problems to the parents or simply out of fear or ignorance.

For Chris, her belief in the church was ultimately replaced by a more personal sense of faith, one that was forged out of a need to understand the meaning behind the pain she and her children had gone through. And much like steel that is made stronger by being brought to its melting point, her faith was strengthened by being continually challenged and tested. Many of the parents interviewed for this book emerged from their experiences with an entirely different idea of faith than the one they were raised with. Everything they suffered guided them to an individual understanding of the reason for their pain and their purpose and role in having to experience the suffering of their child.

When I interviewed Christina, she had survived the chaos and had begun to transform the chaos of Jonathan's childhood into a quest narrative. She was able to find the mercies in her family's pain. She summed up her story in this way:

I give my son a lot of credit for teaching me. Sometimes when I see other parents, I think my experience was really humbling, and I wouldn't trade it for anything.

Getting my face in this stuff and all the things that I've gone through. As embar-rassing and horrific as it's been, I don't think I want to trade it, because it brought me close to a spiritual sense of myself that I didn't have years ago. I am starting to see purpose for my son.

Not only has Christina been able to find a core of personal strength, but she has also discovered a greater gift that she can give to others born out of her experiences:

A lot of healing took place when I started the school of social work. They say that people end up here because of what they've been through in their life—[out of] a great desire to help other people. I thought that I'd be able to help people. And from the beginning class that I had where I studied . . . I began to improve my life. It was so healing, so incredible to me.

Kay Redfield Jamison, a professor of psychiatry at Johns Hopkins School of Medicine, describes in one of the best-known memoirs, *An Unquiet Mind*, how she went from a frightening and deep despair—close to suicide—to a person who has embraced her illness as part of who she is, a part of her identity.[34] The story of survival that Jamison tells sends a powerful message to those who need faith, letting them know that one day they may be able to look back with more perspective and understanding as opposed to only despair. She serves as a model for all mentally ill children and as an example for parents, proving that things can truly get better.

Paul Raeburn describes the painful journey his family takes as they struggle with their son's mental illness (bipolar disorder) and their daughter's depression.[35] While they are caught in the prison of their son's illness, Raeburn, in a brutally honest fashion, describes what the family goes through—including his own failures as a parent. His son fails to obtain the help he desperately needs. Only after many misdiagnoses, seven psychiatrists, and many years does the son reach a level of stability. When you read this narrative, it looks like nothing will ever get better. Indeed, the family is split by a divorce, the mother's depression overshadows the events, and dysfunctional family dynamics are exacerbated by the father's uncontrolled anger—yet somehow they get to the "other side." For many families who suffer, there is the promise of reaching the other side; until you reach it, however, that place can often feel completely unobtainable. As families with mentally ill children will tell you, it isn't a perfect world on the other side, but it is a place where you can accept what life has given you and find faith, hope, and meaning.

FINAL THOUGHTS

The battles that parents of children with mental illnesses must fight extend beyond behavioral health red tape, schools, doctors, their families, and their own children's symptoms and behaviors. Parents engage in a deeply personal and individual fight to find the purpose and hope within their suffering. Dealing with a child in pain brings up the most basic existential questions, and these questions can either contribute to their suffering or, if satisfactorily resolved, provide them with the hope, faith, and sense of meaningfulness that allows them to endure innumerable challenges. So many times parents must walk this path on their own, without any support or guidance, often feeling totally alone. In my interviews, I heard over and over again from parents about the level of despair and loneliness they experienced, yet this issue is rarely addressed in the treatment of the child's illness.[36]

Helping professionals bear a responsibility for finding concrete data about what makes some families persevere in conditions that would make other families collapse in on themselves, and once that link has been determined, to put families on the path to empowerment and resiliency. Unless we acknowledge the immense emotional burden that families with children with mental illnesses must bear, we cannot help them heal. And if the families are toiling in agony, how can their children possibly thrive?

Many of the parents interviewed for this book were still fighting the daily battle, still struggling to gain the perspective needed to ascribe meaning to their suffering. Some parents, such as Chris, were able to find a deeper meaning in their life, and that meaning brought them peace and a sense of hope for the future. Meaning can come from a deeply personal sense of spirituality, a closer connection with a higher power, or it can take the form of a call to action to advocate on behalf of the millions of families struggling with similar concerns. Great things have happened as the result of parents taking on the mantle of advocacy and justice—organizations such as NAMI have emerged, and people such as Judy Robinson have organized parents of mentally ill children. Like the participants in numerous other social justice movements, the parents of children with mental illnesses began fighting the battle for themselves on their own, but continued the battle when they realized that it extended beyond themselves, and decided that perhaps it was the reason they were given this lot in life.

Many parents have found personal meaning in their families' struggles with mental illness and have a deep and unshakable sense of faith. For many, their sense of faith has become a deeply ingrained and highly personal way of looking at the world. Their faith has been strengthened by the process of being tested to the point of breaking. As Phyllis explains:

It's the hardest thing you've ever done. It's the most arduous thing in the world, but it's also the most rewarding thing. You really have to learn how to have faith, and keep the faith in yourself.

CHAPTER 8

Society's Obligation: Doing More for Our Children

Danielle DeMailo and Craig LeCroy

In 1840, the American activist Dorothea Dix surveyed how states were treating mentally disordered individuals and started a campaign for the "moral treatment" of people with mental disorders.[1] It is difficult to look back over more than 100 years and write a book that continues to document the need for better care and treatment of families who have a mentally ill child. Across time, a fundamental question is revealed: What is our nation's social morality? Do we want a "civil society" for America?

At one time, what was unique about America was its civic responsibility for the well-being of the society.[2] When one talks to people in the local community, one is often inspired by untold levels of goodwill—but translating that goodwill into helpful strategies remains a challenge. After hearing from so many parents about their needs and desires, it seems appropriate to end this last chapter with a simple question: What should be society's moral duty to the parents and children who struggle with mental disorders? This chapter frames that question as we examine contemporary issues in the delivery of mental health services to children and families.

CHILDREN'S MENTAL HEALTH: A SIGNIFICANT SOCIAL PROBLEM

Children's mental health disorders are not a specialized subfield that affect a small portion of society. Instead, approximately 20 percent of all children and adolescents in the United States have been assigned a mental health diagnosis—according to the National Mental Health Association, roughly the same percentage as adults. The Department of Health and Human Services

reports that mental illness affects one in every five youth, with commonly identified diagnoses including ADHD, learning disorders, depression, several anxiety disorders, and bipolar disorder. Sometimes one may not even be able to detect that a
child is suffering; in other cases, symptoms become so pervasive that the safety of
that child and those in the child's environment is at risk.[3] For instance, according
to the American Academy of Child and Adolescent Psychiatry, approximately
5,000 youth commit suicide, and suicide is the sixth leading cause of death for
5- to 15 year-olds. In addition, as many as one in 10 youth are diagnosed with conduct disorder, in which the most extreme symptoms include destruction of property
and physical aggression toward both humans and animals.[4]

Despite these significant safety risks that many of our children present to our
society, even today approximately two-thirds of these youth are not getting the
clinical treatment necessary.[5] In 1982, the Children's Defense Fund published a
breakthrough study entitled "Unclaimed Children: The Failure of Public Responsibility to Children and Adolescents in Need of Mental Health Services," calling
national attention to the deficits in children's mental health service delivery and
recommending "best policy practices that support family- and youth-focused,
research-informed, developmentally appropriate, culturally and linguistically competent services and supports."[6] While this report generated widespread attention, it
seems as if policy advocates were making exactly the same requests 20 years later
when President George W. Bush claimed that the U.S. mental health care system
for both children and adults was "fragmented and inadequate and beyond simple
repair."[7] As a result, the Bush administration developed the New Freedom Commission on Mental Health, identifying six goals to improve the quality of services:
(1) refocusing on the family and consumer, (2) increasing understanding about
mental illness, (3) reducing disparities in mental health coverage, (4) improving
technology to increase access to information, (5) improving research, and
(6) increasing early screening and preventive services.[8]

Congress may have had good intentions, yet today, even as health care in general continues to make dramatic strides, the mental health system repeatedly fails
to measure up. Too many children go untreated, too many children and families
are faced with discrimination based on culture and ethnicity, and too many families must shoulder the burden of emotional, social, and financial difficulties. Are
parents solely responsible for making sure their children grow up to be functional
and productive human beings in American society? Do we as a society not have
an obligation to help parents and caregivers provide adequate treatment for their
children and adolescents with mental illness? Perhaps the current policies provide an adequate framework to make this happen, but the implementation of
these policies fails to deliver on these lofty promises.

CHILDREN'S MENTAL HEALTH: SOME BACKGROUND

Even 40 years ago, mental health advocates and politicians were looking for ways
to enhance and streamline the administration of mental health care and treatment. In 1970, the Community Mental Health Centers Act was updated to

include child mental health. The general philosophy behind this transition from institutional care to the communities suggested that recent discoveries in psychiatric medications could improve the stability of mentally ill patients and allow them to live in a less restrictive and more dignified environment. While this shift corresponds with the predominant present-day view that individuals with mental illness deserve the freedom to live as independently as possible, unfortunately decentralized funding prevented this policy from being carried out to its full intent. Congress was forced to accept the fact that communities struggled with securing nonfederal funding sources to substitute for steadily thinning national support.

The Social Security Act has been evolving alongside mental health care legislation, allocating funding integral to the provision of children's mental health services, even though the Social Security Act is not specific to mental health. For instance, Title IV is designed to provide funding to families in financial need so that they can find work and provide sufficient care for their children. Yet, the elements of the Social Security Act that are most closely associated with children's mental health are Supplemental Security Income (SSI), state health insurance or Medicaid, and the State Children's Health Insurance Program (SCHIP).[9] These policies are designed to provide families with children identified as having a mental disability with additional funding to pay for incidentals related to the obstacles associated with these illnesses, as well as offering them medical and mental health insurance free of monthly premiums and with the advantage of little to no co-payments. Unfortunately, many parents today can attest to the fact that state-funded mental health care is far from advantageous. A study from the Urban Institute identified many inconsistencies in how states access Medicaid and SCHIP benefits to meet children's mental health needs.[10]

In addition, due to the increased use of managed care, visit and day limits on mental health services are often commonplace and passively accepted in the world of government-funded care. A recent study found that if states offered full parity to mental health services relative to medical health services, the financial burden on parents would be significantly reduced.[11] In 2008, Congress considered a provision entitled the Paul Wellstone and Pete Domenici Mental Health Parity and Addiction Equity Act, which requires parity in benefits to be provided by insurance companies that offer both physical and mental health services. This law was passed by the House but not the Senate and points to the failure of policies to provide for mental health parity.[12] So far, only 15 states have passed parity laws, and not one of these states requires full mental health benefits parity.

As states sought to maximize their limited resources while upholding the philosophy of providing services in the least restrictive environment, community outpatient clinics and residential treatment centers (RTCs) were developed. Community outpatient clinics provide services in a less costly forum for the community than inpatient treatment and offer a wide range of treatment methods, such as psychiatric and psychological evaluations, individual and family therapy, psychosocial assessments, case management, and crisis intervention. In contrast, most RTCs are filled with children from the child welfare and juvenile justice system. The residential centers were designed to serve as a less restrictive option than inpatient care for children who are unable to function successfully in their natural environments. Although residential treatment centers are being increasingly used to treat mentally ill children, concerns are emerging about their operations because they are often unlicensed and unregulated.[13] Hospitals are now primarily used when safety and medication stability concerns arise with these youth.

Because of the limited options now available for treatment of mentally ill children, agencies providing such services can become overpopulated and over-burdened, and some may be forced to provide less than adequate care. Even as early as the 1980s, when policy analysts were advocating for a reduction in inpatient treatment, thanks to the establishment of RTCs treatment centers, youth inpatient care increased by 87 percent from 1980 to 1985.[14] This growth led states to place restrictions on coverage of RTCs by requiring prior authorizations, carrying out utilization reviews, and, in some cases, issuing a complete denial of services. All of these service delivery options are characterized by unclear eligibility criteria, underdeveloped models of treatment, and few guidelines for proper lengths of stays. There is even some evidence that these restrictive models can actually be harmful for children.[15]

Managed care mandates that all parties in the health care system attempt to maximize cost-effectiveness, and the same review process is often applied to inpatient psychiatric hospitals and even outpatient treatment for mentally ill persons. The consequences of these measures may include premature terminations and discharges, which return children still in need of a mental health treatment home to their parents or guardians. Studies indicate that perhaps managed care is not the sole force that has led to unfinished treatment, however; rather, an underlying flaw exists within the philosophy of children's mental health, reflecting an "inability to hold onto a vision of human interdependence and recognition of the fundamental need for networks of care to sustain people."[16] However, because treatment limitations undermine the need for wraparound mental health services and multidisciplinary coordination, it seems that managed care may perpetuate this flaw.

ONE PROBLEM: MANY SOLUTIONS

As many parents revealed in my interviews, when mental health agencies neglect to provide acceptable treatment, care for mentally ill youth tends to spill over to the juvenile justice system, still often referred to as the "de facto mental health system." This is not counterintuitive, as children in this population may meet their emotional needs through maladaptive and socially unacceptable behaviors. The Department of Justice reports that of the 100,000 teens in juvenile detention in 2010, approximately 60 percent had "behavioral, mental or emotional problems."[17] Policy analysts have concluded that the current health system has chosen to refrain from recognizing flaws in its own system of delivery and would rather shift responsibility and funding for the most severely ill clients, thereby generating a prison system that functions as a mental hospital. The underlying struggle here is prioritizing the needs of the individual versus the safety of society. It appears obvious that policy makers have chosen to favor the safety of society, in turn placing a minimal focus on the improvement of the individual's mental health.

In 1990, the Americans with Disabilities Act (ADA) gave new hope to families, as Congress determined that adults and children with mental disabilities were subjected to discrimination and have the legal right to integrate their daily lives with those of non-disabled individuals.[18] The ADA's intent was to provide opportunities for people with disabilities to participate fully in their communities and society and to lessen the sizable stigma attached to disabilities. However, census data, national polls, and other studies have since documented that people with disabilities continue to maintain inferior status in our society, and are severely disadvantaged socially, vocationally, economically, and educationally.[19]

In legislation geared more specifically toward children and families, the Adoption and Safe Families Act of 1997 (ASFA) placed time limits on the identification and implementation of permanent housing and guardianship for children in foster care, operating under the widely acclaimed theory that safety and permanency in a child's life are essential for healthy attachments and emotional stability. The ASFA requires foster care caseworkers to engage in concurrent planning with the mutually exclusive goals of reunification with the child's biological family and adoption. While this action can be seen as a benefit for children, it has often prevented social workers from making thorough assessments about reunification options before identifying adoption as a permanency plan. A study entitled "Parental Rights and Foster Care" noted that "termination of parental rights decisions require a lower burden of proof and often do not involve a jury decision."[20] Especially in cases in which parents voluntarily and temporarily relinquish custody to secure mental health services for their children, parents may learn that this decision may potentially lead to the permanent termination of custody.

Mental health policy can make service delivery fragmented and confusing, owing to the differing priorities and missions involved in the different systems that interact with mentally ill children, such as the child welfare and juvenile justice systems. After all, a mental health provider focuses on the welfare of both children and their families, the child welfare system's first priority is the care and safety of the child, and the juvenile justice system has a legal responsibility to ensure the safety of society. Professional groups such as the American Psychological Association have ascertained that collaboration between disciplines is a necessary step in providing best practice to youth.[21] Improving the status quo requires four steps: (1) advocating for public policy change, (2) collaborating with state and local governing bodies, (3) providing education and consultation to different disciplines to streamline service goals, and (4) collaborating with all disciplines in the "design, delivery, and evaluation of interventions and services."[22]

LEGAL ISSUES IN CHILDREN'S MENTAL HEALTH

Because some states have experienced the harsh outcomes that can be associated with incomplete mental health treatment, state-level lawsuits have sometimes resulted in legislation designed to enhance the quality of children's mental health services in hopes of preventing future child and family tragedies. In TR v. Dreyfus, a civil rights lawsuit was filed against the state of Washington for failing to provide children with serious mental illnesses needed treatment, leading to the multiple placements and homelessness of 10 youth, whose outcomes includes psychiatric hospitalization and incarceration.[23]

California was hit with a similar lawsuit in Katie A. v. Bonta, in which the state was accused of neglecting to provide a young girl in foster care with mandated mental health services.[24] Although the accusations in this case focused specifically on services for youth in the child welfare system, the legislation ultimately developed out of this lawsuit also identified needs for youth with severe mental illness who are at risk for out-of-home placement. As a result of the lawsuit, California was ordered to ensure that this population of youth receives family-based wraparound services so as to maintain family and home stability and prevent out-of-home placements.

In my own state, Arizona, a significant piece of legislation related to children's mental health care was passed in 2001. Jason K. was a child with serious mental illness, including suicidal ideation. He had difficulties participating in school and was recommended to participate in a day treatment program. Unfortunately, the Medicaid provider denied this recommendation, authorizing only one outpatient therapy session per week. Subsequently, Jason K. ran away from home and school, attempted suicide, and was hospitalized in a psychiatric inpatient unit.

As a result of the lawsuit now known as J.K. v. Eden, Arizona's 12 Principles were born. These guidelines require behavioral health agencies and providers to offer care that includes the following characteristics: (1) collaboration with the child and family, (2) functional outcomes, (3) collaboration with others, (4) accessible services, (5) best practices, (6) most appropriate setting, (7) timeliness, (8) services tailored to the children and family, (9) stability, (10) respect for the child and family's unique cultural heritage, (11) independence, and (12) connection to natural supports.[25] These general principles make sense and have obvious appeal but their implementation has been problematic. Still, I have wondered, if these principles were used as a framework and implemented on a national level, would the United States be fulfilling its obligation to children with mental illness and their families?

Similar principles were developed from the 2002 President's New Commission Freedom on Mental Health.[26] Yet, eight years later, are we truly experiencing the full implementation of this national agenda? Research studies continue to report defects in mental health service delivery, an absence of wraparound services and coordination of care, underutilization of services, and the overrepresentation of minority groups in mental health treatment facilities and the juvenile justice system.

FUNDING: LITTLE HAPPENS WITHOUT MONEY

In a recent North Carolina Family Impact Seminar, advocates identified the need for prevention programs, as to date little funding has been allocated for these services. For example, when they first recognize signs of mental health issues in their children, ideally parents would be taught methods and resources for achieving crisis stabilization. As a result, families who may have been offered such prevention services early on might not need significant mental health interventions such as hospitalization later as children's symptoms may become more severe. This is an example of policies being identified (prevention services) but not prioritized to receive sufficient funding to carry them out. In some cases, funding is provided when it is too late, when the severity of mental illness has reached such a significant level that the safety of the child or the community is at risk. A long-standing problem in children's services is that most of the expenditures continue to be tied up with institutional alternatives of care.

An additional funding issue is related to obtaining evidence-based interventions. Almost all reviews of children's mental health have concluded that mental health policies must take developmental theories into account and utilize evidence-based practice methods for desirable treatment outcomes to be realized.[27] The professional services I encountered when talking with parents were often not developmentally oriented and most certainly were not evidence based. If this country is committed to providing "effective" or evidence-based services, then more effort is needed to train practitioners and promote policies within agencies to administer the most effective treatments.

Many of the existing propositions, combined with the several plans to enhance mental health service delivery, appear philosophically sound. So why do both state and private agencies appear to have difficulty carrying out these objectives? The most obvious answer speaks to what has been acknowledged time and again as the sticking point: money. As the United States continues to suffer the consequences of a struggling economy, states have proposed and followed through with budget cuts in social services and mental health programs just to stay afloat. In reality, times of economic crisis are often when children and families need these services the most. The National Association of State Mental Health Program Directors has reported that 2010 mental health program spending decreased by 5 percent in one year, and noted that 2011 spending may fall by another 8 percent.[28] Some states may feel they have no choice except to cut funds in this area, but if mental health services were truly a priority, could funding in other departments be reduced instead? Perhaps choices in funding allocation reflect a deep-seated philosophy that exists even among mental health providers themselves, that parents are ultimately responsible for the behavior of their children.

PUBLIC AWARENESS: LIMITED AND SKEWED

As revealed by the parents in their moving yet heartbreaking stories, parents often experience strong feelings of guilt in response to the discovery and continued behavioral manifestations of their child's mental illness. Parents often internalize blame and label themselves as "bad parents." Is this truly a parent-invented phenomenon or are societal views about the origins of childhood mental illness eliciting these parental responses? A parent can turn on the TV and watch a program or movie that perpetuates the stereotypes that children with mental illness are products of "neglectful," "permissive," or "authoritarian" parents. The American Psychological Association's summit on children's mental health states the case clearly: "The public has limited awareness of how mental health affects child development and societal well-being in general, how important mental health needs can and should be met, and the scientific basis for promoting mental health and preventing and treating disorders."[29] Peers and acquaintances within a parent's community of support networks may not be properly educated about mental illness and may be influenced by media portrayals. Often individuals who could form an informal support network may shy away from a parent or caregiver with a mentally ill child, leading the parent to feel isolated and abandoned. Without natural supports, parents with children with serious mental illnesses may be unable to attend to daily errands out of fear that their child may become unsafe. A well-founded sentiment is that these parents feel imprisoned in their own homes.

PARENTS AS VICTIMS

While parents may feel like victims in this instance, legal mandates often make them out to be criminals. Consider Denise, an 11-year-old girl who has been diagnosed with bipolar disorder, ADHD, and oppositional defiance disorder. Several times a day, her behaviors vacillate between sadness and tears and physical aggression toward her two siblings and her mother, Mary. Often Denise will kick, hit, punch, and scratch anything or any person in her way, and will not stop without the intervention of her mother. Mary often responds by physically restraining Denise, in an attempt to maintain safety for Denise and her family. However, when Mary shared this strategy with a behavioral health agency and Denise's school, her parenting skills were questioned, and Mary was accused of abusing her child.

It appears that service providers and researchers perpetuate this belief, as evidenced in the literature, which includes a study that evaluated the harms inflicted by parental punishment of children with mental illness.[30] Although the research calls for policies endorsing family therapy and behavior management education, the information is presented in this study with an accusatory tone. The possibility that parents are engaging in physical punishment as a means of self-defense or protection was not identified as an option here, yet Mary's experiences are not at all uncommon.

This study is a reflection of a culture that exists almost in the same manner as institutionalized racism and discrimination. Although many mental health agencies appear to have the whole family's best interests in mind when accepting the child as a client, their actions often speak to the quiet blame of parents as the root of their children's anguish. As I heard from parents in my interviews, social workers and other mental health service providers are quick to make judgments of them, not only for their child's behaviors, but also for their failure to unquestioningly accept the knowledge provided to them by mental health professionals. Even though clinicians may attempt to involve parents in the therapeutic process, parents' own needs often go unnoticed, leaving parents feeling invalidated.

Effective practice with children and parents is focused on improving the welfare of *both* the child and the family; it appears that agencies are failing to uphold this practice. However, is it unclear if agencies perceive the importance of providing services to both parents and children. A situation that encompasses the dilemmas experienced by parents as a result of insufficient provider support involves Katrina, a 10-year-old girl with the diagnosis of bipolar disorder, severe, with psychotic features. Because of Katrina's history of self-mutilation, overdose, and physical violence, her father, Daniel, has resorted to locking his bedroom, where medications, kitchen knives, and any other sharp objects that could be used as a weapon are stored. Daniel has reported that he feels trapped or "imprisoned" in his own home, fearful of Katrina's next move. When Katrina received in-home services through a local behavioral health agency, Daniel's parenting skills were questioned on a weekly basis.

If he was witness to one of Katrina's numerous suicidal gestures or attempts, it was the agency's policy to consider filing a report with Child Protective Services (CPS), claiming that Daniel may be legally unfit to care for Katrina. He would then be assessed by CPS to determine if the charge of "failure to protect" Katrina against personal harm is substantiated. However, the same agency tasked with making these allegations understood first-hand the level of difficulty involved in preventing Katrina from self-harm. During a team staffing, five agency providers met Katrina and Daniel in their home, oblivious to the fact that Katrina had inconspicuously overdosed on her medication in front of their eyes. Yet, the policies in children's mental health serve only to protect the children from harm, not the parents. If this event had occurred in the absence of professionals, it is highly likely that providers would have contacted CPS.

DIFFERENT TREATMENT PERCEPTIONS: DIFFERENT SOLUTIONS

Service providers are required to juggle a number of competing clinical orientations that may contribute to parents feeling as if both their children and the family as a whole are receiving fragmented care. For instance, several community outpatient clinics continue to operate under the medical model, professing that children's mental health problems should be treated with strictly biological interventions. This perspective dictates the need for psychopharmacological treatments while dismissing the impact of the family and environment in the care and management of the child. In their testimony to the White House Conference on Mental Health, Hillary Clinton and Dr. Steven Hyman concluded as early as 1999 that mental illness is a medical disease of the brain that can be treated in the same way as any other medical illness.[31] What are the social and political implications of this discovery? The disease model, in theory, might reduce the stigmatization of mental illness, as people might then compare ADHD to asthma. However, if the family is considered unessential to the treatment of mentally ill youth, it would appear that policies would stray further away from mandating community-based, family-focused care. Moreover, agencies might try to cut costs by limiting service availability to only the child—the target patient carrying the "disease."

Child Protective Services is equipped with services and legislation designed to enhance the welfare and protect the rights of children. Unfortunately, only minimal assistance is provided to the parents, even when a child remains in parental custody. For instance, Kristy, a 16-year-old girl diagnosed with Asperger's disorder, continually threatened to harm her three siblings, her father, and her mother Patty. Kristy often ran away, once with an adult male. Patty resorted to placing restrictions on Kristy in an attempt to assure that she is safe, but this practice caused Kristy to defy her parents' rules even more. Kristy knew that CPS would listen if she made false accusations that her mother was abusive. Even after months of in-home services, Patty felt she could no longer provide Kristy with care sufficient to meet her challenging needs.

With the assistance of her in-home providers, Patty requested assistance from CPS to find respite care or a temporary foster home for Kristy. CPS reported that these services would be available to Kristy only if Patty temporarily relinquished parental custody. CPS did notify Patty that as a result of this decision, Patty would no longer receive in-home services, and CPS could not provide Patty with family therapy, family interventions, or parenting support as long as Kristy was out of her home. This leads to the double bind when parenting mentally ill children: Patty must choose between the temporary safety of her child and the prospect of improving her child's relationship with the family.

Schools also become a critical player in the provision of mental health assessment and treatment. With significant budget cuts resulting in a shortage of teachers and other school staff, it is no wonder schools have difficulty managing the emotional and behavioral needs of children with mental illness. Federal law requires schools to address the needs of children that interfere with learning. The individualized education program (IEP) is the foundation of special education interventions. Schools must pay for any needs identified within an IEP. As a result, many schools limit the identification of emotional and behavioral needs when it becomes fiscally difficult for them to respond to those needs. It also appears that school funding priorities support the philosophy that children with mental illness are ultimately their parents' responsibility. For example, if a child is engaging in physical aggression and destruction of classroom property, the parents are called in to resolve the issue, while the school fails to take action in the setting where the difficulty occurs. There is a critical need in this country to utilize mental health assessment tools and identify the need for mental health services so that school staff can coordinate care with mental health providers.[32]

If school personnel are equipped to manage mental health issues, perhaps they could have handled Denise's physically aggressive behaviors in school before immediately requesting that Mary retrieve her daughter. Surprisingly, this school was designed specifically for youth with serious emotional disturbance (SED). Yet, just like other schools, policy required that parents remove their child from the school if the child becomes a "danger" to others. Understandably, the school seeks to ensure the safety of other students; however, if funding was provided for crisis intervention services, perhaps a team of clinical staff or a special time-out room could be used to deescalate the problematic situations involving Denise. Instead, Mary had to take off another unpaid day from work and spend her "respite time" away from her daughter trying to figure out a way to manage Denise's behaviors. Which actions might school systems take to relieve parents of this burden? Should the school system have any obligation in rectifying this situation?

As if this burden was enough, society bestows parents with additional complications. In today's fast-paced information age, media entities repeatedly advertise the need for perfection, and remain persistent in enticing parents with the notion of "cosmetic psychiatry," in which "society has narrowed its definition of acceptable human variation."[33] Commercials continue to persuade consumers to try to latest drug to relieve "depression" or "anxiety," implying the existence of a miracle elixir that will offer a quick fix to a child's socially unacceptable behaviors. Parents are given false hope of a cure for their child's illness, when they are still trying to come to terms with accepting it. Does the mental health community have a clear conception of what a successful outcome is for children? In the absence of this definition, it is difficult for parents to manage their expectations.

RACIAL DISPARITIES: AN ONGOING CONCERN

If parents already feel stigma associated with their racial, ethnic, or cultural differences, successfully navigating the mental health system may seem improbable. In fact, in my interviews, several parents from minority groups expressed hesitation to seek professional mental health treatment for their children. In some studies, such as in a study of African American caretakers and youth with ADHD, differences among beliefs about the origins of the diagnosis and expectations of the outcomes of treatment were shown to lead to reduced treatment adherence.[34] My own interviews with African American caregivers detected commonly held beliefs that ADHD is not an illness and that children will outgrow the corresponding behaviors in time. Agencies are starting to mandate that all providers receive cultural competency training and receive instruction on how to refrain from making assumptions about the origins of mental health issues.

Some minority populations may believe that mental health treatment ought to be kept within the family and, therefore, may refrain from seeking services to avoid feeling culturally stigmatized. A study in which Korean American parents were asked to participate in a psycho-educational intervention concluded that a culturally relevant parent program designed to increase parental awareness and knowledge about youth mental illness can serve to reduce stigma and enhance treatment utilization within this population.[35] But how can agencies be mandated to provide culturally competent education and treatment to parents of children with mental illness when they are not even consistently including parents in the treatment process?

LIMITED SOLUTIONS FOR COMPLEX CONCERNS

The examples presented earlier in this chapter described the hardships of parents without histories of mental illness, but now let us consider the added encumbrance to those parents who are afflicted with their own mental illness. Is there any hope for these parents in dealing with their own needs as well as the needs of their children? Does society blame them for inflicting their own illnesses on their offspring, either by genetics or based on their parental environment? Sherri is a mother of three, has a diagnosis of bipolar disorder, and recently discovered that her youngest son Jason has been diagnosed with autism. Because of Jason's aggressive outbursts, she is unable to take him shopping, and resorts to asking her other sons to run errands because she must stay at home to care for Jason. Reporting that she has no employable skills, Sherri runs an under-the-table child-care business to provide for the family's basic needs. She admits to claiming only a portion of her income to avoid losing her Medicaid eligibility, which is what provides her and Jason with mental health treatment. She becomes easily frustrated with Jason, and often spends her nights crying, wondering why she has been burdened with a near-unbearable life.

Fortunately, emerging policies and progressive organizations are providing parents like Sherri with hope. In July 2010, the Obama administration released new rules mandating health insurance agencies to provide coverage free of co-payments and other charges for a number of screening and preventive services, to include child and adolescent mental health. In addition, the Children's Defense Fund has pointed out new priorities identified in President Barack Obama's fiscal year 2011 federal budget. For instance, the Obama administration "assumes the passage of health reform and a voluntary quality evidence-based home visiting initiative."[36] This program is designed to improve family functioning and prevent child abuse and neglect. Perhaps it can provide needed mental health screening as well.

NEWER FRAMEWORKS: NEWER MODELS OF HELP

What may be helpful from a policy perspective is Georgetown University's Center for Child and Human Development and National Technical Assistance Center for Children's Mental Health, which recently developed a theoretical framework for regarding mental health as a public health issue.[37] This approach would remove the burden of responsibility of children's mental illness from parents, guardians, and caregivers, and bestow it on society as a whole. In this way, the Center proposes that public policy dictate the careful development of services that balance the promotion of positive mental health with the prevention and treatment of mental illnesses. Services are intended to shape environments so as to provide optimal care while engaging partners from many disciplines. Action steps to carry out this philosophy include identifying both positive mental health and mental health problems as equally essential so that equal time and resources may be devoted to each issue, utilizing collaborative language that incorporates input and perspectives from a variety of sectors, employing policy development as the primary intervention, and designing services that take into account a child's age, culture, and stage of physical, cognitive, and emotional development.

Other agencies throughout the United States have created and executed innovative and influential treatment interventions involving parents on a smaller scale. In Arizona, the Community Partnership of Southern Arizona (CPSA)—a regional behavioral health agency that oversees care and treatment of children's mental health—has mandated that agencies under its jurisdiction create child and family teams (CFTs) for children identified with severe mental health problems. These teams include mental health professionals as well as parents, guardians, other family members, relatives, and representatives from other collaborating agencies. CFTs are required to meet a minimum of every three months and address a written agenda that includes the identification of the child and family's current strengths, needs, progress toward goals, and tasks for each participant to complete prior to the next meeting. All attendees are strongly encouraged to participate and share their successes as well as ongoing concerns and recent challenges. When implemented with fidelity, the team concept can work effectively, but many teams follow the rhetoric and miss the needed substance for providing real help. Nonetheless, this policy represents a step in the right direction.

Families have been influential in the legal decision-making processes of child placement in New Zealand since 1989, developing the Family Group Conference Model. Casey Family Programs' Cheyenne Division was one of the first organizations to adopt this model, administering family group conferences to assist families with identifying and developing permanency planning for children in the foster care system. Within this model, professionals serve only as neutral facilitators, allowing family members, relatives, family friends, and other informal supports to decide where and under which conditions a child should live. Basic beliefs that underlie this process include the notion that "families can make safe decisions for their children, families are experts on their strengths, needs, and resources, and families and the Child Welfare System can make more progress on behalf of the child working together cooperatively."[38] Would this model be feasible in the larger children's mental health system? If these values were widely held, supported, and enforced throughout the nation's child mental health system, a more effective and humane system of care might be one step closer.

To incorporate parents and caregivers in the assessment and treatment of youth with mental illness, what better environment could be conducive to family-centered interventions than the child's own home or community? Some state and county governments now require that intensive in-home services be made available to children with severe mental and behavioral health concerns, and private agencies are adopting this policy as well. Intensive in-home services include a combination of individual and family counseling, crisis intervention, behavior modification, and case management. The first principle of the President's New Freedom Commission on Mental Health identified the need for home- and community-based services so as to provide youth with the least restrictive environment of care and accentuate the importance of a child's natural environment and informal supports, including families, school, day care, primary care outpatient clinics, and other systems serving youth.[39]

Evidence of principles being used from this national policy has been sighted in state and local agencies as well. Such is the case with the Virtual Residential Program.[40] This program offers a cost-effective alternative to inpatient care and residential treatment. It seeks to minimize or even eliminate the placement of youth with severe mental illness into psychiatric hospitals, juvenile correctional facilities, and residential treatment centers. In a program designed to take place within the child and family system, clinicians provide an average of 35 hours per week of intensive services within the child's home and community. Parents are regarded as treatment team members and experts in the child's behavior and family dynamics. Weekly treatment team meetings allow parents and youth to participate in strength-based discussions of weekly successes and challenges. The child engages in a five-phase system, and parental agreement is necessary for a child to advance through the phases, ideally resulting in graduation and the transition to lower-intensity services.

Other innovative programs are being implemented that incorporate roles for both parent and child. One such program designed to supplement home- and community-based family interventions is the Outdoor Education Program developed by For Love of Children, a private child and family service program.[41] This program offers child and family retreats in which children with emotional and behavioral problems join with parents, guardians, caregivers, or foster parents at an outdoor campsite. Participants engage in therapeutic activities that facilitate the development of teamwork, communication, problem solving, and trust. Unlike with services provided exclusively to the child or identified client, parents and caregivers are provided with an experiential medium in which to enhance their parenting skills and release their frustrations associated with raising children who present with considerable challenges.

Fortunately, Mary, exhausted from trying to manage her daughter Denise's violent outbursts without losing her job or her sanity, sought intensive in-home services through a local private agency. The mental health clinician met with Denise and her family at least three times per week in their home, providing crisis intervention services, skills training, parenting education, respite care, behavioral modification, and team building. Both Mary and Denise participated in goal identification, treatment planning, and reassessments of the family's progress. The clinician helped Denise identify a more restrictive yet appropriate school setting that could adequately care for Denise's needs and manage behavioral crises within the school's own walls. After approximately one year of treatment, Mary and Denise were proud to say that the violence that was once commonplace in Mary's home was significantly reduced, and eventually eliminated.

In addition to family-focused interventions, state and national policies have emphasized the need for services specifically for parents, such as parenting classes, psycho-educational groups, and parent support groups. So far, a few agencies have been identified as meeting these objectives, in hopes that they might serve as models for further policy and program development. For instance, the Triple P Positive Parenting Program originating in Australia is being implemented across the United States because of positive results from outcome studies.[42] Triple P specialists have been training service providers in the delivery of this program, which is grounded in the belief that individuals can develop the capacity for self-sufficiency. Triple P offers a range of parent services, from educational classes to process groups. It also operates on a macro level in which interventions involve working with parents to coordinate media and health awareness campaigns to raise awareness of parenting issues and encourage program participation. Although the program has a broad focus, Triple P's mission and intervention strategies appear to address the challenges that parents with mentally ill youth endure.

Because of parent services offered to Katrina's father Daniel to assist him with caring for a child with severe mental illness, the story of Katrina and Daniel turned in a more encouraging direction. Daniel was able to partake in parenting classes emphasizing the importance of a child's need for self-determination and choices as well as behavior management strategies. He also attended psycho-educational groups describing typical symptoms and behaviors in children with bipolar disorder, and parent support groups in which Daniel and other parents had the opportunity to share their stories without judgment. After Daniel was able to reduce his need to control the outcomes of Katrina's behaviors, Katrina was able to significantly reduce the frequency with which she engaged in defiance and rebellion.

Armed with parental participation and policies identifying parents as experts on their children, policy makers and administrators have begun to develop programs in which parents are granted the opportunity to share their wisdom with other parents. One such treatment modality that facilitates this process is Multi-Family Group Therapy (MFGT).[43] A particularly impressive aspect of this approach is that the model has been tested with a low-income urban population and found to be effective. This model revolves around four broad conceptual categories that are related to parenting skills and family processes: rules, responsibility, relationships, and respectful communication. It also addresses issues that are related to early dropout from treatment and factors that interfere with achieving desired outcomes for youth, such as stress, negative peer group influence, and negative attitudes toward mental health care. Analysts in the field have determined that the most effective therapeutic tenets of MFGT include the therapist's development of a safe and trusting environment and each client's willingness to participate in the change process.[44]

One well-designed study using a randomized controlled trial tested the efficacy of a multifamily psycho-educational group in reducing the severity of children's mental health symptoms. One important part of the study found that multifamily group participation positively enhanced parental beliefs about the outcomes of treatment, thereby improving service utilization. A policy maker or program developer could conclude that the development of policies and programs to enhance parents' knowledge about how their child's mental illness will be treated could lead to a reduction in the need for long-term youth mental health services. Unfortunately, most studies focusing on child mental health issues test the effectiveness of a novel treatment modality rather than examining how interventions work through the influence of parent factors.

Multifamily models can work when appropriately implemented and supported within the organization and community. Such a program was implemented on the child and adolescent unit in an inpatient psychiatric hospital in Arizona, in which parents and youth have been able to share their experiences as well as offer advice and assistance to other parents and children about effective ways to manage and overcome family crises.

PARENT ADVOCACY, PARENT SUPPORT

Also noteworthy are the parent advocate roles being developed in many states. Many mental health agencies have hired "Family Support Partners," positions designed specifically for parents with first-hand knowledge and experience in caring for a child with mental illness, to provide parents seeking services with peer support.[45] Existing separately from therapeutic support, this kind of peer support values personal tribulations and success stories that Family Support Partners can share in the service of making parents feel they are not alone. Family Support Partners can also model appropriate parenting skills, identify community resources, and act as living proof that success is achievable. In New York, for example, Kimberly Hoagwood and associates have developed a parent empowerment program by working with parents to systematically identify barriers and gaps present when parents attempt to access services.[46] This research-based model is moving the field as a whole forward by advancing parents as change agents.

On a larger scale, parents have joined together to cultivate parent advocacy groups designed to increase public awareness of childhood mental illness and to educate and persuade legislators to allocate more resources for mental health services. Perhaps one of the best-known advocacy groups is the National Alliance on the Mentally Ill (NAMI). NAMI New Hampshire developed a parent-run advocacy group responsible for the passage of state mental health parity legislation and restored financial support for community mental health centers. In addition, NAMI New Hampshire's Family Partner Program allows trained parents and family members to become mentors for other families, teaching those families to advocate for the services that parents and children require. Furthermore, NAMI's Family to Family program offers a 12-week structured course on advocating for the development and improvement of mental health services for children and families. More research is needed to support these parent advocacy efforts and help them obtain greater funding and support.

One barrier to effective advocacy is that this population of parents can be characterized as isolated, tired, and disempowered, lacking the confidence and motivation to successfully lobby for augmented mental health services. To start, the mental health system can assist these parents in regaining their power by promoting policies designed to support the rights of parents. Child Protective Services was founded to hold society accountable for its failure to provide children with a safe and stable home environment. The community mental health system should hold society accountable for the humane treatment and safety of parents as well. Rather than just encourage parents' involvement, perhaps policies should mandate parental participation in the decision-making process related to their child's treatment and hold agencies accountable when they fail to do so. When mental illness is identified, parents should be active participants at intake meetings, during assessments, during development of treatment plans, and during medication and psychiatric evaluations.

PART OF THE SOLUTION: IMPROVING ASSESSMENT AND TREATMENT

Mental health agencies could vastly improve the quality of their work if they adopted the use of valid and reliable assessment tools to assist with diagnosis and treatment planning. For example, if a child is suspected of having ADHD, an assessment instrument like the Connors Parent Form to test for ADHD could be used.[47] Even though such instruments are widely available, the majority of agencies do not make use of assessment tools for assistance in assessment and diagnosis. In addition, agencies should be required to include parents in treatment team meetings, giving weight to their voices and recommendations as experts on their children. Parents who are unwilling or unavailable to partake in these meetings should be given copies of meeting minutes, outcomes, and action plans. Perhaps behavioral and mental health agencies could even designate clinical teams that are designed specifically to address parents' needs and work to overcome barriers in meeting these needs.

Mental health professionals should be held accountable for their failure to recognize the hardships these parents face and the many hats these parents wear. After all, parents of children with mental illness are not only parents—they are mentors, teachers, counselors, maids, and police officers. Efforts to construct these policies must consider the role of supportive listening in providing assistance to parents, and examine the role of parental blame in inhibiting favorable outcomes. The significance of this aspect of care is often overlooked.

The Huerta family was able to reap the benefits of a local program that upheld fundamental principles promoting respect, involvement, and parent collaboration. Accessing a continuum of care ensured that this foster family of four children received what they needed, and they were able to provide their expertise with mental health professionals in a manner that kept this family functioning together, as a family, in their own home.

An important factor in the Huerta family's success was their Family Support Partner, also a foster parent, who shared her experiences taking in foster children and the coping strategies and resources she used to help manage children's behaviors as well as her own distress. Both Mr. and Mrs. Huerta participated in parenting classes geared toward parents of children with mental illness to assist them with utilizing appropriate communication and problem-solving tools, as well as parent management strategies to meet their foster children's needs. Several months later, after the Huerta family successfully adopted two of the four children, they were able to share their story with other parents in a documentary outlining the long-term benefits of the services and programs they accessed.

To communicate information like the Huerta family's story and the difficulties they faced on a larger scale, the general public needs to be educated about the severity of this social problem, via resources such as those provided by the National Alliance on the Mentally Ill. In addition, parent advocacy groups should seek media attention for their cause through the development of campaigns and public service announcements outlining the need for more advanced and comprehensive policies, funding, and programming in mental health care systems. Advertising agencies in support of this media campaign should work to shift the media focus away from "bad" parents who have been abusive or neglectful to stressed parents in need—in need of society's help to provide mentally ill children with the opportunity to function in their communities and lead productive lives.

ADULT MENTAL HEALTH: A ROLE MODEL

The children's mental health system may have something to learn from the adult mental health system as a model, particularly in terms of the widespread media attention devoted to mental health recovery. For example, mental health consumers have been successful in sharing their personal stories by publishing first-hand accounts of their experiences. A popular example is *The Quiet Room: A Journey Out of the Torment of Madness*, written by Lori Schiller and Amanda Bennett, about Ms. Schiller's battle with schizoaffective disorder.[48] Another example is Kay Redfield Jamison's popular book *An Unquiet Mind: A Memoir of Moods and Madness*, which is an autobiography that depicts not only consumers of mental illness, but also consumers who become professionals within the field. Mental health consumers have looked to Jamison's "life example" as a person who has a diagnosis of bipolar disorder, yet has successfully completed a Ph.D. in psychology and become a well-regarded university professor in a Department of Psychiatry.[49] More recently the success of *A Beautiful Mind* as both a book and a movie shattered many stereotypes of individuals with mental illness.[50] There are some analogous life stories written by parents, such as *Hurry Down Sunshine* and *Crazy: A Father's Search Through America's Mental Health Madness*, but there are still too few to raise substantial public awareness and elicit responsiveness to change efforts addressing children's mental health issues.

After all of the policies, legislation, programs, and services have been identified and implemented to address the needs and concerns of this disenfranchised group of parents, if only one recommendation can be made, let it be that these parents share their wisdom and teach others. Moreover, they should teach not only other parents with mentally ill children, but also parents without mentally ill children, mental health professionals, and society at large. Certainly there is much to be learned from this "pedagogy of faithful caring." The fate of parents with mentally ill children resides like a carefully constructed bird's nest in a tree that can easily be toppled by strong winds. To keep the nest safe, society must revisit its moral obligations to help those in need. The nest sits in a vulnerable position and can be easily destroyed, but with the proper care and support we can strengthen it and keep it safe.

Appendix: Resources for Parents of Children and Adolescents with Mental Illnesses

Among the many children and adolescents living in the United States today with a mental illness, fewer than one in three receives adequate treatment for his or her disorders. However, when children with mental illnesses do receive treatment and support, many of their symptoms can be eased and their struggles lessened. This appendix provides a list of resources to assist you and your family in obtaining the necessary support, treatment, and services.

FIRST STEPS WHEN YOUR CHILD HAS BEEN DIAGNOSED WITH A MENTAL ILLNESS

1. Begin the process by meeting with your child's primary care provider. Ask for a full physical examination of your child. For your child to be accurately diagnosed, ruling out any potential physical conditions that might be causing his or her problems is imperative. Your primary care provider can also refer your child to a qualified mental health professional.
2. After a primary care provider has ruled out potential medical conditions, meet with a children's mental health professional. If your primary care provider is unable to provide a recommendation, go to the American Academy of Child and Adolescent Psychiatry website (www.aacap.org) and click on "Child and Adolescent Psychiatrist Finder."

Christina Leber, MSW, contributed significantly to this appendix.

3. When working with a mental health professional, be aware that a diagnosis for your child should be based on a comprehensive examination of your child's life, behavioral patterns, and full range of symptoms. This examination should include professional observation and evaluation, collateral information provided by your family and other people close to your child, and the criteria from the *Diagnostic and Statistical Manual of Mental Disorders* (DSM). It may take time for a mental health professional to complete a full assessment of your child and, therefore, the process may take multiple visits. Do not hesitate to seek a second opinion if you do not feel satisfied with the evaluation your child has received.

4. Remember to include your child's school in the process. It may be a good idea to meet with your child's teacher or other school personnel to discuss how to best meet your child's individual needs. Also, co-occurring conditions, such as learning disabilities, may be present for your child; the school should be able to help you identify if any such issues exist.

5. Keep accurate and detailed records of your child's history, including all emotional, behavioral, social, and developmental concerns. These records can help mental health professionals make a diagnosis or can be used to gauge whether a child's symptoms have changed or developed over time. In particular, keep records of your family's history of mental illness (sometimes mental illness runs in families), the challenges the child faced in school, interventions that have successfully helped your child, any changes in your child's life that have been particularly upsetting, significant mood instability or unusual sleep patterns, and any specific factors that may exacerbate your child's condition.

For further information regarding first steps when your child has a new diagnosis of mental illness, visit the Child and Adolescent Action Center at the National Alliance on Mental Illness at http://www.nami.org/caac.

RESIDENTIAL TREATMENT FACILITIES

While most children do best when they live in the comfort and security of their own homes, the reality of caring for a child with a mental illness can be exhausting for a family, causing problems with marriages and other family relationships. If your child is not responding to treatment and the strain on your family is too great, residential treatment programs do exist to relieve this burden. Special care should be taken when selecting such a program, as many of the private residential treatment facilities in the United States are not healthy or constructive environments for children with mental illnesses. Many of these facilities do not adhere to any state licensing or monitoring systems, and some promote practices—such as extreme discipline and separation from family—that can be extremely harmful to children and adolescents. Quality residential programs exist but should be considered only as a last resort, when all community resources and family supports have been exhausted.

For further information regarding treatment centers as well as information about licensing and accreditation, visit the Child and Adolescent Action Center at the National Alliance on Mental Illness at http://www.nami.org/caac.

USE OF PSYCHOTROPIC MEDICATION BY CHILDREN AND ADOLESCENTS

The use of psychotropic medications by children and adolescents with mental illnesses is complex and controversial. While the use of medication in treatment for children with mental illnesses can often be effective, care should be taken with its prescription. Parents need to be aware of both the benefits and the risks of medication when making such a decision, and psychotropic medication should be prescribed only when the anticipated benefits outweigh the potential risks. If your child is prescribed psychotropic medication, he or she should be monitored closely to identify side effects that could pose serious health risks to the child. It is helpful to keep a log of your child's behavioral and emotional responses to medications, and report back to your child's psychiatrist on these responses.

For further information regarding the use of medication for children and adolescents, visit the Child and Adolescent Action Center at the National Alliance on Mental Illness at http://www.nami.org/caac.

BOOK RESOURCES

Books for Parents

General

Dulcan, Mina, Richard Martini, & Mary Beth Lake. (2003). *Concise Guide to Child and Adolescent Psychiatry*, 3rd ed. Washington, DC: American Psychiatric Publishing.

Koplewicz, Harold S. (1997). *It's Nobody's Fault: New Hope and Help for Difficult Children and Their Parents*. New York: Three Rivers Press.

Naseef, Robert A. (2001). *Special Children, Challenged Parents: The Struggles and Rewards of Raising a Child with a Disability*. Baltimore, MD: Brookes.

Attention-Deficit/Hyperactivity Disorder

Barkley, Russell A. (2000). *Taking Charge of ADHD: The Complete Authoritative Guide for Parents*, rev. ed. New York: Guilford Press.

Dendy, Chris A. Zeigler. (2006). *Teenagers with ADD and ADHD: A Guide for Parents and Professionals*, 2nd ed. Washington, DC: Woodbine House.

Fowler, Mary C. (1996). *Maybe You Know My Kid: A Parent's Guide to Identifying, Understanding, and Helping Your Child with ADHD*, 3rd ed. New York: Birch Lane Press.

Jensen, Peter S. (2004). *Making the System Work for your Child with ADHD*. New York: Guilford Press.

Autism and Asperger's Syndrome

Exkorn, K. S. (2005). *The Autism Sourcebook: Everything You Need to Know About Diagnosis, Treatment, Coping, and Healing*. New York: HarperCollins.

Myles, Brenda Smith, & Jack Southwick. (1999). *Asperger Syndrome and Difficult Moments: Practical Solutions for Tantrums, Rage, and Meltdowns*. Shawnee Mission, KS: Autism Asperger Publishing.

Ozonoff, Sally, Geraldine Dawson, & James McPartland. (2002). *A Parent's Guide to Asperger Syndrome and High-Functioning Autism: How to Meet the Challenges and Help Your Child Thrive*. New York: Guilford Press.

Stillman, W. (1999). *Empowered Autism Parenting: Celebrating (and Defending) Your Child's Place in the World*. Hoboken, NJ: Wiley.

Early-Onset Bipolar Disorder

Evans, Dwight L., & Linda Wasmer Andrews. (2005). *If Your Adolescent Has Depression or Bipolar Disorder: An Essential Resource for Parents*. New York: Oxford University Press.

Lombardo, Gregory T. (2007). *Understanding the Mind of Your Bipolar Child: The Complete Guide to the Development, Treatment, and Parenting of Children with Bipolar Disorder*. New York: St. Martin's Press.

Miklowitz, David J., & Elizabeth L. George. (2008). *The Bipolar Teen: What You Can Do to Help Your Child and Your Family*. New York: Guilford Press.

Depression

Evans, D. L., & Andrews, L. W. (2005). *If Your Adolescent Has Depression or Bipolar Disorder: An Essential Resource for Parents*. New York: Oxford University Press.

Fassler, David, & Lynne S. Dumas. (1997). *Help Me, I'm Sad: Recognizing, Treating, and Preventing Childhood and Adolescent Depression*. New York: Penguin Putnam.

Koplewicz, Harold S. (2003). *More Than Moody: Recognizing and Treating Adolescent Depression*, reissue ed. New York: Perigee Trade.

Oster, Gerald D., & Sarah S. Montgomery. (1995). *Helping Your Depressed Teenager: A Guide for Parents and Caregivers*. New York: John Wiley & Sons.

Drug Abuse and Dual Diagnosis

Babbit, N. (2000). *Adolescent Drug and Alcohol Abuse: How to Spot It, Stop It, and Get Help for Your Family*. Patient Centered Guides.

Ryglewicz, Hilary, & Bert Pepper (1996). *Lives at Risk: Understanding and Treating Young People with Dual Diagnosis*. Washington, DC: Free Press.

Eating Disorders

Lock, James, & Daniel Le Grange. (2005). *Helping Your Teenager Beat an Eating Disorder*. New York: Guilford Press.

Walsh, Timothy B., & V. L. Cameron. (2005). *If Your Adolescent Has an Eating Disorder: An Essential Resource for Parents*. New York: Oxford University Press.

Obsessive–Compulsive Disorder

March, John S., & Christine M. Benton, (2007). *Talking Back to OCD*. New York: Guilford Press.

Wagner, Aureen Pinto. (2002). *What to Do When Your Child Has Obsessive–Compulsive Disorder: Strategies and Solutions*. Mobile, AL: Lighthouse Press.

Schizophrenia

Gur, R. W., & Johnson, A. B. (2006). *If Your Adolescent Has Schizophrenia: An Essential Resource for Parents*. New York: Oxford University Press.

Medications

Dulcan, Mina, & Claudia Lizarralde. (2003). *Helping Parents, Youth and Teachers Understand Medications for Behavioral and Emotional Problems: A Resource Book of Medication Information Handouts*, 2nd ed. Washington, DC: American Psychiatric Publishing.

Preston, John, John H. O'Neal, & Mary C. Talaga. (2006). *Child and Adolescent Clinical Psychopharmacology Made Simple*. Oakland, CA: New Harbinger.

Wilens, Timothy E. (2002). *Straight Talk About Psychiatric Medications for Kids*, rev. ed. New York: Guilford Press.

Books for Children with Mental Illnesses

General

Catch a Falling Star: A Tale from the Iris the Dragon Series

This illustrated book by Gayle Grass and Coral Nault (Illustrator) explores the topic of mental illness through a fairy tale about a young boy called Fish and his dragon friend, Iris. This book deals with the early symptoms of a mental disorder in a nonthreatening way. (Iris the Dragon, Inc., 2003, 50 pages)

The Face at the Window

In this illustrated children's book, written by Regina Hanson with illustrations by Linda Saport, a young Jamaican girl learns about mental illness through the strange behavior of her neighbor Miss Nella. Colorful illustrations help to tell a reassuring story about the rift mental illness often creates between people. Dialogue is written in the local dialect. (Clarion Books, 1997, 22 pages)

Childhood ADD and ADHD

Lucky Horseshoes: A Tale from the Iris the Dragon Series

Gayle Grass and illustrator Linda Crockett recount the story of Skippy, a young girl living with ADHD who overcomes challenges with her school and home with the friendship of a dragon named Iris. (Iris the Dragon Inc., 2006, 46 pages)

The Best of Brakes: An Activity Book for Kids with ADD

This book contains all of the best games, puzzles, activities, tips, and resources from the popular newsletter *Brakes*, for kids with ADD and ADHD. It includes articles by teachers, counselors, and children about the experience of living with ADD or ADHD. (IMagination Press, 2000, 94 pages)

Taking ADD to School: A School Story about Attention Deficit Disorder and/or Attention Deficit Hyperactivity Disorder

This colorfully illustrated book by Ellen Weiner and illustrator Terry Ravanelli tells the story of Ben, an eight-year-old boy with ADD who is struggling in school. (Jayjo Books, 1999, 25 pages)

Childhood Autism

Taking Autism to School

This wonderful book by Andreanna Edwards and Tom Dineen (illustrator) is an educational tool about autism to be used with school children. It is appropriate for children aged 5 to 10 years. (JayJo Books, 2002, 32 pages)

Childhood Bipolar Disorder

Brandon and the Bipolar Bear: A Story for Children with Bipolar Disorder

This story by Tracy Anglada gives children a glimpse into the feelings and fears of a child with bipolar disorder through the experiences of Brandon as he cycles between depression and mania. Brandon and his readers come to understand what his illness is all about and learn that he is not to blame for his disorder. This booklet is appropriate for children aged 4 to 11 years. (See www.bipolar-children. Bigstep.com for ordering information, booklet, 20 pages)

The Storm in My Brain

This small, soft, colored booklet includes sections that teach a child how it feels to have a mood disorder through a question-and-answer format. Questions include: What is a mood disorder? Can I feel better? Does this mean I am a bad person? The book also offers tips for parents and teachers. This is a new publication from the Depression and Bipolar Support Alliance (DBSA) and the Child and Adolescent Bipolar Foundation (CABF). (Booklet, 18 pages)

Childhood Obsessive–Compulsive Disorder

Polly's Magic Games: A Child's View of OCD

This children's book, written by Constance H. Foster and Edwin A. Chase, tells the story of Polly, a 10-year-old girl with OCD. The book describes common symptoms and treatment options. It is appropriate for children aged 8 to 12 years. (Dilligaf Publishing, 1994, 24 pages)

Kissing Doorknobs

Terry Spencer Hesser tells the story of a 14-year-old girl who is diagnosed with OCD and overcomes the challenges associated with the disorder. (Laure Leaf, 1999, 160 pages)

Up and Down the Worry Hill: A Children's Book About Obsessive–Compulsive Disorder and Its Treatment

This story, written by Aureen Pinto Wagner and illustrated by Paul A. Jutton, tells the experience of a young boy named Casey in his struggle with OCD. (Lighthouse Press, 2000, 42 pages)

Books for Adolescents with Mental Illnesses

Adolescent ADD and ADHD

A Bird's-Eye View of Life with ADD and ADHD: Advice from Young Survivors

This reference book, written by Chris Zeigler Dendy and Alex Zeigler, includes stories from 12 teens and a young adult who are living with ADD and ADHD. It offers factual information and practical strategies in words that are easy for young people to understand. (Cherish the Children Publisher, 2003, 164 pages)

Adolescent Autism

Your Life Is Not a Label

Authors Jerry Newport and Ron Bass offer advice about how to handle autism in this encouraging and educational guide for teens with Asperger syndrome or high-functioning autism. (Future Horizons, 2001, 317 pages)

Adolescent Bipolar Disorder

Mind Race: A Firsthand Account of One Teenager's Experience with Bipolar Disorder

This novel by Patrick E. Damieson, PhD, and Moira A. Rynn, MD, gives a firsthand account of one adolescent's struggles with bipolar disorder. It offers advice and resources to help other adolescents who are experiencing this disorder. (Oxford University Press, 2006, 156 pages)

Adolescent Depression

The Depression Solutions Workbook

Written by mental health expert Jacqueline Corcoran, this book aims to help adolescents who are depressed, sad, angry, or thinking about hurting themselves find help and get focused on building strengths, motivation, and skills to promote positive and lasting change. (New Harbinger Publications, 2009, 214 pages)

Monochrome Days: A Firsthand Account of One Teenager's Experience with Depression

Author Cait Irwin, with assistance from Dwight Evans and Linda Wasmer Andrews, describes her personal journey through adolescent depression. This book offers tips for handling this disorder as well as treatment options. (Oxford University Press, 2007, 208 pages)

Adolescent Eating Disorders

Next to Nothing: A Firsthand Account of One Teenager's Experience with an Eating Disorder

The author of this memoir, Carrie Arnold (with Timothy Walsh), describes her experience battling anorexia as a teenager and explains how she eventually found help. She offers practical advice about both anorexia and bulimia in easy-to-understand language. (Oxford University Press, 2007, 146 pages)

Adolescent Obsessive–Compulsive Disorder

Free from OCD: A Workbook for Teens with Obsessive–Compulsive Disorder

The activities in this book help teens and parents learn new skills to manage OCD. (Instant Self Help Books, 2010, 135 pages)

Adolescent Social Anxiety Disorder

What You Must Think of Me: A Firsthand Account of One Teenager's Experience with Social Anxiety Disorder

This memoir, written by Emily Ford with Michael Liebowitz and Linda Wasmer Andrews, chronicles the author's struggles with social anxiety. It includes an account of her obstacles and her eventual triumph over her disorder through therapy and determination. (Oxford University Press, 2007, 133 pages)

INTERNET RESOURCES

Children's Mental Health and Advocacy Organizations

About Our Children

The NYU Child Study Center produces a large amount of information about child mental health disorders as well as ideas about how best to parent children with the accompanying disorders.
Web address: www.aboutourkids.org

Autism Society of America

Information and resources about autism.
Web address: www.autism-society.org

Child Advocate

This website is committed to providing information about child mental health, including educational, legal, and medical issues, and strives to meet the needs of children, families, and professionals regarding emotional and behavioral disorders.
Web address: www.ChildAdvocate.net

Child and Adolescent Bipolar Foundation (CABF)

This organization provides support for families raising children with early-onset bipolar disorder. The website includes information and resources on this form of bipolar disorder.
Web address: www.bpkids.org

Children and Adults with Attention-Deficit/Hyperactivity Disorder (CHADD)

CHADD is a national organization for people with ADHD that provides education, advocacy, and support to individuals and families. The organization publishes an informative website as well as a variety of printed materials for professionals, families, and others affected by ADHD.
Web address: www.chadd.org

Child Welfare League of America (CWLA)

CWLA is the oldest membership-based child welfare/advocacy organization in the United States. It is devoted to educating the public about child welfare issues, maintaining child safety and keeping children free from harm, and enhancing the lives or children and their families.
Web address: www.cwla.org

Federation of Families for Children's Mental Health

This organization provides information and support for families of children with mental illnesses as well as for the children themselves.
Web address: www.ffcmh.org

Juvenile Bipolar Research Foundation

The Juvenile Bipolar Research Foundation is the first charitable organization dedicated to the support of research for the study of early-onset bipolar disorder.
Web address: www.bpchildresearch.org

National Alliance on Mental Illness (NAMI)

NAMI is the United States' largest grassroots mental health organization dedicated to improving the lives of children and adults living with mental illness and their families. Founded in 1979, it has become the nation's voice on mental illness. The national organization includes NAMI organizations in every state and in more than 1,100 local communities across the country, whose members join together to meet the NAMI mission through advocacy, research, support, and education. Go to the Child and Teen Support section for fact sheets, family guides, advocacy tips, and more.
Web address: www.nami.org

National Mental Health Consumers' Self-Help Clearing House

Run by consumers, this site includes resources and services for people who want to start self-help groups.
Web address: www.mhselp.org/program.html

National Mental Health Information Center

The National Mental Health Information Center was developed for users of mental health services and their families as well as the general public. The center has staff to answer calls and identify relevant federal, state, and local organizations involved in mental health treatment and prevention.
Web address: www.mentalhealth.org

OCD Resource Center

Information and resources on obsessive–compulsive disorder.
Web address: www.ocdresource.com

Parents of Autistic Children (POAC)

While many organizations exist to find a cause and cure for this developmental disability, POAC has focused its attention and resources on how best to help the children and families who are struggling with autism today.
Web address: www.poac.net

SAMHSA's National Mental Health Information Center

This website provides healthcare providers, community organizers, and children and families with information about mental health organizations on the local, state, and national levels, as well as updates on federal grants and relevant mental health awareness and advocacy events.
Web address: www.mentalhealth.org

Federal Agencies

Center for Mental Health Services (CMHS)

CMHS provides resources for children, adolescents, and families.
Web address: www.mentalhealth.samhsa.gov/cmhs

Centers for Disease Control and Prevention (CDC)

The CDC has data and statistics on suicide and mental illnesses.
Web address: www.cdc.gov

Centers for Medicare & Medicaid Services (CMS)

CMS administers the Medicare, Medicaid, and State Children's Health Insurance Program (SCHIP) programs.
Web address: www.cms.hhs.gov

National Institute of Mental Health (NIMH)

The mission of NIMH is to diminish the burden of mental illness through research.
Web address: www.nimh.nih.gov

National Mental Health Association (NMHA)

NMHA advocates for federal legislation and funding for mental health programs and disperses educational information on the local and national level. Local chapters also provide support groups and other mental health services.
Web address: www.nmh.org

Office of the U.S. Surgeon General

In 1999, the Surgeon General issued *A Comprehensive Report on Mental Health*. The third chapter covers children and adolescents with mental illnesses.
Web address: www.surgeongeneral.gov/index.html

Organizations Focused on Special Education and School-Based Mental Health Services

IDEA Partnership

The IDEA Partnership is dedicated to improving outcomes for students and youth with disabilities by joining state agencies and stakeholders through shared work and learning. Its website includes resources for schools, families, and advocates.
Web address: www.ideapartnership.org

SchoolMentalHealth.org

This side offers school mental health resources not only for clinicians, but also for educators, administrators, parents/caregivers, families, and students. The resources included in the site emphasize practical information and skills based on current research, including prominent evidence-based practices, as well as lessons learned from local, state, and national initiatives.
Web address: www.schoolmentalhealth.org

School Psychiatry Program and the Mood and Anxiety Disorders Institute (MADI) Resource Center

This site was created for parents, educators, and clinicians working together to support children and teens with mental health conditions. It is intended to help meet the needs of young people with depression, bipolar disorder, ADHD, autism spectrum disorders, and anxiety disorders.
Web address: www.schoolpsychiatry.org

National Information Center for Children and Youth with Disabilities (NICHCY)

This site provides services to assist those helping children with disabilities. Information, assistance, and referrals are provided.
Web address: www.nichcy.org

Professional Organizations

American Academy of Child and Adolescent Psychiatry (AACAP)

Web address: www.aacap.org

American Psychiatric Association (APA)

Web address: www.psych.org

American Psychological Association (APA)

Web address: www.apa.org

National Association of Social Workers (NASW)

Web address: www.naswdc.org

Websites for Children and Adolescents

KidsHealth

KidsHealth has separate categories for children, teens, and parents. Each of these sections includes its own design, age-appropriate content, and tone. There are many in-depth features, articles, animations, games, and resources developed by experts in the health of children and teens.
Web address: www.kidshealth.org

Mindzone: Cope. Care. Deal.

Mindzone is a mental health website for teens that offers ideas for learning the facts and ways to cope with mental illness.
Web address: www.copecaredeal.org

Step Out of the Silence

This online community for middle school, high school, and college-age youth enables them to share their experiences with mental illness through artwork, creative writing, poetry, art, and photography. The website aspires to assist youth in learning to deal with their emotions effectively and productively by giving youth a creative outlet for their emotions and fostering a sense of community.
Web address: www.stepoutofthesilence.org

Parental Support Websites

Parent to Parent USA

This website provides information and emotional support to parents who have a child or adolescent with a disability, chronic illness, or other special health care need (including mental illness). The program connects two parents in a one-to-one relationship, consisting of a parent with personal experience and training who assists another parent seeking support.
Web address: www.p2pusa.org

MOVIES

Day for Night: Recognizing Teenage Depression

Produced by Depression and Related Affective Disorders Association in association with the Johns Hopkins School of Medicine (1996)
VHS, 28 minutes, Contact 410-987-7447 or write DRADA, Meyer 3-0181, 600 N. Wolfe St., Baltimore, MD 21287-7381 for ordering information.
As part of an effort to help teens gain a better understanding of depression, *Day for Night: Recognizing Teenage Depression* is intended to build awareness of the illness and, in the process, save lives. Offering an in-depth look at the signs, symptoms, and treatment of teenage depression, this video includes interviews with young people who are dealing with clinical depression and bipolar disorder. Featuring their families and friends, as well as interviews with health professionals, the video's goal is to provide education, support, and hope to those suffering from this debilitating, yet treatable disease.

Depression: On the Edge

Produced by PBS (1997)
VHS, 30 minutes, order online at www.castleworks.com
Depression: On the Edge is co-hosted by the musical group Third Eye Blind. It addresses teen angst—from normal "blues" to clinical depression to suicide—and shows how and where youth can get help if they need it. *On the Edge* stresses early identification and treatment as the best weapon in the fight against the national epidemic of teen depression and suicide. It also aims to break down the social stigma of depression that leads many teens to deny and hide the problem. By speaking candidly and personally, *On the Edge* shows young people that the sooner they learn the facts, the sooner they can help themselves and their peers.

Hope and Solutions for OCD

Produced by the Awareness Foundation for OCD (1999)
VHS (four 20-minute tapes)
To order, write AFOCD, c/o Gail Adams, 3N374 Limberi Lane, St. Charles, IL 60175, Tel: 630-513-9234
This four-part series is intended to educate viewers about the characteristics of OCD, its causes, treatment, strategies for recovery, OCD in the schools, and OCD in the family.

In Our Own Words: Teens with Bipolar Disorder

Produced by The Jocelyn Center, 405 Central Ave., Northfield, IL (2001)
Call 847441.5600 for ordering information
VHS, 25 minutes

In this insightful video program, a group of teens and young adults tell their compelling stories of self-discovery and functioning as bipolar individuals. The video provides an inside glimpse into the lives and emotions of these young people through revealing first-person accounts of awareness and management of their illness. The video, which is accompanied by an educator's guide, helps teens with this disorder know they are not alone. It also promotes understanding among family members, caregivers, educators, and mental health professionals.

MAGAZINE RESOURCES

The National Alliance on Mental Illness publishes *NAMI Beginnings*, a free, quarterly magazine developed by the Child and Adolescent Action Center that provides articles on children and adolescent mental health issues. To sign up for a free subscription to *NAMI Beginnings*, contact Bianca Ruffin at biancar@ nami.org or visit the NAMI store at http://www.nami.org/template.cfm?section =NAMI_Store. Online versions of the magazine as well as previous issues can be found at NAMI's website: http://www.nami.org/caac.

Notes

CHAPTER 1

1. Although I am using the first person to write this book, not all of the interviews were conducted by me. Eric Bradley, who was at the time an MSW student, worked closely with me on this project and conducted a number of the interviews and contributed immensely to the background research used in this book.

2. J. Knitzer, *Unclaimed Children: The Failure of Public Responsibility to Children and Adolescents in Need of Mental Health Services* (Washington, DC: Children's Defense Fund, 1982).

3. Department of Health and Human Services, *Report of the Surgeon General's Conference of Children's Mental Health: A National Action Agenda* (Washington, DC, 1999).

4. Ibid.

5. Ibid.

6. A. E. Kazdin, *Psychotherapy for Children and Adolescents: Directions for Research and Practice* (London: Oxford University Press, 2000).

7. Even more alarming evidence for the prevalence of mental disorders in youth comes from Alan Kazdin, who is one of the leading researchers on child and adolescent mental health. In his recent work *Psychotherapy for Children and Adolescents*, Kazdin provides some basic statistics concerning the prevalence of mental illness among children and adolescents. He explains that to date there has been no large-scale, nationwide study of psychiatric disorders among children and adolescents in the United States and, therefore, it is difficult to pin down the exact prevalence rate. Yet, as he explains, several studies have provided estimates of the disorders using current diagnostic criteria and rigorous assessment methods. Such studies included children and adolescents (4 to 18 years old) and found that 17 to 22 percent suffer significant developmental, emotional, or behavioral problems. Kazdin cautions that the prevalence rates ought to be viewed as general patterns rather than conclusions about the "real" rates of disorders among children, in part due to the fact that diagnostic systems and definitions of disorders have changed considerably over the past two decades.

Consequently, even when the diagnostic criteria are the same, different methods of assessment can lead to quite different results. While there is still a great deal of ambiguity and lack of consensus regarding the actual number of youth in the United States who suffer from mental illness, it is reasonable to state that at least 10 percent have a serious mental disorder and that the actual incidence may be 20 percent or higher. One of our greatest challenges as a nation, then, is to develop and provide appropriate mental health services for these children and their parents.

8. World Health Organization, *Caring for Children and Adolescents with Mental Disorders* (Geneva: World Health Organization, 2002).

9. Ibid., p. 1.

10. I discovered the significance of storytelling when I wrote my last book, C. W. LeCroy, *The Call to Social Work* (Thousand Oaks, CA: Sage), which presents the life stories of social workers. A readable book about the importance of storytelling is R. N. Remen, *Kitchen Table Wisdom* (New York: Riverhead Books, 1996).

11. A. W. Frank, *The Wounded Storyteller: Body, Illness, and Ethics* (Chicago: University of Chicago Press, 1995, p. 17). Frank has outlined this notion of how storytelling and listening to stories is a responsible moral act and represents a "mutuality of need, when each is *for* the other" (p. 25). G. Becker, *Disrupted Lives: How People Create Meaning in a Chaotic World* (Berkeley, CA: University of California Press, 1999), sees people's narratives of disruption as moral accounts of their lives.

12. In particular, E. Mishler, *Research Interviewing* (Cambridge, MA: Harvard University Press, 1986), believes there is an empowering capacity of narrative and provides a framework for the interviewer's role in facilitating empowerment. As specific examples, see R. L. Rubinstein, "Nature, Culture, Gender, Age." In *Anthropology and Aging*, R. L. Rubinstein, ed. (Dordrecht, Netherlands: Kluwer, 1990); G. Becker, *Disrupted Lives*.

13. Frank, in *The Wounded Storyteller*, discusses the use of storytelling by people who suffer from physical ailments. He suggests three types of narratives emerge from people who have such illnesses. The *restitution story* is often told but makes illness only transitory. *Chaos stories* are embedded in the crisis of the illness and cannot get beyond that aspect. *Quest stories* address suffering directly and are motivated by the person's belief that something is to be gained by the experience. Restitution and quest stories are most often found in published accounts. Indeed, many of the stories I heard from the parents I interviewed qualify as quest stories. For example, some of the parents have joined or even helped start parent advocacy groups that are one form of the quest story.

14. Frank provides an eloquent description of this process: "Realizing who they always have been, truly been, each becomes or prepares to become the re-created, moral version of that self. In this display of character, memory is revised, interruption assimilated, and purpose grasped. 'Whatever has happened to me or will happen,' the storyteller as hero implicitly claims, 'the purpose remains mine to determine'" (p. 131).

15. G. Becker, *Disrupted Lives*, addresses in great detail how narrative or stories become the pathway for examining a period of disruption and continuity. The stories people tell about themselves (the narratives) reflect their experiences. The notion is that narratives are a way to resolve the core issues that can heal a person's discontinuities. "Through stories people organize, display, and work through their experiences" (p. 25). Becker has examined many aspects of disruption using narrative analysis. including infertility, midlife, stroke, late-life transitions, and ethnic minorities.

16. A. Frank, *The Wounded Storyteller*, p. 101.

17. M. Bornstein, *Handbook of Parenting* (2nd ed.): *Volume 1: Children and Parenting; Volume 2: Biology and Ecology of Parenting; Volume 3: Being and Becoming a Parent; Volume 4:*

Social Conditions and Applied Parenting; Volume 5: Practical Issues in Parenting (Mahwah, NJ: Lawrence Erlbaum Associates, 2002).

18. H. Blumer, *Symbolic Interactionism: Perspective and Method* (Englewood Cliffs, NJ: Prentice Hall, 1969), succinctly states the case for such empirical observation of experience: "no theorizing, however ingenious, and no observance of scientific protocol, however meticulous, are substitutes for developing a familiarity with what is actually going on in the sphere of life under study" (p. 39). His whole approach focused on examining the social world of people. Any understanding of people had to account for the actions and experience of people as they meet the situations that arise in their worlds.

19. L. Slater, *Welcome to My Country* (New York: Random House, 1966); S. Plath, *The Bell Jar* (New York: Bantam, 1972); W. Styron, *Darkness Visible: A Memoir of Madness* (New York: Random House, 1990); E. Wurtzel, *Prozac Nation* (Boston: Houghton Mifflin, 1994); A. Solomon, *Depression: The Noonday Demon* (New York: Simon & Schuster, 2002); S. Kaysen, *Girl, Interrupted* (New York: Random House, 1994); K. Jamison, *An Unquiet Mind* (New York: Knopf, 1995). For memoirs of individuals who have experienced another person's mental illness directly, see J. Neugeburen, *Imagining Robert: My Brother, Madness and Survival* (New York: William Morrow, 1996); C. Simon, *Mad House* (New York: Random House, 1999); P. Duke, *A Brilliant Madness: Living with Manic Depressive Illness* (New York: Bantam Books, 1992); J. Thordike, *Another Way Home: A Family's Journey Through Mental Illness* (New York: Penguin, 1997); C. Maurice, *Let Me Hear Your Voice: A Family's Triumph over Autism* (New York: Random House, 1994); E. R. Fling, *Eating an Artichoke: A Mother's Perspective on Asperger Syndrome* (London: Jessica Kingsley, 2000); S. Hammer, *By Her Own Hand: Memoirs of a Suicide's Daughter* (New York: Vintage Books, 1991); M. Moorman, *My Sister's Keeper: Learning to Cope with a Sibling's Mental Illness* (New York: W. W. Norton, 1999); P. Stacey, *The Boy Who Loved Windows: Opening the Heart and Mind of a Child Threatened with Autism* (New York: DaCapo Press, 2003); R. Hughes, *Running with Walker: A Memoir* (London: Jessica Kingsley, 2003).

20. S. Kvale, *InterViews: An Introduction to Qualitative Research Interviewing* (Thousand Oaks, CA: Sage, 1996).

21. Ibid.

22. This framework is directly from Kvale's book.

23. This notion is attributed to Kierkeg.

CHAPTER 2

1. V. Paradiz, *Elijah's Cup: A Family's Journey into the Community and Culture of High-Functioning Autism and Asperger's Syndrome* (London: Jessica Kinglsey, 2005).

2. Ibid., p. 18.

3. A. Deveson, *Tell Me I'm Here: One Family's Experience with Schizophrenia* (New York: Penguin Books, 1991).

4. C. Simon, *Mad House: Growing Up in the Shadow of Mentally Ill Siblings* (New York: Doubleday, 1997). As quoted in R. E. Gur and A. B. Johnson, *If Your Adolescent Has Schizophrenia* (New York: Oxford University Press, 2006), an excellent parent guidebook that deals specifically with schizophrenia.

5. Deveson, *Tell Me*.

6. P. Wyden, *Conquering Schizophrenia: A Father, His Son, and a Medical Breakthrough* (New York: Alfred Knopf, 1998).

7. P. Raeburn, *Acquainted with the Night: A Parent's Quest to Understand Depression and Bipolar Disorder in His Children* (New York: Broadway Books, 2004).

8. Raeburn, *Acquainted with the Night.*

9. P. Buck, *The Child Who Never Grew* (New York: Woodbine House, 1992).

10. Parent quote is from a review of N. Miller and C. Sammons, *Everybody's Different* (New York: Paul Brooks, 1999), posted on Amazon.com.

11. Ibid.

12. S. Pinker, *The Blank Slate: The Modern Denial of Human Nature* (New York: Penguin, 2002).

13. Ibid., p. ix.

14. Ibid., p. x.

15. Ibid., p. 261.

16. These notions come from psychoanalytic theory. In particular, Frieda Fromm-Reichmann in 1948 introduced the term "schizonogenic mother," suggesting this personality type could cause schizophrenia. Later, Gregory Bateson examined communication patterns and paradoxes and introduced his notion of the "double bind." The effort was criticized because it was never a very testable idea in the first place.

17. *Refrigerator Mothers*, produced by David Simpson, J. J. Hanley, and Gordon Quinn, Kartemquin Educational Films; available at www.fanlight.com.

18. A. Rubin, J. Cardenas, K. Warren, C. K. Pike, and K. Wambach, "Outdated practitioner views about family culpability and severe mental disorders," *Social Work*, 5, 412–422, 1998.

19. See H. P. Lefley, "Family burden and family stigma in major mental illness," *American Psychologist*, 44, 556–560, 1989.

20. W. R. McFarlane, "Families in the treatment of psychotic disorders," *Harvard Mental Health Letter News*, 10, 12, October 1995.

21. J. R. Harris, *The Nuture Assumption: Why Children Turn Out the Way They Do* (New York: Free Press, 1998).

22. Pinker, *The Blank State*, p. 12.

23. Harris, *The Nurture Assumption*, p. 291.

24. D. Karp, *Burden of Sympathy: How Families Cope with Mental Illness* (New York: Oxford University Press, 2001), discusses this notion.

25. D. L. Rosenhan, "On being sane in insane places." In C. Clark and H. Robboy (eds.), *Social Interaction* (New York: St. Martin's Press, 1992).

26. Ibid.

27. K. Temerlin, "Suggestion effects in psychiatric diagnosis," *Journal of Nervous and Mental Disease*, 147, 349–353, 1968.

28. This thesis is discussed in detail in H. S. Becker, *Outsiders: Studies in the Sociology of Deviance* (New York: Free Press, 1963).

29. D. Noonan, "Why don't we call them quirky," *Newsweek Health*, (2004), http://msnbc.msn.com/id/4824772/.

30. C. W. Mills, "Situated actions and vocabularies of motive." In J. Manis and B. Meltzer (eds.), *Symbolic Interaction* (Boston: Allyn and Bacon, 1972), p. 209.

31. Karp, *Burden of Sympathy.*

32. Ibid., p. 84.

33. For a recent and detailed look at the research on childhood mental illness and diagnosis, see *Journal of Clinical Child and Adolescent Psychology*, 34, 2005; the whole issue is devoted to diagnosis.

34. P. Conrad, "Discovery of hyperkinesis: Notes on the medicalization of deviant behavior," *Social Problems, 23*, 12–21, 1975.

35. H. Kutchins and S. A. Krik, *Making Us Crazy: The Psychiatric Bible and the Creation of Mental Disorders* (New York: Free Press, 2003). The authors also wrote *The Selling of DSM: The Rhetoric of Science in Psychiatry* (New York: Aldine, 1992).

36. J. J. Arnett, "Adolescent storm and stress, reconsidered," *American Psychologist, 54*, 317–326, 1999.

37. G. S. Hall, *Adolescence: Its Psychology and Its Relation to Physiology, Anthropology, Sociology, Sex, Crime, Religion, and Education (Vols. I & II)* (Englewood Cliffs, NJ: Prentice-Hall, 1904).

38. This general point is becoming a hot topic. For a fascinating look into this subject, see A. V. Horwitz and J. C. Wakefield, *The Loss of Sadness: How Psychiatry Transformed Normal Sorrow into Depressive Disorder* (New York: Oxford, 2007), in which the authors argue that the psychiatric profession has understood and reclassified normal human sadness as an abnormal experience. Like Kutchins and Kirk, they argue that the *DSM* is extremely flawed.

39. Data are from S. Satel, "Mind over manual" [op-ed], *The New York Times*, http://www.nytimes.com/2007/09/13/opinion/13satel.html.

40. Ibid.

CHAPTER 3

1. E. Bradley contributed significantly to this section. As part of his master's thesis, Eric used the interviews from this study and focused on parents' experience of burden. I am grateful for Eric's contribution.

2. S. C. Reinhard, "Perspectives on the family's caregiving experience in mental illness," *Journal of Nursing Scholarship, 26*, 70–74, 1994; J. Greenberg, R. Greenley, D. McKee, R. Brown, and C. Griffin-Francell, "Mothers caring for an adult child with schizophrenia: The effects of subjective burden on maternal health," *Family Relations, 42*, 205–211, 1993.

3. D. T. Marsh and H. P. Lefley, "The family experience of mental illness: Evidence for resilience," *Psychiatric Rehabilitation Journal, 20*, 3–13, 1996.

4. M. Yarrow, J. Clausen, and P. Robbins, "The social meaning of mental illness," *Journal of Social Issues, 11*, 33–48, 1955.

5. C. Creer, E. Sturt, and T. Wykes, "The role of relatives." In J. K. Wing (ed.), *Long Term Community Care: Experience in a London Borough* (Cambridge, MA: Cambridge University Press, 1982), pp. 29–39.

6. H. P. Lefley, "Behavioral manifestations of mental illness." In A. B. Hatfield and H. P. Lefley (eds.), *Families of the mentally ill* (New York: Guilford Press, 1987), pp. 107–127.

7. Ibid., 1997.

8. S. Noh and R. J. Turner, "Living with psychiatric patients: Implications for the mental health of family members," *Social Science and Medicine, 25*, 263–271, 1987.

9. H. Gravitz, "The binds that tie—and heal: How families cope with mental illness," *Psychology Today, 34*, 70, 2001.

10. Ibid., p. 73.

11. D. Karp, *The Burden of Sympathy: How Families Cope with Mental Illness* (New York: Oxford University Press, 2001).

12. Marsh and Lefley, "The family experience of mental illness."

13. P. MacGregor, "Grief: The unrecognized parental response to mental illness in a child," *Social Work*, 39, 160–166, 1994.

14. Ibid., p. 161.

15. Ibid., p. 163.

16. Ibid., p. 164.

17. P. Boss, *Ambiguous Loss* (New York: Harvard University Press, 1999).

18. Ibid., p. 22.

19. C. Malacrida, "Motherhood, resistance and attention deficit disorder: Strategies and limits," *Canadian Review of Sociology and Anthropology*, 38, 141–165, 2001. For an extended report and analysis of this topic, see Claudia Malacrida, *Cold Comfort: Mothers, Professionals, and Attention Deficit Disorder* (Toronto: University of Toronto Press, 2003).

20. Ibid.

21. M. Devault, *Feeding the Family: The Social Organization of Caring as Gendered Work* (Chicago: University of Chicago Press, 1991).

22. J. Baker, "The heroine's odyssey: The child's service system through the eyes of parents." In R. Cohen & J. Cohen (eds.), *Chiseled in Sand: Perspectives on Change in Human Services Organizations* (Belmont, CA: Brooks Cole/Wadsworth, 2001).

23. Ibid., p. 167.

24. Ibid., p. 557.

25. P. MacGregor, "Grief."

26. H. P. Lefley, "Family burden and family stigma in major mental illness," *American Psychologist*, 44, 558, 1989.

27. P. Macgregor, "Grief," p. 160.

28. A. Rubin, J. Cardenas, K. Warren, C. Pike, and K. Wambach, "Outdated practitioner views about family culpability and severe mental disorders," *Social Work*, 45, 412–422, 1998.

29. Ibid., p. 412.

30. P. Belluck, "Troubled children: Living with love, chaos, and Haley," *New York Times*, October 22, 2006. This is an excellent introduction to current issues in addressing children's mental illness.

31. National Institute of Mental Health, *Blueprint for Change: Research on Child and Adolescent Mental Health* (Washington, DC: Author, 2001); P. Armburster and T. Fallon, "Clinical, sociodemographic, and system risk factors for attrition in a children's mental health clinic," *American Journal of Orthopsychiatry*, 64, 577–586, 1994; A. E. Kazdin, "Family experience of barriers to treatment and premature termination from child therapy," *Journal of Consulting and Clinical Psychology*, 65, 1453–463, 1997.

32. A. E. Kazdin, "Family experience of barriers to treatment."

33. L. Chavez and L. E. Barnes, "Issues in psychiatric caregiving," *Archives of Psychiatric Nursing*, 3, 61–68, 1989; P. MacGregor, "Grief."

34. *Report of the Surgeon General's Conference on Children's Mental Health* (Washington, DC: Author, 1999).

35. Ibid., p. 19.

36. K. Delaney and B. Engels-Scianna, "Parents' perceptions of their child's emotional illness and psychiatric treatment needs," *Journal of Child and Adolescent Psychiatric Nursing*, 9, 15–27, 1996.

37. L. Chavez and L. E. Barnes, "Issues in psychiatric caregiving," p. 162.

38. P. MacGregor, "Grief," p. 163.

CHAPTER 4

1. C. W. LeCroy, *The Call to Social Work: Life Stories* (Thousand Oaks, CA: Sage, 2002).

2. A. W. Frank, *The Renewal of Generosity* (Chicago: University of Chicago Press, 2004).

3. Ibid.

4. This point is made by Abraham Verghese, *The Tennis Partner: A Doctor's Story of Friendship and Loss* (New York: Harper Collins, 1998).

5. B. Ehrenreich, *Bright-Sided: How the Relentless Promotion of Positive Thinking Has Undermined America* (New York: Henry Holt, 2009).

6. B. Ehrenreich, *Bright-Sided*, p. 12.

7. A related virtue in Ehrenreich's book is that by analyzing positive thinking, she helps us reflect on the value of thinking about our lives and the society in which we live in a realistic rather than idealistically selfish ways.

8. J. Hoffman, "When thumbs up is no comfort: Treating illness with a smile and metaphor," *The New York Times*, June 1, 2008.

9. For an in-depth perspective and history of faith and healing see, A. Harrington, *The Cure Within: A History of Mind–Body Medicine* (New York: W. W. Norton, 2009). In this book Harrington investigates the alternative medicine industry but also helps us understand the human need to make personal sense of illness and suffering.

10. Ibid.

11. D. M. Rauner, *The Role of Caring in Youth Development and Community Life* (New York: Columbia University Press, 2000).

12. The difficulty that the United States has encountered in creating an effective "system of care" or system of coordinated services for children is well known. Many children have multiple needs and require care across different bureaucratic structures, such as mental health services, specially designed educational services, health care difficulties, and so forth. See B. J. Friesen and J. Poertner, *From Case Management to Service Coordination for Children with Emotional, Behavioral, or Mental Disorders* (Baltimore: Brooks, 1995); L. Bickman and D. J. Rog (eds.), *Children's Mental Health Services* (Thousand Oaks, CA: Sage, 1995).

13. See, for example, P. L. Berger and J. Neuhaus, *To Empower People: The Role of Mediating Structures in Public Policy* (Washington, DC: American Enterprise Institute, 1977).

14. Original work by E. Durkheim, *Suicide* (Glencoe, IL: Free Press, 1957).

15. R. Bellah, R. Madsen, W. Sullivan, A. Swidler, and S. Tipton, *Habits of the Heart: Individualism and Commitment in American Life* (3rd ed.) (Berkeley, CA: University of California Press, 2007).

16. A. Gartner and F. Riessman, *Self-help in the Human Services* (San Francisco: Jossey-Bass, 1977).

17. P. R. Silverman, "Mutual aid groups," *Encyclopedia of Social Work* (18th ed.). Silver Spring, MD: National Association of Social Workers, 1987.

18. E. F. Torrey, *Surviving Schizophrenia: A Manual for Families, Consumers, and Providers* (New York: Quill, 2001).

19. E. Swados, *The Four of Us: A Family Memoir* (New York: Farrar, Straus, and Giroux, 1991).

20. Karp in *Burden of Sympathy* also discusses this but as the four C's, where he adds "All I can do is cope with it" (p. 153).

21. V. Tarico, B. P. Low, E. Trupin, and A. Forsythe-Stevens, "Children's mental health services: A parent perspective," *Community Mental Health Journal, 25,* 313–326, 1989.

22. K. Delaney and B. Engels-Scianna, "Parents' perceptions of their child's emotional illness and psychiatric treatment needs," *Journal of Child and Adolescent Psychiatric Nursing,* 9, 15–27, 1996.

23. D. B. Nevas and B. A. Farber, "Parents' attitudes toward their child's therapist and therapy," *Professional Psychology: Research and Practice, 32,* 165–170, 2001.

24. S. Vitanza and R. Cohen, *Perspectives on Treatment and Services: Results of a National Survey of Parents and Caregivers of Children with Serious Mental Illnesses.* Paper presented at the Building on Family Strengths: Research and Services in Support of Children and Their Families Conference, Portland, OR, 2001, p. 3.

25. P. Raeburn, *Acquainted with the Night: A Parent's Quest to Understand Depression and Bipolar Disorder in His Children* (New York: Broadway Books, 2004).

26. Ibid.

27. L. Margolin, *Under the Cover of Kindness: The Invention of Social Work* (Charlottesville, VA: University of Virginia Press, 1997). Jerry Floersch provides an excellent critique of this book and finds a lack of real evidence to support Margolin's argument; see J. Floersch, "*Under the Cover of Kindness* book review," *American Journal of Sociology, 104,* 1197, 2000.

28. L. Armstrong, *And They Call It Help: The Psychiatric Policing of America's Children* (New York: Deane, 1993).

29. Review from Amazon.com.

30. R. A. Winett and R. Winkler, "Current behavior modification in the classroom: Be still, be quiet, be docile," *Journal of Applied Behavior Modification, 5,* 499–504, 1972.

31. G. Harris, "Proof is scant on psychiatric drug mix for young," *The New York Times,* November 23, 2006.

32. Ibid.

33. Thomas Insel made this statement, as reported in G. Harris, "Proof is scant."

34. P. S. Jensen, L. E. Arnold, J. Swanson, B. Vitiello, et al., "Follow-up of the NIMH MTA study at 36 months after randomization," *Journal of the American Academy of Child and Adolescent Psychiatry, 46,* 2007; J. M. Swanson, G. R. Elliott, L. L. Greenhill, T. Wigal, et al., "Effects of stimulant medication on growth rates across 3 years in the MTA follow-up," *Journal of the American Academy of Child and Adolescent Psychiatry, 46,* 2007.

35. P. Raeburn, *Acquainted with the Night,* p. 302.

36. D. Karp, *Speaking of Sadness: Depression, Disconnection, and the Meanings of Illness* (New York: Oxford University Press, 1996).

37. D. Karp, *Is It Me or My Meds?* (New York: Harvard University Press, 2006).

38. E. Parens and J. Johnston, "Mental health in children and adolescents," Hastings Center, 2010, www.hastingscenter.org/.

39. Ibid.

40. For a summary of these issues, see S. Satel, "Suicide risks and SSRIs: New data should change the equation," *Medical Progress Today.Com,* 2007, http://www.medicalprogresstoday.com.

CHAPTER 5

1. P. Raeburn, *Acquainted with the Night: A Parent's Quest to Understand Depression and Bipolar Disorder in His Children* (New York: Broadway Books, 2004).

2. B. Collins and T. Collins, "Parent–professional relationships in the treatment of seriously emotionally disturbed children and adolescents," *Social Work*, 35, 522, 1990.

3. Ibid., 525.

4. J. Lyons, *Redressing the Emperor: Improving Our Children's Public Mental Health System* (Westport, CT: Praeger, 2004).

5. Ibid., p. 524.

6. S. Young, "An overview of issues in research on consumer satisfaction with child and adolescent mental health services," *Journal of Child and Family Studies*, 4, 234, 1995.

7. V. Tarico, B. P. Low, E. Trupin, and A. Forsythe-Stevens, "Children's mental health services: A parent perspective," *Community Mental Health Journal*, 25, 313–326, 1989.

8. President's New Freedom Commission on Mental Health, "Achieving the promise: Transforming mental health care in America," www.mentalhealthcommission.gov/reports/finalreport/toc.html.

9. B. Friensen, "The concept of recovery: 'Value added' for the children's mental health field?" *Focal Point*, 5–8, Summer 2005.

10. B. A. Stroul and R. M. Friedman, *A System of Care for Severely Emotionally Disturbed Children and Youth* (Washington, DC: Georgetown University, Child and Adolescent Service System Program Technical Assistance Center, 1986).

11. See B. J. Burns, E. J. Costello, A. Angold, D. Tweed, D. Stangl, E. M. Farmer, and A. Erkanli, "Children's mental health service use across service sectors," *Health Affairs*, 14, 147–159, 1995; B. A. Stroul and R. E. Friedman, *System of Care for Children and Youth with Severe Emotional Disturbance* (Report SOC2, reprint of July 1986 rev. ed.). (Washington, DC: Georgetown University Center for Child and Human Development, National Technical Assistance Center for Children's Mental Health, 1994); S. M. Horwitz, K. Hoagwood, R. A. Stiffman, T. Summerfeld, J. R. Weisz, E. J. Costello, K. Rost, D. L. Bean, L. Cottler, P. J. Leaf, M. Roper, and G. Norquist, "Reliability of the services assessment for children and adolescents," *Psychiatric Services*, 52, 1088–1094, 2001.

12. J. Lyons, *Redressing the Emperor*, p. 29.

13. For additional information on the system of care model, see http://systemsofcare.samhsa.gov/Publications/index.aspx; for a list of the 10 principles, see http://www.tapartnership.org/SOC/SOCprinciples.php.

14. R. Donner, B. Huff, M. Gentry, D. McKinney, J. Duncan, S. Thompson, and P. Silver, "Expectations of case management for children with emotional problems: A parent perspective." In B. J. Friesen and J. Poertner (eds.), *From Case Management to Service Coordination for Children with Emotional, Behavioral, or Mental Disorders* (Baltimore: Paul Brookes, 1995).

15. A. Nelson, "Surviving the system," *Focal Point*, 19, Summer 2005.

16. Information about the center can be found at http://www.rtc.pdx.edu/index.php.

17. "Can Jason live at home? Yes—with wraparound services," *Focal Point*, Portland Research and Training Center, 14–15, 2006.

18. Ibid., p. 15.

19. M. McKay and W. Bannon, "Evidence update: Engaging families in child mental health services," *Child and Adolescent Psychiatry: Clinics of North America*, 13, 905–921, 2004.

20. D. T. Marsh and M. A. Fristad, *Handbook of Serious Emotional Disturbance in Children and Adolescents* (New York: Wiley, 2002). See also E. Farmer, "Issues confronting effective services in systems of care," *Child and Youth Services Review*, 22, 627–650, 2000.

21. S. Hollandsworth, "Their last good chance to get better," *Texas Monthly*, November 2003.

22. A. J. Pumariega and N. C. Winters, *The Handbook of Child and Adolescent Systems of Care: The New Community Psychiatry* (New York: Jossey-Bass, 2003).

23. Karen Nielsen commenting on P. Belluck, "Troubled children: Living with love, chaos, and Haley," *New York Times*, October 22, 2006.

24. Comment regarding P. Belluck, "Troubled children."

25. American Academy of Child and Adolescent Psychiatry, "Child and adolescent psychiatry workforce crisis: Solutions to improve care," 2009, www.aacap.org.

26. A. Frank, *The Wounded Storyteller* (Chicago: University of Chicago Press, 1995), discusses this notion, p. 10.

27. K. R. Delaney and B. Engels-Scianna, "Parents' perceptions of their child's emotional illness and psychiatric treatment needs," *Journal of Child and Adolescent Psychiatric Nursing*, 9, 15–26, 1996.

28. A. Hochschild, "Emotion work, feeling rules, and social structure," *American Journal of Sociology*, 85, 551–575, 1979; A. Hochschild, *The Managed Heart: Commercialization of Human Feeling* (Berkeley, CA: University of California Press, 1983).

29. D. Karp, *Burden of Sympathy: How Families Cope with Mental Illness* (New York: Oxford University Press, 2001), p. 73.

30. In psychology, this is sometimes referred to as the "recovery model" and was emphasized in President George W. Bush's New Freedom Commission on Mental Health.

31. S. Twedt, "It's a crime: How mentally ill teens are trapped in lockups," *Pittsburgh Gazette*, July 15, 2001.

32. Ibid. The following data on hospitals and detention centers are taken from S. Twedt's article.

33. Ibid.

34. Ibid. In some states, after one hour restraints have to come off, children can be isolated in time-out for only one hour at a time, and centers cannot sedate a child unless a psychiatrist is present.

35. A. Cusac, "Arrest my kid: He needs mental health care," *The Progressive*, 22–26, July 2001.

36. National Alliance for the Mentally Ill, "Families on the brink: The impact of ignoring children with serious mental illness," 1999.

37. J. Katz-Leavy, I. S. Lourie, and R. Kaufmann, "Meeting the mental health needs of severely emotionally disturbed minority children and adolescents," *Children Today*, 16, 10–14, 1987.

38. T. Cross, "Services to minority populations," *Focal Point*, 1–4, Fall 1988.

39. This and other studies from various years can be found at http://www.oas.samhsa.gov/nsduh.htm.

40. Department of Health and Human Services, *Report of the Surgeon General's Conference on Children's Mental Health: A National Action Agenda* (Washington, DC: Author, 1999).

41. A. McLean, "'Recovering' consumers and a broken mental health system in the United States: Ongoing challenges for consumers/survivors and the New Freedom Commission on Mental Health," *International Journal of Psychosocial Rehabilitation*, 8, 58–70, 2003.

42. Ibid.

43. D. Jasper, "An offer to help, take it or leave it," *The Enquirer*, March 22, 2004.

44. As reported in A. Cusac, "Arrest my kid."

45. Ibid.

46. National Federation of Families for Children's Mental Health, *Working Definition of Family-Driven Care* (Rockville, MD: Author, 2008).

47. B. Ramos, G. Burton, K. E. Hoagwood, and P. Jensen, "Introduction and background information." In P. J. Jenson and K. E. Hoagwood (eds.), *Improving Children's Mental Health Through Empowerment: A Guide to Assisting Families* (New York: Oxford University Press, 2008), pp. 3–7.

48. V. Robbins, J. Johnston, H. Barnett, W. Hobstetter, K. Kutash, A. Duchnowski, et al., *Parent to Parent: A Synthesis of the Emerging Literature* (Tampa, FL: University of South Florida, Louis de la Parte Florida Mental Health Institute, Department of Child and Family Studies, 2008).

49. A. Krivelyova, C. Stormann, T. King, D. Hussey, and E. Montgomery, *Employment Outcomes of Caregivers in Systems of Care*. Presentation at the 20th Annual Research Conference—A System of Care for Children's Mental Health: Expanding the Research Base, Tampa, FL, March 4–7, 2007.

50. J. Lyons, *Redressing the Emperor*.

51. The bill of rights can be found at http://www.aacap.org/cs/root/resources_for_families/patient_bill_of_rights.

52. The most recent evidence for this is from "Science updates: Task force finds cognitive behavioral therapy effective for children and adolescents exposed to trauma," National Institute of Mental Health, October 29, 2008.

53. A. E. Kazdin, *Psychotherapy for Children and Adolescents: Directions for Research and Practice* (London: Oxford University Press, 2000).

54. C. LeCroy, "Enhancing the delivery of effective mental health services to children," *Social Work*, 37, 225–231, 1992.

55. C. LeCroy, *Handbook of Evidence Based Treatment Manuals for Children and Adolescents* (New York: Oxford University Press, 2009).

56. S. Fritz, "Daniel, 1988–2000: A child's suicide, unending grief and lessons learned," *St. Petersburg Times*, November 16, 2003.

57. Ibid.

58. E. Werner and R. S. Smith, *Journeys from Childhood to Midlife: Risk, Resilience and Recovery* (Ithaca, NY: Cornell University Press, 2001).

59. This notion about moral commitment is discussed in detail by A. Frank, *The Wounded Storyteller*.

60. A. Frank, *The Wounded Storyteller*, p. 159.

61. Ibid., p. 163.

CHAPTER 6

1. C. Sheilds, *Unless* (New York: Harper Perennial, 2003), p. 1.

2. D. Marsh and H. P. Lefley, "The family experience of mental illness," *Psychiatric Rehabilitation Journal*, 20, 3–13, 1996.

3. J. M. Rosenzweig, E. M. Brennan, and M. Ogilvie, "Work–family fit: Voices of parents of children with emotional and behavioral disorders," *Social Work*, 47, 2002.

4. R. Tessler, *Family Experiences with Mental Illness* (Westport, CT: Auburn House, 2000); D. Karp, *Burden of sympathy* (New York: Oxford University Press, 2004).

5. V. Cicerelli, "An examination of the trajectory of the adult child's caregiving for an elderly parent," *Family Relations*, 49, 169–176, 2000; A. C. Mui, "Caregiving for frail

elderly parents," *Gerontologist*, 35, 86–94, 1995; R. R. Hansson and E. Nelson, "Adult children with frail elderly parents," *Family Relations*, 39, 153–159, 1990; R. Rubinstein, *The
Many Dimensions of Aging* (New York: Spring, 2000).

6. Studies supporting this point are reviewed in World Health Organization, *Caring for
Children and Adolescents with Mental Disorders* (Geneva: Author, 2003).

7. Ibid.

8. Ibid.

9. American Academy of Pediatrics. The guidelines appear in the journal *Pediatrics*,
108, 2002.

10. D. Karp, *The Burden of Sympathy*.

11. E. Goffman, *Stigma: Notes on Management of Spoiled Identity* (Englewood Cliffs, NJ:
Prentice Hall, 1963).

12. Goffman was astute to recognize that important things happen in the interaction
of social situations and personality. His contribution was to help us examine the importance of situations and encounters.

13. P. W. Corrigan, "How clinical diagnosis might exacerbate the stigma of mental illness," *Social Work*, 52, 131–138, 2007.

14. A. M. Freedman, H. I. Kaplan, and B. J. Sadock, *Modern Synopsis of Comprehensive
Handbook of Psychiatry* (2nd ed.) (Baltimore: Williams & Wilkins, 1976), p. 449.

15. Hinshaw states, "There is an absence of research on the impact of stigma on children and adolescents who have experienced it themselves" (p. 723). See S. P. Hinshaw,
"The stigmatization of mental illness in children and parents: Developmental issues, family concerns, and research needs," *Journal of Child Psychology and Psychiatry*, 46, 714–734,
2005.

16. D. Kranke and J. Floersch, "Mental health stigma among adolescents: Implications
for social workers," *School Social Work Journal*, 34, 28–42, 2009.

CHAPTER 7

1. C. S. Lewis, *Mere Christianity: A Revised and Amplified Edition, with a New Introduction, of the Three Books, Broadcast Talks, Christian Behaviour, and Beyond Personality* (San
Francisco: Harper, 2001).

2. S. Salzberg, *Faith: Trusting Your Own Deepest Experience* (New York: Riverhead
Books, 2002).

3. M. Greenberg, *Hurry Down Sunshine* (New York: Random House, 2008).

4. Ibid., p. 128.

5. P. Early, *Crazy: A Father's Search Through American's Mental Health Madness*
(New York: Putnam, 2006).

6. A. Frank, *The Wounded Storyteller* (Chicago: University of Chicago Press, 1995).

7. D. Karp, *The Burden of Sympathy: How Families Cope with Mental Illness* (New York:
Oxford University Press, 2001).

8. C. Mattingly, "Hope, willing, and narrative re-envisioning," *The Hedgehog Review*,
8, 33, 2006.

9. Ibid., p. 35.

10. R. Ellmann, *James Joyce* (New York: Oxford University Press, 1959), p. 38.

11. C. Castaneda, *The Teachings of Don Juan* (New York: Square Press, 1968).

12. *Medieval Sourcebook: Jalal ad-Din Rumi (1207–1273 ce): From The Masnavi, c. 1250 ce*,
www.fordham.edu/halsall/source/1270rumi-poems1.html.

13. V. Frankl, *Man's Search for Meaning* (New York: Washington Square Press, 1985), p. 74.

14. This conclusion is from K. Brehony, *After the Darkest Hour: How Suffering Begins the Journey to Wisdom* (New York: Henry Holt, 2000).

15. A. Morrow Lindbergh. Quotes found at www.annemorrowlindbergh.com/Quotes/index.html.

16. R. Ellmann, *James Joyce*.

17. D. Karp, *Burden of Sympathy*, p. 57. This notion comes from A. Strauss, "Turning points in identity." In C. Clark and H. Robby (eds.), *Social Interaction* (New York: St. Martin's Press, 1992).

18. M. Greenberg, *Hurry Down Sunshine*, p. 169.

19. P. Early, *Crazy*, p. 361.

20. T. N. Hanh, *The Miracle of Mindfulness* (Boston, MA: Beacon Press, 1975).

21. Ibid., p. 5.

22. M. H., "Parenting a bipolar child," National Alliance on Mental Illness (NAMI) website, http://www.nami.org.

23. P. Early, *Crazy*, p. 235.

24. M. Seligman, *Authentic Happiness* (New York: Free Press, 2004). Seligman identifies and values a set of nearly universal virtues that he believes lead to deep and lasting gratification. These virtues include wisdom and knowledge, courage, love and humanity, justice, temperance, spirituality, and transcendence. "The good life," he writes, "is using your signature strengths every day to produce authentic happiness and abundant gratification."

25. For an in-depth commentary on this topic, see A. V. Horwitz and J. C. Wakefield, *The Loss of Sadness: How Psychiatry Transformed Normal Sorrow into Depressive Disorder* (New York: Oxford University Press, 2007).

26. C. W. Belser, *Larry the Penguin Searches for the Meaning of Life* (United Kingdom: Misaki Books, 2009).

27. V. Frankl, *Man's Search for Meaning*, p. 56.

28. K. Brehony, *After the Darkest Hour*.

29. Ibid., p. 49.

30. S. Salzberg, *Faith: Trusting Your Own Deepest Experience* (New York: Riverhead Books, 2002), p. xiv.

31. Ibid.

32. Ibid., p. 12.

33. Ibid., p. 22.

34. K. R. Jamison, *An Unquiet Mind* (New York: Vintage, 1997).

35. P. Raeburn, *Acquainted with the Night: A Parent's Quest to Understand Depression and Bipolar Disorder in His Children* (New York: Broadway Books, 2004).

36. Mahoney makes this same point in his critique of the field of psychotherapy, when discussing the need for a deeper recognition of the role of compassion in the face of human suffering, See M. Mahoney, "Suffering, philosophy, and psychotherapy," *Journal of Psychotherapy Integration*, 15, 337–352, 2005; and R. B. Miller, "Suffering in psychology: The demoralization of psychotherapeutic practice," *Journal of Psychotherapy Integration*, 15, 299–336, 2005.

CHAPTER 8

1. M. Muckenhoupt, *Dorothea Dix: Advocate for Mental Health Care* (New York: Oxford University Press, 2003).

2. See, for example, the Declaration of Independence: http://www.earlyamerica.com/earlyamerica/freedom/doi/text.html.

3. Department of Health and Human Services, "Factsheet: Children's mental health statistics," http://www.nmha.org.

4. Ibid.

5. Department of Health and Human Services, *Report of the Surgeon General's Conference of Children's Mental Health: A National Action Agenda* (Washington, DC: Author, 1999).

6. J. Knitzer, *Unclaimed Children: The Failure of Public Responsibility to Children and Adolescents in Need of Mental Health Services* (Washington, DC: Children's Defense Fund, 1982).

7. C. S. Redhead, *President's New Freedom Commission on Mental Health: Recommendations for Screening and Treating Children and Subsequent FY2005 Appropriations* (Washington, DC: Congressional Research Service, 2004).

8. President's New Freedom Commission on Mental Health, "Achieving the promise: Transforming mental health care in America," 2003, www.mentalhealthcommission.gov/reports/finalreport/toc.html.

9. Titles XVI, XIX, and XXI of the Social Security Act are what this section refers to as most closely associated with children's mental health. Title XVI, "Supplemental Security Income for the Aged, Blind, and Disabled," is relevant because it offers additional income to individuals younger than age 18 who have a mental (or physical) impairment determined by a medical professional, resulting in significant limitations to the child's functioning in at least one of the four life domains, to include home, school, peers, and the community. Title XIX, "Grants to States for Medical Assistance Programs," provides federal specifications for monies given to states to fund state medical insurance. In 49 states, this program is referred to as "Medicaid"; Arizona has termed its state medical program "Arizona Health Care Cost Containment System" (AHCCCS). Qualifying for this health insurance requires means testing related to family income. Coverage for mental health services is based on state-determined provisions and limitations. Title XXI, "State Children's Health Insurance Program," was developed to provide quality child health assistance to low-income and/or uninsured youth, and is often reserved for children in state care. In this way, children in current custody of the state as a result of the loss of their parents or guardians by death or imprisonment, temporary removal due to abuse and/or neglect, placement in long-term foster care, temporary or permanent voluntary relinquishment of custody related to parental hardship and/or unmanageable child behavioral problems, or permanent termination of parental rights are able to receive coverage for medical and mental health services. Retrieved May 2010 from http://www.ssa.gov.

10. E. Howell, "Access to children's mental health services under Medicaid and SCHIP," The Urban Institute, 2004, http://www.urban.org/uploadedPDF/311053_B-60.pdf.

11. C. Barry, R. G. Frank, and T. G. McGuire, "The costs of mental health parity: Still an impediment?", *Health Affairs*, 25, 623–634, 2006.

12. The Paul Wellstone and Pete Domenici Mental Health Parity Act is "Subtitle B" of the Mental Health Parity and Addiction Equity Act of 2008 (HR 1424); it requires insurance companies that provide both medical and mental health/substance abuse services to use the same financial requirements and treatment limitations for both medical coverage and mental health coverage. Information on this act was cited in the National Conference of State Legislation, July 2010, http://www.ncsl.org.

13. R. M. Friedman, A. Pinto, L. Behar, et al., "Unlicensed residential programs: The next challenge in protecting youth," *American Journal of Orthopsychiatry*, 76, 295–303, 2006.

14. C. A. Kiesler and C. Simpkins, "The de facto national system of psychiatric inpatient care," *American Psychologist*, 46, 582, 1991.

15. J. S. Lyons, *Redressing the Emperor: Improving Our Children's Public Mental Health System* (Westport, CT: Praeger, 2004).

16. E. P. Coffey, M. E. Olson, and P. Sessions, "The heart of the matter: An essay about the effects of managed care on family therapy with children," *Family Process*, 40, 397, 2001.

17. Department of Justice, "Factsheet: Children's mental health statistics," 2010, http://www.nmha.org.

18. The Americans with Disabilities Act of 1990 was based on Congress's decision that physical or mental disabilities do not hinder a person's right to partake in all aspects of society, as well as historical documentation reporting several recorded acts of discrimination. This legislation applies to children's mental health, as it was designed to protect children with mental illness from discrimination in areas such as education, communication, housing, transportation, health services, and access to public services. This act was amended in 2008, and became effective in 2009, providing clearer specifications on the degree to which an individual's disability "substantially limits" the person's ability to participate in aspects of society without accommodations in response to Supreme Court cases such as *Sutton v. United Airlines, Inc.* (1999) and *Toyota Motor Manufacturing, Kentucky, Inc. v. Williams* (2002). This information was retrieved April 2010 from http://www.ada.gov.

19. P. D. Blanck, *Employment, Disability, and the American Disabilities Act* (Chicago: Northwestern University Press, 2001).

20. L. M. McWey, T. L. Henderson, and J. B. Alexander, "Parental rights and the foster care system: A glimpse of decision-making in Virginia," *Journal of Family Issues*, 29, 1049, 2008.

21. B. F. Fuemmeler, "Bridging disciplines: An introduction to the special issue on public health and pediatric psychology," *Journal of Pediatric Psychology*, 29, 405–414, 2004.

22. M. Hansen, A. Litzelman, D. T. Marsh, and A. Milspaw, "Approaches to serious emotional disturbance: Involving multiple systems," *Professional Psychology: Research and Practice*, 35, 463, 2004.

23. In this case, the plaintiffs had mental health diagnoses such as schizophrenia, bipolar disorder, and major depressive disorder, and indicated that they were reportedly ineligible to access clinically indicated services from Washington's state mental health system. The plaintiffs also claimed that youth across Washington undergo significant impairment from multiple placements such as psychiatric hospitalizations and incarcerations. Information retrieved June 2010 from the National Center for Youth Law website: http://www.youthlaw.org.

24. The settlement, negotiated in 2003, requires that Los Angeles County implement several comprehensive reforms, such as improved detection of the mental health needs of youth, more effective permanency planning, and timely development of services catering to individual needs to support the care and stability of children in state custody. In conjunction with its execution of family-based wraparound services, the settlement commanded the immediate closure of the MacLaren Children's Center, shifting its funding to community- and family-based services. Information retrieved June 2010 from the National Center for Youth Law website: http://www.youthlaw.org.

25. Lawyers representing Arizona's AHCCCS-eligible children filed *J. K. v. Dillenberg*, a class-action lawsuit seeking improved access to behavioral health care. The agreement commits the state of Arizona to a wholesale redevelopment of its children's behavioral health system according to a set of principles that put child and family needs first. See http://www.youthlaw.org.

26. L. Huang, B. Stroul, R. Friedman, P. Mrazek, B. Friesen, S. Pires, and S. Mayberg, "Transforming mental health care for children and their families," *American Psychologist*, 60, 615–627, 2005. Principal values identified in this research include "1) comprehensive home- and community-based services and supports, 2) family partnerships and support, 3) culturally competent care, 4) individualized care, 5) evidence-based practices, 6) coordination of services, responsibility, and funding, 7) prevention, early identification, and early intervention, 8) early childhood education, 9) mental health services in schools, and 10) accountability" (p. 618).

27. C. LeCroy, *Handbook of Evidence Based Treatment Manuals* (New York: Oxford University Press, 2009).

28. C. Vestal, "As economy takes toll, mental health budgets shrink," Stateline.org, Pew Center on the States, 2010.

29. American Psychological Association, "Report on Healthy Development: A Summit on Young Children's Mental Health," 2010, http://www.apa.org/pi/families/summit-report.aspx.

30. M. O'Reilly, "'I didn't violent punch him': Parental accounts of punishing children with mental health problems," *Journal of Family Therapy: Association for Family Therapy and Systemic Practice*, 30, 272–295, 2008.

31. T. L. Roleff and L. K. Egendorf, *Mental Illness Is a Disease: Hillary Rodham Clinton and Steven Hyman: Opposing Viewpoints: Mental Illness* (San Diego: Greenhaven Press, 2000). Hillary Rodham Clinton, then First Lady, and Dr. Steven Hyman, Director of the National Institute of Mental Health (NIMH), discussed the benefits of identifying mental illnesses as medical illnesses with genetic origins at the White House Conference on Mental Health, June 7, 1999.

32. R. Nemeroff, J. M. Levitt, L. Faul, A. Wonpat-Borja, S. Bufferd, S. Setterberg, and P. S. Jensen, "Establishing ongoing, early identification programs for mental health problems in our schools: A feasibility study," *Journal of the American Academy of Child and Adolescent Psychiatry*, 47, 2008. School counselors and other mental health service providers were trained and supervised to administer an evidence-based mental health assessment tool, the "Voice Diagnostic Interview Schedule for Children IV," as students were assessed and diagnosed with mental illnesses such as ADHD and oppositional defiance disorder. Researchers concluded that the use of this assessment tool was effective and helpful in providing continuity of care between the school system and the mental health arena.

33. D. A. Karp, *Is It Me or My Meds?* (Cambridge, MA: Harvard University Press, 2007), p. 225. Karp has predicted that if this mentality with respect to psychiatric medications continues, the recognition of diversity will be minimized, because the development of a restricted number of feelings and behaviors will dictate what is socially appropriate.

34. M. P. Mychailyszyn, S. DosReis, and M. Myers, "African American caretakers' views of ADHD and use of outpatient mental health care services for children," *Families, Systems, & Health*, 26, 2008.

35. S. Shin, "Effects of culturally relevant psychoeducation for Korean American families of persons with chronic mental illness," *Research on Social Work Practice*, 14, 2004. In this study, Korean Americans with at least one child with mental illness were assigned randomly to either the control group providing supportive therapy or the experimental

group facilitating a psychoeducation group that was culturally sensitive. Results indicated that the experimental group reported clinically significant reductions in stigma related to mental illness, improved coping strategies, and enhanced abilities to independently manage family crises.

36. *Children's Defense Fund (CDF) Priorities for America's Children*, retrieved from: http://www.childrensdefense.org, June, 2010. Other funding priorities identified in President Obama's FY2011 Federal Budget for children and families include: "funding for extension of ARRA (The American Recovery and Reinvestment Act of 2009)'s Temporary FMAP (Federal Medical Assistance Percentage) increase in Medicaid, prevention and wellness activities, Children's Health Insurance Program (CHIP), and the Maternal and Child Health Block Grant."

37. National Technical Assistance Center for Children's Mental Health, Georgetown University Center for Child and Human Development, "A public health approach to children's mental health: A conceptual framework," http://gucchdtacenter.georgetown .edu/public_health.html

38. *History of the Family Decision Making Program*, handout obtained at foster parent training at For Love of Children, Washington, DC, 2003, p. 3. Other beliefs that guide the work of facilitators of the Family Decision Making Model include "all children are entitled to be free from harm, children are best raised in families, families should be respected, and children should not be removed from their family unless there is a significant risk of harm to the child, family, or community that cannot be eliminated."

39. President's New Freedom Commission on Mental Health, "Achieving the promise: Transforming mental health care in America," www.mentalhealthcommission.gov/ reports/finalreport/toc.html.

40. Providence Service Corporation, "Virtual residential programs," http:// www.provcorp.com/Services/VirtualResidentialPrograms.asp.

41. "Love for Children" Program Headquarters: 671 FLOC Way, Harpers Ferry, WV 25425.

42. M. R. Sanders, C. Markie-Dadds, L. A. Tullyl, and W. Bor, "The Triple P—Positive Parenting Program: A comparison of enhanced, standard, and self-directed behavioral family intervention for parents of children with early onset conduct problems," *Journal of Consulting and Clinical Psychology*, 68, 624–640, 2000.

43. L. M. Franco, K. M. Dean-Assael, and M. M. McKay, "Multiple family groups to reduce youth behavioral disorders." In C. W. LeCroy (ed.), *Handbook of Evidence Based Treatment Manuals* (New York: Oxford University Press, 2008). This chapter describes the application of this model in detail and has a bibliography of the research studies.

44. S. A. Edwards, *The Essential Elements of a Multi-Family Group Therapy: A Delphi Study*, Ph.D. dissertation, Virginia Polytechnic Institute and State University, April 9, 2001. In his Ph.D. dissertation in family and child development, Edwards combined the beliefs of a panel of experts in the field identifying key elements of Multi-Family Group Therapy that contribute to the effectiveness of this therapeutic modality.

45. J. VanDenBerg. *Wraparound Facilitator and Family Support Partner*, 2007. In his educational handout, VanDenBerg identifies the numerous roles of Family Support Partners (FPPs) as including "engagement through education and direct support, helping carry out crisis stabilization, modeling strengths-based approaches and sharing experiences, being team members as needed, carrying out plan strategies, [linking] to natural supports and community resources, [providing] direct support to youth and parents, [helping] families with paperwork, [providing] support in court, and [modeling] parenting skills."

46. S. S. Olin, K. E. Hoagwood, J. Rodreguez, B. Ramos, G. Burton, M. Penn, M. Crowe, M. Radigan, and P. S. Jensen, "The application of behavior change theory to family-based services: Improving parent empowerment in children's mental health," *Journal of Child and Family Studies*, 19, 462–470, 2010. For a comprehensive review of family support programs, see K. E. Hoagwood, M. A. Cavaleri, S. Olin, B. J. Burns, E. Slaton, D. Gruttadaro, and R. Hughes, "Family support in children's mental health: A review and synthesis," *Clinical Child Family Psychology Review*, 13, 1–45, 2010.

47. C. K. Conners, *Conners' Rating Scales—Revised Technical Manual* (Toronto, Ontario: Multi-Health Systems Inc., 1997). The Parent Form is designed to assess concerning behaviors, including symptoms of ADHD, learning deficits, social challenges, and verbal/physical aggression in 16- to 18-year-olds from the parent/guardian perspective. These data are combined with information from teacher and self-report forms to comprehensively assess each child.

48. L. Schiller and A. Bennett, *The Quiet Room: A Journey Out of the Torment of Madness* (New York: Warner Books, 1994). Schiller and Bennett, a *Wall Street Journal* reporter, describe from Schiller's perspective what it is like to feel out of control of one's life, battling command auditory hallucinations that have told Schiller to commit suicide, living in a mental hospital, and then learning to cope with her mental illness as she is reintegrated into the community. Schiller's story, as the protagonist, allows readers to view her as a human being rather than a mental patient. This first-person account serves to reduce stigma and solicit collective interest to view treatment for mental illnesses as a societal priority.

49. K. R. Jamison, *An Unquiet Mind: A Memoir of Moods and Madness* (New York/ Canada: Random House, 1995). Dr. Kay Redfield Jamison, a psychiatry professor at the Johns Hopkins School of Medicine, describes her battle with bipolar disorder. Her book profiles her erratic lifestyle, resistance to therapy and psychotropic medications, and professional achievements. Jamison depicts individuals with mental illness not only as human, but also as intelligent and exceptional. Her esteemed writing has the potential to help dispel the myth that mentally ill persons are incapable of experiencing career successes, especially in the field of mental health.

50. S. Nasar, *A Beautiful Mind: The Life of Mathematical Genius and Nobel Laureate* (New York: Touchstone, 2001).

References

Active Minds. Retrieved July 21, 2010, from http://www.activeminds.org.

American Psychiatric Association. (2000). *Diagnostic and Statistical Manual of Mental Disorders* (4th ed.). Washington, DC: Author.

American Psychological Association. (2010). Report on Healthy Development: A Summit on Young Children's Mental Health. http://www.apa.org/pi/families/summit-report.aspx.

Armburster, P., & Fallon, T. (1994). Clinical, sociodemographic, and system risk factors for attrition in a children's mental health clinic. *American Journal of Orthopsychiatry, 64*, 577–586.

Armstrong, L. (1993). *And They Call It Help: The Psychiatric Policing of America's Children.* New York: Deane.

Arnett, J. J. (1999). Adolescent storm and stress, reconsidered. *American Psychologist, 54*, 317–326.

Austin, C. (1983). Case management in long-term care: Options and opportunities. *Health and Social Work, 8*, 16–30.

Baker, J. (2001). The heroine's odyssey: The child's service system through the eyes of parents. In R. Cohen & J. Cohen (eds.), *Chiseled in Sand: Perspectives on Change in Human Services Organizations.* Belmont, CA: Brooks Cole/Wadsworth.

Barry, C., Frank, R. G., & McGuire, T. G. (2006). The costs of mental health parity: Still an impediment? *Health Affairs, 25*, 623–634.

Bean, D. (2000). False-negative reporting and mental health services utilization: Parents' reports about child and adolescent services. *Mental Health Services Research, 2*, 239–249.

Becker, G. (1999). *Disrupted Lives: How People Create Meaning in a Chaotic World.* Berkeley, CA: University of California Press.

Becker, H. S. (1963). *Outsiders: Studies in the Sociology of Deviance.* New York: Free Press.

Bellah, R. N., Madsen, R., Sullivan, W. M., Swidler, A. and Tipton, S. M. (2007). *Habits of the Heart: Individualism and Commitment in American Life* (3rd ed.). Berkeley, CA: University of California Press.

Belluck, P. (October 22, 2006). Troubled children: Living with love, chaos, and Haley. *New York Times*.

Belser, C. W. (2009). *Larry the Penguin Searches for the Meaning of Life*. UK: Misaki Books.

Berger, P. L., & Neuhaus, J. (1977). *To Empower People: The Role of Mediating Structures in Public Policy*. Washington, DC: American Enterprise Institute.

Bernheim, K. F. (1990). Family provider relationships: Charting a new course. In H. P. Lefley & D. L. Johnson (eds.), *Families as Allies in Treatment of the Mentally Ill: New Directions for Mental Health Professionals* (pp. 99–113). Washington, DC: American Psychiatric Association.

Bickman, L., Foster, E. M., & Lambert, E. W. (1996). Who gets hospitalized in a continuum of care? *Journal of the American Academy of Child and Adolescent Psychiatry, 35*, 74–80.

Bickman, L., & Rog, D. J. (eds.). (1995). *Children's Mental Health Services*. Thousand Oaks, CA: Sage.

Blanck, D. (2001). *Employment, Disability, and the American Disabilities Act*. Chicago: Northwestern University Press.

Blumer, H. (1969). *Symbolic Interactionism: Perspective and Method*. Englewood Cliffs, NJ: Prentice Hall.

Bornstein, M. (2002). *Handbook of Parenting* (2nd ed.): *Volume 1: Children and Parenting; Volume 2: Biology and Ecology of Parenting; Volume 3: Being and Becoming a Parent; Volume 4: Social Conditions and Applied Parenting; Volume 5: Practical Issues in Parenting*. Mahwah, NJ: Lawrence Erlbaum Associates.

Bradley, E. (2003). *The Experience of Burden: Families with Mentally Ill Children*. Master's in social work thesis, Tempe, AZ.

Brannan, A. M., Heflinger, C. A., & Bickman, L. (1997). The caregiver strain questionnaire: Measuring the impact on the family of living with a child with serious emotional disturbance. *Journal of emotional and behavioral disorders, 5*, 212–222.

Brehony, K. A. (2000). *After the Darkest Hour: How Suffering Begins the Journey to Wisdom*. New York: Henry Holt.

Buck, P. (1992). *The Child Who Never Grew*. New York: Woodbine House.

Burns, B. (1999). Effective treatment for mental disorders in children and adolescents. *Clinical Child and Family Psychology Review, 2*, 199–254.

Burns, B. J., Costello, E. J., Angold, A., Tweed, D., Stangl, D., Farmer, E. M., & Erkanli, A. (1995). Children's mental health service use across service sectors. *Health Affairs, 14*, 147–159

Burns, B. J., & Goldman, S. K. (eds.). (1999). *Promising Practices in Wraparound for Children with Severe Emotional Disturbance and Their Families. Systems of Care: Promising Practices in Children's Mental Health* (1998 Series, Vol. IV). Rockville, MD: Center for Mental Health Services.

Burns, B., & Hoagwood, K. (2002). *Community Treatment for Youth*. London: Oxford University Press.

Burns, B. J., Hoagwood K., & Maultsby, L. T. (1998). Improving outcomes for children and adolescents with serious emotional and behavioral disorders: Current and future directions. In M. H. Epstein, K. Kutash, & A. J. Duchnowski (eds.), *Outcomes for Children and Youth with Emotional and Behavioral Disorders and Their Families: Programs and Evaluation Best Practices* (pp. 685–707). Austin, TX: Pro-ED.

Burns, D. E. (2009). *Saving Ben: A Father's Story of Autism*. Denton, TX: University of North Texas Press.

Canino, G. (2002). Methodological challenges in assessing children's mental health services utilization. *Mental Health Services Research, 4*, 97–107.

Castaneda, C. (1968). *The Teachings of Don Juan*. New York: Square Press.

Chavez, L., & Barnes, L. E. (1989). Issues in psychiatric caregiving. *Archives of Psychiatric Nursing, 3*, 61–68.

Cicerelli, V. (2000). An examination of the trajectory of the adult child's caregiving for an elderly parent. *Family Relations, 49*, 169–176.

Clark, E. (1999). *Biting the Stars*. Toronto: HarperCollins Canada.

Coffey, E. P., Olson, M. E., & Sessions, P. (2001). The heart of the matter: An essay about the effects of managed care on family therapy with children. *Family Process, 40*, 397.

Collins, B., & Collins, T. (1990). Parent–professional relationships in the treatment of seriously emotionally disturbed children and adolescents. *Social Work, 35*, 522–527.

Colt, G. H. (2006). *November of the Soul: The Enigma of Suicide*. New York: Scribner.

Conners, C. K. (1997). *Conner's Rating Scales—Revised Technical Manual*. Toronto, Ontario: Multi-Health Systems.

Conrad, P. (1975). Discovery of hyperkinesis: Notes on the medicalization of deviant behavior. *Social Problems, 23*, 12–21.

Corbin, J., & Strauss, A. (1990). Grounded theory research: Procedures, canons, and evaluative criteria. *Qualitative Sociology, 13*(1), 3–21.

Corrigan, P. W. (2007). How clinical diagnosis might exacerbate the stigma of mental illness. *Social Work, 52*, 131–138.

Costello, E. J., Angold, A., Burns, B. J., Stangl, D. K., Tweed, D. L., Erkanli, A., & Worthman, C. M. (1996). The Great Smoky Mountains study of youth: Goals, design, methods, and prevalence of DSM-II-R disorders. *Archives of General Psychiatry, 53*, 1129–1136.

Courneyor, D. E., & Johnson, H. C. (1991). Measuring parents' perceptions of mental health professionals. *Research on Social Work Practice, 1*, 399–415.

Creer, C., Sturt, E., & Wykes, T. (1982). The role of relatives. In J. K. Wing (ed.), *Long Term Community Care: Experience in a London Borough* (pp. 29–39). Cambridge, UK: Cambridge University Press.

Cross, T. (Fall 1988). Services to minority populations. *Focal Point*, 1–4.

Delaney, K., & Engels-Scianna, B. (1996). Parents' perceptions of their child's emotional illness and psychiatric treatment needs. *Journal of Child and Adolescent Psychiatric Nursing, 9*, 15–27.

Department of Health and Human Services. (1999). *Report of the Surgeon General's Conference on Children's Mental Health: a National Action Agenda*. Washington, DC: Author.

Department of Health and Human Services. (1999). *Surgeon General's Report on Mental Health*. Washington, DC: Author.

Department of Health and Human Services. (n.d.). Factsheet: Children's mental health statistics. http://www.nmha.org

Department of Justice. (2010). http://www.nmha.org.

Devault, M. (1991). *Feeding the Family: The Social Organization of Caring as Gendered Work*. Chicago: University of Chicago Press.

Deveson, A. (1991). *Tell Me I'm Here: One Family's Experience with Schizophrenia*. New York: Penguin Books.

Donner, R., Huff, B., Gentry, M., McKinney, D., Duncan, S., Thompson, S. & Silver, P. (1995). Expectations of case management for children with emotional problems: A parent perspective. In B. J. Friesen & J. Poertner (eds.), *From Case Management to Service Coordination for Children with Emotional, Behavioral, or Mental Disorders* (pp. 43–62). Baltimore, MD: Paul Brookes.

Duke, P. (1992). *A Brilliant Madness: Living with Manic Depressive Illness.* New York: Bantam Books.

Durkheim, E. (1966). *Suicide.* Glencoe, IL: Free Press.

Early, P. (2006). *Crazy: A Father's Search Through American's Mental Health Madness.* New York: Putnam.

Edwards, S. A. (2001). *The Essential Elements of a Multi-Family Group Therapy: A Delphi Study.* Blacksburg, VA: Virginia Polytechnic Institute and State University.

Ehrenreich, B. (2010). *Bright-Sided: How the Relentless Promotion of Positive Thinking Has Undermined America.* New York: Henry Holt.

Ellmann, R. (1959). *James Joyce.* New York: Oxford University Press.

Farmer, E. (2000). Issues confronting effective services in systems of care. *Child and Youth Services Review, 22,* 627–650.

Fling, E. R. (2000). *Eating an Artichoke: A Mother's Perspective on Asperger Syndrome.* London: Jessica Kingsley.

Floersch, J. (2000). *Under the Cover of Kindness* book review. *American Journal of Sociology, 104,* 1197.

Franco, L. M., Dean-Assael, K. M., & McKay, M. M. (2008). Multiple family groups to reduce youth behavioral disorders. In C. W. LeCroy (ed.), *Handbook of Evidence Based Treatment Manuals* (pp. 546–590). New York: Oxford University Press.

Frank, A. (1995). *The Wounded Storyteller.* Chicago: University of Chicago Press.

Frank, A. (2004). *The Renewal of Generosity.* Chicago: University of Chicago Press.

Frankl, V. E. (2006). *Man's Search for Meaning.* Boston, MA: Beacon Press.

Freedman, A. M., Kaplan, H. I., & Sadock, B. J. (1981). *Modern Synopsis of Comprehensive Handbook of Psychiatry* (2nd ed.). Baltimore, MD: Williams & Wilkins.

Friedman, R. M., Pinto, A., Behar, L., et al. (2006). Unlicensed residential programs: The next challenge in protecting youth. *American Journal of Orthopsychiatry, 76,* 295–303.

Friensen, B. (Summer 2005). The concept of recovery: "Value added" for the children's mental health field? *Focal Point, 8,* 3.

Friesen, G. B. J., & Poertner, J. (1995). *From Case Management to Service Coordination for Children with Emotional, Behavioral, or Mental Disorders.* Baltimore, MD: Brooks.

Fuemmeler, B. F. (2004). Bridging disciplines: An introduction to the special issue on public health and pediatric psychology. *Journal of Pediatric Psychology, 29,* 405–414.

Gartner, A., & Riessman, F. (1977). *Self-help in the human Services.* San Francisco: Jossey-Bass.

Goffman, E. (1963). *Stigma: Notes on Management of Spoiled Identity.* Englewood Cliffs, NJ: Prentice Hall.

Gravitz, H. (2001). The binds that tie—and heal: How families cope with mental illness. *Psychology Today, 34,* 70–76.

Greenberg, J., Greenley, J. R., McKee, D., Brown, R., & Griffin-Francell, C. (1993). Mothers caring for an adult child with schizophrenia: The effects of subjective burden on maternal health. *Family Relations, 42,* 205–211.

Greenberg, J. S., Kim, W. H., & Greenley, J. R. (2010). Factors associated with subjective burden in siblings of adults with severe mental illness. *American Journal of Orthopsychiatry, 67,* 231–214.

Greenberg, M. (2008). *Hurry Down Sunshine.* New York: Random House.

Hall, G. S. (1904). *Adolescence: Its Psychology and Its Relation to Physiology, Anthropology, Sociology, Sex, Crime, Religion, and Education (Vols. I & II).* Englewood Cliffs, NJ: Prentice-Hall.

Hammer, S. (1991). *By Her Own Hand: Memoirs of a Suicide's Daughter.* New York: Vintage Books.

Hanh, T. N. (1975). *The Miracle of Mindfulness.* Boston, MA: Beacon Press.

Hansen, M., Litzelman, A., Marsh, D. T., &. Milspaw, A. (2004). Approaches to serious emotional disturbance: Involving multiple systems. *Professional Psychology: Research and Practice, 35,* 463.

Hansson, R., & Nelson, E. (1990). Adult children with frail elderly parents. *Family Relations, 39,* 153–159.

Harrington, A. (2009). *The Cure Within: A History of Mind–Body Medicine.* New York: W. W. Norton.

Harris, J. R. (1998). *The Nature Assumption: Why Children Turn Out the Way They Do.* New York: Free Press.

Hinshaw, S. P. (2005). The stigmatization of mental illness in children and parents: Developmental issues, family concerns, and research needs. *Journal of Child Psychology and Psychiatry, 46,* 714–734.

Hoagwood, K. E., Cavaleri, M. A., Serene Olin, S., Burns, B. J., Slaton, E., Gruttadaro, D., & Hughes, R. (2010). Family support in children's mental health: A review and synthesis. *Clinical Child and Family Psychology, 13,* 1–45.

Hoagwood, K., & Erwin, H. (1997). Effectiveness of school-based mental health services for children: A 10-year research review. *Journal of Child and Family Studies, 6,* 435–451.

Hochschild, A. (1979). Emotion work, feeling rules, and social structure. *American Journal of Sociology, 85,* 551–575.

Hochschild, A. (1983). *The Managed Heart: Commercialization of Human Feeling.* Berkeley, CA: University of California Press.

Hoffman, J. (June 1, 2008). When thumbs up is no comfort: Treating illness with a smile and metaphor. *The New York Times.*

Horwitz, A. V., & Wakefield, J. C. (2007). *The Loss of Sadness: How Psychiatry Transformed Normal Sorrow into Depressive Disorder.* New York: Oxford University Press.

Horwitz, S. M., Hoagwood, K., Stiffman, A. R., Summerfeld, T., Weisz, J. R., Costello, E. J., Rost, K., Bean, D. L., Cottler, L., Leaf, P. J., Roper, M., & Norquist, G. (2001). Reliability of the services assessment for children and adolescents. *Psychiatric Services, 52,* 1088–1094.

Howell, E. (2004). Access to children's mental health services under Medicaid and SCHIP. The Urban Institute. http://www.urban.org/uploadedPDF/311053 _B-60.pdf.

Huang, L., Stroul, B., Friedman, R., Mrazek, P., Friesen, B., Pires, S., & Mayberg, S. (2005). Transforming mental health care for children and their families. *American Psychologist, 60,* 615–627.

Hughes, R. (2003). *Running with Walker: A Memoir.* London: Jessica Kingsley.

Jamison, K. R. (1997). *An Unquiet Mind.* New York: Vintage.

Jensen, A., & Weisz, J. R. (2002). Assessing the match and mismatch between practitioner-generated and standardized interview-generated diagnoses for clinic referred for children and adolescents. *Journal of Clinical and Consulting Psychology, 70*, 158–168.

Jensen, P. (1999). Are stimulants overprescribed? Treatment of ADHD in four U.S. communities. *Journal of the American Academy of Child and Adolescent Psychiatry, 38*, 797–804.

Jensen, P. (2004). Making the system work for your child with ADHD. New York: Guilford Press.

Jensen, P. S., Arnold, L. E., Swanson, J. M., Vitiello, B., Abikoff, H. B., Greenhill, L. L., et al. (2007). Three-year follow-up of the NIMH MTA study. *Journal of the American Academy of Child and Adolescent Psychiatry, 46*, 989–1002.

Karp, D. (1996). *Speaking of Sadness: Depression, Disconnection, and the Meanings of Illness.* New York: Oxford University Press.

Karp, D. (2001). *Burden of Sympathy: How Families Cope with Mental Illness.* New York: Oxford University Press.

Karp, D. (2006). *Is It Me or My Meds?* New York: Harvard University Press.

Katz-Leavy, J., Lourie, I. S., & Kaufmann, R. (1987). Meeting the mental health needs of severely emotionally disturbed minority children and adolescents. *Children Today, 16*, 10–14.

Kaysen, S. (1994). *Girl, Interrupted.* New York: Random House.

Kazdin, A. E. (1989). Hospitalization of antisocial children: Clinical course, follow-up status, and predictors of outcome. *Advances in Behaviour Research and Therapy, 11*, 1–67.

Kazdin, A. E. (1997). Family experience of barriers to treatment and premature termination from child therapy. *Journal of Consulting and Clinical Psychology, 65*, 453–463.

Kazdin, A. E. (2000). *Psychotherapy for Children and Adolescents: Directions for Research and Practice.* London: Oxford University Press.

Kazdin, A. E., Holland, L., & Breton, S. (1991). *Barriers to Participation in Treatment Scale—Parent and Therapist Versions.* New Haven, CT: Yale University Press.

Kazdin, A. E., Holland, L., & Crowley, M. (1997). Family experience of barriers to treatment and premature termination from child therapy. *Journal of Consulting and Clinical Psychology, 65*, 453–463.

Kiesler, C. A., & Simpkins, C. (1991). The de facto national system of psychiatric inpatient care. *American Psychologist, 46*, 582.

Knitzer, J. (1982). *Unclaimed Children: The Failure of Public Responsibility to Children and Adolescents in Need of Mental Health Services.* Washington, DC: Children's Defense Fund.

Kranke, D., & Floersch, J. (2009). Mental health stigma among adolescents: Implications for social workers. *School Social Work Journal, 34*, 28–42.

Krivelyova, A., Stormann, C., King, T., Hussey, D., & Montgomery, E. (2007). *Employment Outcomes of Caregivers in Systems of Care.* Presentation at the 20th Annual Research Conference—A System of Care for Children's Mental Health: Expanding the Research Base, Tampa, FL, March 4–7, 2007.

Kutash, K., & Rivera, V. R. (1995). Effectiveness of children's mental health services: A review of the literature. *Education and Treatment of Children, 18*, 443–477.

Kutchins, H., & Kirk, S. A. (1992). *The Selling of DSM: The Rhetoric of Science in Psychiatry.* New York: Aldine.

Kutchins, H., & Kirk, S. A. (2003). *Making Us Crazy: The Psychiatric Bible and the Creation of Mental Disorders.* New York: Free Press.

Kvale, S. (1996). *InterViews: An Introduction to Qualitative Research Interviewing*. Thousand Oaks, CA: Sage.

Lambert, E. W., Brannan, A. M., Heflinger, C. A., Breda, C., & Bickman, L. (1997). Common patterns of service use in children's mental health. *Evaluation and Program Planning*, 21, 47–47.

LeCroy, C. (1992). Enhancing the delivery of effective mental health services to children. *Social Work*, 37, 225–231.

LeCroy, C. (2007). *The Call to Social Work*. Newbury Park, CA: Sage.

LeCroy, C. (2009). *Handbook of Evidence Based Treatment Manuals for Children and Adolescents*. New York: Oxford University Press.

Lefley, H. P. (1987). Behavioral manifestations of mental illness. In A. B. Hatfield & H. P. Lefley(eds.), *Families of the Mentally Ill* (pp. 107–127). New York: Guilford Press.

Lefley, H. P. (1989). Family burden and family stigma in major mental illness. *American Psychologist*, 44, 556–560.

Lewis, C. S. (2001). *Mere Christianity: A Revised and Amplified Edition, with a New Introduction, of the Three Books, Broadcast Talks, Christian Behaviour, and Beyond Personality*. San Francisco: HarperSanFrancisco.

Lincoln, Y. S., & Guba, E. G. (1985). *Naturalistic Inquiry*. Beverly Hills, CA: Sage.

Lyons, J. (2004). *Redressing the Emperor: Improving Our Children's Public Mental Health System*. Westport, CT: Praeger.

Macgregor, P. (1994). Grief: The unrecognized parental response to mental illness in a child. *Social Work*, 39, 160–166.

Mahoney, M. (2005). Suffering, philosophy, and psychotherapy. *Journal of Psychotherapy Integration*, 15, 337–352.

Malacrida, C. (2001). Motherhood, resistance and attention deficit disorder: Strategies and limits. *Canadian Review of Sociology and Anthropology*, 38, 141–165.

Malacrida, C. (2003). *Cold Comfort: Mothers, Professionals, and Attention Deficit Disorder*. Toronto: University of Toronto Press

Margolin, L. (1997). *Under the Cover of Kindness: The Invention of Social Work*. Charlottesville, VA: University of Virginia.

Marsh, D. T., & Fristad, M. A. (2002). *Handbook of Serious Emotional Disturbance in Children and Adolescents*. New York: Wiley.

Marsh, D. T., & Lefley, H. P. (1996). The family experience of mental illness: Evidence for resilience. *Psychiatric Rehabilitation Journal*, 20, 313.

Mattingly, C. (2006). Hope, willing, and narrative re-envisioning. *Hedgehog Review*, 8, 21–35.

Maurice, C. (1994). *Let Me Hear Your Voice: A Family's Triumph Over Autism*. New York: Random House.

McFarlane, W. R. (1995). Families in the treatment of psychotic disorders. *Harvard Mental Health Letter News*, 10, 12.

McKay, M., & Bannon, W. (2004). Evidence update: Engaging families in child mental health services. *Child and Adolescent Psychiatry Clinics of North America*, 13, 201–210.

McLean, A. (2003). "Recovering" consumers and a broken mental health system in the United States: Ongoing challenges for consumers/survivors and the New Freedom Commission on Mental Health. *International Journal of Psychosocial Rehabilitation*, 8, 58–70.

McWey, L. M., Henderson, T. L., & Alexander, J. B. (2008). Parental rights and the foster care system: A glimpse of decision-making in Virginia. *Journal of Family Issues*, 29, 1049.

Medieval Sourcebook: Jalal ad-Din Rumi (1207–1273 CE): From The Masnavi, c. 1250 CE, www.fordham.edu/halsall/source/1270rumi-poems1.html.

Miller, N., & Sammons, C. (1999). *Everybody's Different*. New York: Paul H.Brooks.

Miller, R. B. (2005). Suffering in psychology: The demoralization of psychotherapeutic practice. *Journal of Psychotherapy Integration, 15,* 299–336.

Mills, C. W. (1972). Situated actions and vocabularies of motive. In J. Manis & B. Meltzer (eds.), *Symbolic Interaction* (pp. 23–46). Boston: Allyn and Bacon.

Mishler, E. (1986). *Research Interviewing*. Cambridge, MA: Harvard University Press.

Moorman, M. (1999). *My Sister's Keeper: Learning to Cope with a Sibling's Mental Illness*. New York: W. W. Norton.

Muckenhoupt, M. (2003). *Dorothea Dix: Advocate for Mental Health Care*. New York: Oxford University Press.

Mui, A. C. (1995). Caregiving for frail elderly parents. *Gerontologist, 35,* 86–94.

Mychailyszyn, M. P., DosReis, S., & Myers, M. (2008). African American caretakers' views of ADHD and use of outpatient mental health care services for children. *Families, Systems, & Health, 26,* 210–221.

Nasar, S. (2001). *A Beautiful Mind: The Life of Mathematical Genius and Nobel Laureate*. New York: Touchstone.

National Center for Youth Law. (2010). http://www.youthlaw.org.

National Federation of Families for Children's Mental Health. (2008). *Working Definition of Family-Driven Care*. Rockville, MD: Author.

National Institute of Mental Health. (2001). *Blueprint for Change: Research on Child and Adolescent Mental Health*. Washington, DC: Author.

National Technical Assistance Center for Children's Mental Health, Georgetown University Center for Child and Human Development. (2010). A public health approach to children's mental health: A conceptual framework, http://gucchdtacenter.georgetown.edu/public_health.html.

Nelson, A. (Summer 2005). Surviving the system. *Focal Point, 19,* 5–6.

Nemeroff, R., Levitt, J. M., Faul, L., Wonpat-Borja, A., Bufferd, S., Setterberg, S., & Jensen, P. S. (2008). Establishing ongoing, early identification programs for mental health problems in our schools: A feasibility study. *Journal of the American Academy of Child and Adolescent Psychiatry, 47,* 12–24.

Neugeburen, J. (1996). *Imagining Robert: My Brother, Madness and Survival*. New York: William Morrow.

Nevas, D. B., & Farber, B. A. (2001). Parents' attitudes toward their child's therapist and therapy. *Professional Psychology: Research and Practice, 32,* 165–170.

Noh, S., & Turner, R. J. (1987). Living with psychiatric patients: Implications for the mental health of family members. *Social Science and Medicine, 25,* 263–271.

Olin, S. S., Hoagwood, K. E., Rodriguez, J., Ramos, B., Burton, G., Penn, M., Crowe, M., Radigan M., & Jensen, P. S. (2010). The application of behavior change theory to family-based services: Improving parent empowerment in children's mental health. *Journal of Child and Family Studies, 19,* 462–470.

Paradiz, V. (2005). *Elijah's Cup: A Family's Journey into the Community and Culture of High-Functioning Autism and Asperger's Syndrome*. London: Jessica Kingsley.

Parens, E., & Johnston, J. (2010). Mental health in children and adolescents. Hastings Center.www.hastingscenter.org/.

Pinker, S. (2002). *The Blank Slate: The Modern Denial of Human Nature*. New York: Penguin.

Plath, S. (1972). *The Bell Jar*. New York: Bantam.

President's New Freedom Commission on Mental Health. (2003). Achieving the promise: Transforming mental health care in America. www.mentalhealthcommission.gov/reports/finalreport/toc.html.

Pumariega, A. J., & Winters, N. C. (2003). *The Handbook of Child and Adolescent Systems of Care: The New Community Psychiatry*. New York: Jossey-Bass.

Raeburn, P. (2004). *Acquainted with the Night: A Parent's Quest to Understand Depression and Bipolar Disorder in His Children*. New York: Broadway Books.

Ramos, B., Burton, G., Hoagwood, K. E., & Jensen, P. (2008). Introduction and background information. In P. J. Jenson & K. E. Hoagwood (eds.), *Improving children's mental health through empowerment: A guide to assisting families* (pp. 3–7). New York: Oxford University Press.

Rauner, D. M. (2000). *The Role of Caring in Youth Development and Community Life*. New York: Columbia University Press.

Redhead, C. S. (2004). *President's New Freedom Commission on Mental Health: Recommendations for Screening and Treating Children and Subsequent FY2005 Appropriations*. Washington, DC: Congressional Research Service.

Reinhard, S. C. (1994). Perspectives on the family's caregiving experience in mental illness. *Journal of Nursing Scholarship, 26*, 70–74.

Remen, R. N. (1996). *Kitchen Table Wisdom*. New York: Riverhead Books.

Robbins, V., Johnston, J., Barnett, H., Hobstetter, W., Kutash, K., Duchnowski, A., et al. (2008). *Parent to Parent: A Synthesis of the Emerging Literature*. Tampa, FL: University of South Florida, Louis de la Parte Florida Mental Health Institute, Department of Child and Family Studies.

Roleff, T. L., & Egendorf, L. K. (2000). *Mental Illness Is a Disease: Hillary Rodham Clinton and Steven Hyman*. San Diego: Greenhaven Press.

Rosenhan, D. L. (1992). On being sane in insane places. In C. Clark & H. Robboy (eds.), *Social Interaction* (pp. 595–605). New York: St. Martin's Press.

Rosenzweig, J. M., Brennan, E. M., & Ogilvie, M. (2002). Work–family fit: Voices of parents of children with emotional and behavioral disorders. *Social Work, 47*, 415–424.

Rubin, A. (1992). Is case management effective for people with serious emotional mental illness? A research review. *Health and Social Work, 17*, 138–150.

Rubin, A., Cardenas, J., Warren, K., Pike, C., & Wambach, K. (1998). Outdated practitioner views about family culpability and severe mental disorders. *Social Work, 45*, 412–422.

Rubinstein, R. L. (1990). Nature, culture, gender, age. In R. L. Rubinstein (ed.), *Anthropology and Aging* (pp. 11–38). Dordrecht, Netherlands: Kluwer.

Rubinstein, R. (2000). *The Many Dimensions of Aging*. New York: Spring.

Salzberg, S. (2002). *Faith: Trusting Your Own Deepest Experience*. New York: Riverhead Books.

Sanders, M. R., Markie-Dadds, C., Tullyl, L. A., & Bor, W. (2002). The Triple P—Positive Parenting Program: A comparison of enhanced, standard, and self-directed behavioral family intervention for parents of children with early onset conduct problems. *Journal of Consulting and Clinical Psychology, 68*, 624–640.

Satel, S. (September 13, 2007). Mind over manual [op-ed]. *The New York Times*. http://www.nytimes.com/2007/09/13/opinion/13satel.html.

Satel, S. (2007). Suicide risks and SSRIs: New data should change the equation. *Medical Progress Today.Com*. http://www.medicalprogresstoday.com.

Schiller, L., & Bennett, A. (1994). *The Quiet Room: A Journey Out of the Torment of Madness*. New York: Warner Books.

Schoenwald, S. K. (1998). Multisystemic therapy: Changing the natural and service ecol-
ogies of adolescents and families. In M. H. Epstein & K. Kutash (eds.), *Outcomes
for Children and Youth with Emotional and Behavioral Disorders and Their Families:
Programs and Evaluation Best Practices* (pp. 485–511). Austin, TX: Pro-Ed.
Seligman, M. (2004). *Authentic Happiness*. New York: Free Press.
Sheilds, C. (2003). *Unless*. New York: Harper Perennial.
Shin, S. (2004). Effects of culturally relevant psychoeducation for Korean American
families of persons with chronic mental illness. *Research on Social Work Practice,
14,* 334–346.
Silverman, P. R. (2008). Mutual aid groups. In *Encyclopedia of Social Work* (18th ed.)
(pp. 1121–1134). ilver Spring, MD: National Association of Social Workers.
Simon, C. (1997). *Mad House: Growing up in the Shadow of Mentally Ill Siblings*. New York:
Doubleday.
Slater, L. (1966). *Welcome to My Country*. New York: Random House.
Solomon, A. (2002). *Depression: The Noonday Demon*. New York: Simon & Schuster.
Stacey, P. (2003). *The Boy Who Loved Windows: Opening the Heart and Mind of a Child
Threatened with Autism*. New York: DaCapo Press.
Strauss, A. (1992). Turning points in identity. In C. Clark & H. Robby (eds.), *Social Inter-
action* (pp. 77–98). New York: St. Martin's Press.
Stroul, B. A. (1995). Case management in a system of care. In B. J. Friesen & J. Poertner
(eds.), *From Case Management to Service Coordination for Children with Emotional,
Behavioral, or Mental Disorders: Building on Family Strengths* (pp. 3–25). Baltimore,
MD: Paul H. Brooks.
Stroul, B. A., & Friedman, R. M. (1986). *A System of Care for Seriously Emotionally Dis-
turbed Children and Youth*. Washington, DC: CASSP Technical Assistance Center,
Georgetown University Child Development Center.
Stroul, B. A., & Friedman, R. M. (1988). Caring for severely emotionally disturbed chil-
dren and youth: Principles for a system of care. *Child Today, 17,* 11–15.
Stroul, B. A., & Friedman, R. M. (1996). *A System of Care for Seriously Emotionally Dis-
turbed Children and Youth* (rev. ed.). Washington, DC: CASSP Technical Assis-
tance Center, Georgetown University Child Development Center.
Styron, W. (1990). *Darkness Visible: A Memoir of Madness*. New York: Random House.
Swados, E. (1991). *The Four of Us: A Family Memoir*. New York: Farrar, Straus, and
Giroux.
Swanson, J. M., Elliott, G. R., Greenhill, L. L., Wigal, T., Arnold, L. E., Vitiello, B.,
Hechtman, L., Epstein, J., Pelham, W. E., Abikoff, H. B., Newcorn, J., Molina,
B. S. G., Hinshaw, S., Wells, K., Hoza, B., Jensen, P. S., Gibbons, R., Hur, K.,
Stehli, A., Davies, M., March, J., Conners, C. K., Caron, M., & Volkow, N. D.,
for the MTA Cooperative Group. (2007). Effects of stimulant medication on
growth rates across 3 years in the MTA follow-up. *Journal of the American Academy
of Child and Adolescent Psychiatry, 46,* 1015–1027.
Tarico, V., Low, B. P., Trupin, E., & Forsythe-Stevens, A. (1989). Children's mental
health services: A parent perspective. *Community Mental Health Journal, 25,*
313–326.
Temerlin, K. (1968). Suggestion effects in psychiatric diagnosis. *Journal of Nervous and
Mental Disease, 147,* 349–353.
Tessler, R. (2000). *Family Experiences with Mental Illness*. Westport, CT: Auburn House.
Thordike, J. (1997). *Another Way Home: A Family's Journey Through Mental Illness*.
New York: Penguin.

Torrey, F. (2001). *Surviving Schizophrenia: A Manual for Families, Consumers, and Providers.* New York: Quill.

Traustadottir, R. (1991). Mothers who care: Gender, disability, and family life. *Journal of Family Issues, 12,* 211–228.

VanDenBerg, J. (2007). *Wraparound Facilitator and Family Support Partner.* Vroon VanDenBerg.

Verghese, A. (1998). *The Tennis Partner: A Doctor's Story of Friendship and Loss.* New York: Harper Collins.

Vestal, C. (2010). As economy takes toll, mental health budgets shrink. Stateline.org, Pew Center on the States.

Vitanza, S., & Cohen, R. (2001). *Perspectives on Treatment and Services: Results of a National Survey of Parents and Caregivers of Children with Serious Mental Illnesses.* Paper presented at the Building on Family Strengths: Research and Services in Support of Children and Their Families Conference, Portland, OR.

Weil, M., & Karls, J. M. (1985). *Case Management in the Human Services.* San Francisco: Jossey-Bass.

Weisz, J. R., Weiss, B., Alicke, M. D., & Klotz, M. L. (1987). Effectiveness of psychotherapy with children and adolescents: A meta-analysis for clinicians. *Journal of Consulting and Clinical Psychology, 55,* 542–549.

Weisz, J. R., Weiss, B., & Donenberg, G. R. (1992). The lab versus the clinic: Effects of child and adolescent psychotherapy. *American Psychologist, 47,* 1578–1585.

Werner, E., & Smith, R. S. (2001). *Journeys from Childhood to Midlife: Risk, Resilience and Recovery.* Ithaca, NY: Cornell University Press.

Winett, R. A., & Winkler, R. (1972). Current behavior modification in the classroom: Be still, be quiet, be docile. *Journal of Applied Behavior Modification, 5,* 499–504.

World Health Organization. (2002). *Caring for Children and Adolescents with Mental Disorders.* Geneva: Author.

Wurtzel, W. (1994). *Prozac Nation.* Boston: Houghton Mifflin.

Wyden, P. (1998). *Conquering Schizophrenia: A Father, His Son, and a Medical Breakthrough.* New York: Alfred Knopf,

Yarrow, M., Clausen, J., & Robbins, P. (1955). The social meaning of mental illness. *Journal of Social Issues, 11,* 33–48.

Young, S. (1995). An overview of issues in research on consumer satisfaction with child and adolescent mental health services. *Journal of Child and Family Studies, 4,* 219–238.

Index

About the Author

CRAIG WINSTON LECROY, PhD, is Professor of Social Work at Arizona State University. He is the author of more than 100 scholarly publications. His 10 previous books include *Handbook of Evidence Based Treatment Manuals for Children and Adolescents; Case Studies in Child, Adolescent, and Family Treatment;* and *Empowering Adolescent Girls*. Professor LeCroy has directed numerous child and adolescent projects, including a National Institute of Mental Health Training Grant for improving social work practice with children, a substance abuse prevention program, a universal prevention program for girls, and an ongoing investigation into the impact of home-based intervention for at-risk families.